THE POWER OF MEDITATION

The Wisdom Culture Series

The *Wisdom Culture Series* is published by Wisdom Publications in association with the Foundation for the Preservation of the Mahayana Tradition (FPMT). Under the guidance of Lama Zopa Rinpoche, the series provides English-language readers with key works for the study and cultivation of the Mahayana Buddhist path, especially works of masters within the lineage of Lama Tsongkhapa and the Geluk school of Tibetan Buddhism. "Wisdom culture," an expression frequently used by Lama Yeshe, is a Dharma culture rooted in wisdom and compassion. The *Wisdom Culture Series* is intended to support this vision by transmitting the timeless wisdom of the Dharma through authoritative and accessible publications.

Volumes:

The Middle-Length Treatise on the Stages of the Path to Enlightenment, Tsongkhapa

The Power of Mantra, Lama Zopa Rinpoche

The Swift Path, Paṇchen Losang Yeshé

Perseverance, Lama Zopa Rinpoche

The Power of Meditation, Lama Zopa Rinpoche

More volumes to come!

THE POWER OF MEDITATION

*A Complete Guide to
Transforming Your Mind*

Lama Zopa Rinpoche

Compiled and Edited by Gordon McDougall

Wisdom Publications
132 Perry Street
New York, NY 10014 USA
wisdomexperience.org

Library of Congress Cataloging-in-Publication Data is available.
LCCN 2023047981

ISBN 978-1-61429-788-8   ebook ISBN 978-1-61429-812-0

28 27 26 25 24   5 4 3 2 1

Cover design by Jess Morphew.
Interior design by Tony Lulek.

Printed on acid-free paper that meets the guidelines for permanence and durability of
the Production Guidelines for Book Longevity of the Council on Library Resources.

Printed in the United States of America.

Please visit fscus.org.

CONTENTS

Part II. Developing a Meditation Practice

EDITOR'S PREFACE

D URING HIS INCREDIBLE LIFE, Lama Zopa Rinpoche was a
great meditator. I suspect that everything he did was a meditation. He was not a conventional teacher; his words seemed to come
from a deeper space, giving us, his students, exactly what we needed to
hear. I have been so fortunate, as his student for decades, to have seen
Rinpoche not only in his role as a teacher but also as the head of a great
octopus of an organization, the Foundation for the Preservation of the
Mahayana Tradition, where his decisions seemed to also come from that
deeper space, some inner voice that arose from a profound meditative
stability. What I never saw was Rinpoche not working tirelessly for
others.

How was it, after hours and hours of teaching, he would still be fresh,
whereas we were a sea of droopy jellyfish, flopping all over our cushions?
The teachings say that when you attain *shamatha*, calm abiding, you
have a sense of mental and physical pliancy, with its accompanying bliss.
I cannot even think what that might be like, but Rinpoche seemed to
demonstrate this is possible.

Searching for teachings on meditation to create this book, I was stuck
with the disconnect between what we Western students in the early
days thought of as meditation and what Rinpoche means by the term.
In the 1970s, when the young headed for India and Nepal, looking for
something missing in the West, they were lured to Kopan Monastery's
famous one-month meditation course. They wanted to learn sitting
meditation but what they got from Rinpoche was *lamrim*, the graduated path to enlightenment, the vital teachings on how to change their
lives. They wanted bliss and got the hard work of mind transformation.
Many fled. But many more stayed, and their lives were utterly changed.

The transcripts of the early Kopan courses are filled with Rinpoche talking about "how to practice Dharma, to practice meditation," tying the two terms together to emphasize that these terms are synonyms. Meditation is much more than watching the breath; it is becoming familiar with what is virtuous. And because we are definitely not familiar with the virtuous, moving the mind from its habitual confused state is a big undertaking. For that, we need inspiration and determination. It's not enough to buy a meditation cushion and light a stick of incense. When we fully understand the need to transform the mind, we can slowly rearrange our life so that it is simpler and more virtuous. As our lifestyle changes, we will find our meditations become richer and more rewarding. That is why, as well as knowing the mechanics of meditating, we need to know how to create a daily routine that includes preliminary practices and all-important elements such as purifying our negative tendencies and enhancing our positive ones. When that is an integral part of our life, our meditation will surely bear fruit.

In this book, Rinpoche explains the necessary daily preparations as well as those we need to do before a retreat. He shows us how to develop shamatha as well as how to meditate on lamrim subjects. And because the majority of our life is not spent on a meditation cushion, he explains what to do "between sessions," where we can turn our daily life into a meditation.

This is not a thin book. There is a lot to learn if we want our meditation to be our life and not just a hobby. But if we can really see how essential transforming our mind is, we will have the energy to tackle our negativities and develop our meditation practice. Rinpoche cites three vital attributes: being far sighted, being determined, and being relaxed. We must keep the long view, motivating everything we do with the wish for enlightenment; we must have the strong determination to do whatever is needed to succeed; and with these two, we must not become tight but maintain a relaxed, light attitude. We are in for the long haul. We just have to look at the great masters like His Holiness the Dalai Lama and Lama Zopa Rinpoche to see how they embody these three vital attributes.

In general, quotations in this book have been taken from published texts such as Shantideva's *A Guide to the Bodhisattva's Way of Life* and have been cited accordingly, but some are Rinpoche's own translations, which I have taken from the transcripts.

To compile this book, I have used teachings stored in the Lama Yeshe Wisdom Archive, which have been lovingly recorded, transcribed, and checked by a vast number of people, all working to preserve the precious words of a great teacher. I would like to thank everybody who contributed to this book: those at LYWA, the audio team who recorded the teachings, and the team at Wisdom Publications, who are an inspiration to work with.

I apologize for any errors found in this book; they are a hundred percent mine. May this book be a tool to allow people to transform their life into one of meditation, where helping others motivates every thought and action. May whatever merit gained from the creation of this book be dedicated to the swift return of our beloved teacher, Lama Zopa Rinpoche; to peace in this troubled world; to the long life, well-being, and fulfillment of the wishes of all our holy teachers, especially His Holiness the Dalai Lama; and to the flourishing of the Foundation for the Preservation of the Mahayana Tradition and of the Dharma throughout the world.

Gordon McDougall
Bath, England

PART I

MEDITATION AND THE MIND

1. BECOMING FAMILIAR WITH VIRTUE

SUBDUING THE MIND

Meditation is primarily concerned with caring for the mind. Although our body and our mind are intimately related and interconnected, they are quite different types of phenomena. Our body is an object we can see with our eyes, a physical thing, but not so the mind. To use meditation purely to benefit our body, for worldly ends, is to waste its potential. It would be like the aspirin we take to be rid of a headache; the pain may go away, but we are not cured because the real cause has not been addressed. We should not squander the power of meditation on such limited aims. Meditation should have a higher, more valuable purpose.

Because we have been born as a human being, we each have the potential to give our life meaning. But to take full advantage of it, we must actualize our potential by engaging fully in a spiritual path. One of the first and most important subjects in the graduated path to enlightenment—the *lamrim*, which is how the entire Buddhist path is explained within Tibetan Buddhism—is the perfect human rebirth, showing how rare and special our current life is. By utilizing our human rebirth properly and gaining control over our mind, we can sever the root of all suffering completely. And we can even go beyond that.

This is the true purpose of meditation. It has the power to bring us liberation, freedom from all suffering, but it also can help us to attain full enlightenment, an attainment that enables us to fulfill not only our own aims but also those of all others. This should be our sole reason for engaging in meditation. The great yogis and meditation masters of the past have practiced the Dharma with just this purpose in mind. Like-wise, when we meditate—and in Buddha's teachings there are literally hundreds of different meditations to choose from, depending on our level of realization—we should do so with this same motivation.

We are not compelled to meditate by some outside agent, by other people, or by God. Rather, just as we are responsible for our own suffering, so are we solely responsible for our own happiness. It is entirely up to us. At present, all kinds of suffering permeate our life to a greater or lesser extent. In common language, the English word "suffering" seems to specifically refer to manifest physical and mental pain. I have heard many students say, "I'm not suffering," meaning they are not currently ill or depressed, or suffering in some obvious way. The term used most often in Buddhism is the Pali word *dukkha*,[1] which refers to all levels of suffering. Perhaps we can use the word "dissatisfaction." It really means to have a mind disturbed by delusions.

Unless we do something about it, we will continue to suffer. Therefore, we must undertake some spiritual practice, which means looking inward, to the mind. If we disregard the role the mind has in our happiness and suffering and continue to expend all our energy on arranging and rearranging the external aspects of our existence, then our suffering will continue. Our suffering had no beginning, and if we do not adopt an effective spiritual practice, neither will it have an end.

That means we must subdue our mind through meditation. Whether or not we sit with our legs in a perfect meditation posture is unimportant. What is important is to check whether the meditation we do is an actual remedy for our suffering. Does it effectively eliminate the delusions obscuring our mind? Does it combat our ignorance, hatred, and greed? If it does, it is a perfect meditation. If, on the other hand, it merely serves to generate and increase our negativities, such as pride, then it is only another cause of suffering. In such a case, even though we may say we are meditating, we are not actually following a spiritual path or practicing Dharma at all.

We must understand our mind in order to transform it; therefore learning how to meditate is of prime importance. All over the world now there are many places called meditation centers where we can learn mindfulness meditation—watching the breath, being aware of the body, and things like that. It tends to be the first thing people encounter when they become interested in meditation. Generally, when we first go to a meditation center, there is a genuine motivation to do something different. We are looking for something we can't find in our normal daily life.

This initial response to meditation is excellent, breaking us free from our fixed ideas, showing us a glimpse of the much better way there can be to live our life. To even have an interest in meditation is like a miracle. From there, everything starts. People in the West generally have a high intelligence and a good education, but they tend to have very fixed concepts about life. In a very materialistic society, ideas tend to be quite closed, quite narrow. So, to go against this way of thinking and give freedom to ourselves to explore much deeper truths is marvelous.

By exploring our mind, we can discover the cause of happiness and suffering. We can discover the continuity of the mind and develop an understanding of future lives and how working for the happiness beyond this life is so important. We can come to realize the possibility of total freedom from all suffering, discovering liberation from samsara—the recurring cycle of death and rebirth that keeps us trapped in suffering. When we explore even further, we realize the potential we have to attain full enlightenment, where we overcome even the most subtle obscurations of the mind in order to help free all sentient beings. In short, from that initial interest in meditation we bring great meaning into our life.

It is very good to meditate, but unless we know how to meditate properly, we waste our time. Our meditation can become just another hobby, like playing football or decorating the house. There are so many types of meditation; it's like trying to choose from all the items in a department store. Perhaps we are attracted to Zen meditation; we like the idea we can just stop thinking, like giving the mind a holiday. If so, we must be intelligent and consider whether, in doing that, we also give our compassion and wisdom a holiday as well.

We need to choose a meditation that will transform our mind. Our meditation should not just be to attain some temporary happiness, not even the bliss of shamatha.[2] We should use it to attain the true peace of mind that has been missing for beginningless lifetimes. We suffer because of the delusions that plague our mind and rob us of peace. Since delusions are the root, the only way to attain any true happiness is to overcome them. To try to have a happy life without addressing these delusions—in fact while cherishing them as our best friend as so many of us do—can never work. It is like rubbing ointment onto a foot that has a thorn in it to relieve the pain without pulling the thorn out. Just as the only way to stop the pain is to remove the thorn, the only way to overcome problems is to subdue our mind.

Subduing the mind is the job of meditation. In fact, anything that helps to subdue the mind is meditation, whether it is focusing on the breath, studying the Dharma, saying prayers, reciting mantras, or any of the many techniques within the various Buddhist traditions. One of those many techniques is best suited for our own personal disposition. Some, such as tantric meditations, are said to be faster or more profound, but the aim is the same. If we wish to destroy an enemy, whether we use a bow and arrow, a gun, or even an atomic bomb, the target is the same, our enemy, and the goal is the same, their destruction. Whatever method we use in Buddhism, the enemy is the unsubdued mind and the goal is to totally subdue it.

Meditation Is Becoming Familiar with a Virtuous Object

In the *Adornment of Mahayana Sutras*, Maitreya defines meditation as making the mind familiar with the object. In particular, we familiarize our mind with a virtuous object. For instance, to achieve bodhichitta, the altruistic mind that seeks enlightenment in order to lead all beings out of suffering, it is necessary to train the mind with various meditations such as looking at the kindness of others, how they have all been our mother, and so forth. Only through slowly habituating our mind with such virtuous thoughts can we increase and stabilize them. It cannot be achieved immediately or within a few days. As we train the mind, the virtuous state starts to arise more naturally, and we move closer and closer to having the actual realization, where the mind and its object become indistinguishable. In the case of bodhichitta, the mind moves from meditating on bodhichitta—exploring the techniques to become this wonderful mind—to becoming bodhichitta, where we spontaneously and continuously think only of the welfare of all other sentient beings.

Whether we call it meditation or not, this familiarization to virtuous objects is the real meditation we must do. It might sound like it has nothing to do with our life, just something made up, but it is not. For instance, to progress quickly along the spiritual path, we need to see what great potential we have. When we explore the perfect human rebirth as a virtuous object of meditation, this initial lamrim topic shows us the usefulness of having the particular type of life we now have, how difficult it is to attain, and how rare and fragile it is. We don't feel our life is so special now only because we have not explored its nature.

The objects we need to focus on in our meditations must be virtuous ones. We have no problem focusing on nonvirtuous ones. For countless lifetimes we have been making the mind familiar with all sorts of nonvirtuous thoughts. Somebody angers us and we are unable to move our mind away from how they have harmed us. Our minds go back to the object—the harmer and the harm done to poor us—again and again. "They did this to me. They did that to me. They stared at me in that horrible way." Dwelling on our enemy in that way, we see all the reasons we hate them. Our face turns red; our veins stand out. We have to hold ourselves back from doing something violent to them. In that way, we have utterly perfected the meditation on anger, habituating ourselves to the angry state so that it becomes second nature to us.

The meditation we should be doing, however, is the complete opposite of this. Rather than letting the mind come under the control of delusions and allowing them to grow, we train to keep our delusions under control and to slowly subdue them. With meditation, we move the mind away from disturbing thoughts toward positive ones. For instance, the angry, impatient mind can be tamed by training in patience.

Siblings can have very different personalities, one patient and compassionate, the other angry and selfish. This doesn't come from the parents or the environment but from habituation from previous lifetimes.

As soon as any human or animal is born, it instinctively knows to go to its mother's breast for milk. I once saw on television how immediately a tiny baby kangaroo, a joey, was born, it crawled into the mother's pouch. Nobody taught it that! In the West, this is called instinct, but Buddhism explains this as the ripening of past lives' imprints, seeds left on the mental continuum from having done such an action countless times in the past.

That is why generating compassion and loving-kindness seems to come so easily to some people, whereas most of us have to work hard at overcoming our selfishness. Just as some people are naturally contented, others are constantly dissatisfied. These traits show that habituations build up over lifetimes.

The strongest habituation most of us have is the attachment that clings to the happiness of this life. This is the biggest obstacle to meditating and developing a contented mind. Therefore, doing meditations that slowly move our mind away from attachment to this life's mundane pleasures to a greater happiness, the happiness of future lives, is considered the first Dharma. Meditations such as on impermanence and death and the shortcomings of desire are vital, but they rarely come easily. Our mind resists them because it has not been habituated to renunciation. Even when we persist in our meditations, it's a difficult struggle, whereas we fall into attachment for a desirable object effortlessly. Attachment comes like a waterfall, like a heavy shower of rain.

Through meditation, however, as the mind becomes increasingly purified and clear, those very heavy deluded thoughts that obscure us will diminish. Then, as mind become subtler and clearer, positive states of mind like loving-kindness will become natural to us, and as a byproduct we will be able to remember past lives and see future lives, of ourselves and others.

We Are Under the Control of the Delusions

Because few people are aware that the real purpose of meditation is to transform the mind by subduing it, they don't actively try to do this, even though they might work hard at a meditation practice. Subduing the mind is essential because at present our mind is controlled by our delusions, not by us, and it has been for beginningless lifetimes.

We can define delusions (*klesha, nyönmong*) as any mental state, such as attachment, anger, or jealousy, that obscures the essentially pure nature of the mind and hence causes suffering. Also called obscurations, afflictions, destructive emotions, or disturbing thoughts, they are any state of mind that disturbs the mental continuum rather than bringing it peace. "Obscurations" is a very nice translation, indicating that the delusions obscure us from seeing the situation as it really is and therefore bring us great harm.

Karma (*lé*), literally "action," comes from this obscuring, disturbing attitude. When we act due to a deluded mind, a seed or imprint (*vasana, bakchak*) is left on our mental continuum that stays there until it ripens when the right conditions occur. A positive imprint can be destroyed by anger and the like, and a negative imprint can be purified by specific purification practices, but, unless that happens, a karmic seed will always ripen as a positive or negative experience, causing us to act and create more imprints. Our current incarnation, which comes from such a karmic seed, is the product of karma and delusions, and in turn it is then the cause of karma and delusions. This is why we experience suffering, and this is how our suffering is perpetuated.

Of the countless delusions, the main ones are the three poisons: attachment, anger, and ignorance. When we suddenly feel irrationally angry at somebody, although it might seem causeless, there is definitely a cause, possibly from our connection with them in a previous life.

The principal cause of delusions is misunderstanding the fundamental nature of how things exist. What is impermanent we see as permanent, and what is dependent we see as independent. Most importantly, we mistakenly see things as existing from their own side, rather than as mere designations, which is how they actually exist. From that, attachment arises for what we take to be an inherently beautiful thing (which doesn't exist like that) and aversion arises for what we take to be an inherently repulsive thing (which also doesn't exist like that). Our delusion sinks into the object, making it difficult to separate from it, like oil sinking into cloth. The problem is not in the object but in our attitude to it.

Using meditation first to observe how we have been controlled by delusions for countless lifetimes, we then use our meditation to protect ourselves from those delusions—which is the complete opposite to our habitual attitude. It is crucial that we understand that this is the purpose of meditation. Otherwise, we can spend our life in a cave in the mountains, sitting cross-legged, believing we are a great meditator, and never realize that nothing we do separates us from our delusions at all. Unless meditation has the power to transform the mind so that it becomes free of the poisons of attachment, anger, and ignorance, it is not a spiritual practice. On the other hand, somebody working in the city, with a busy life, a family, and possessions, who actively tries to become a better person by working on their delusions, *is* a spiritual person.

We Can Definitely Transform Our Mind

In meditation we have control over the sensory input so external sense objects no longer overwhelm us. This is how we get inner peace and happiness. The difference between the peace we gain through meditation and the uncontrolled mind, always chasing external objects, is like the difference between the sky and the earth.

Even if we are not familiar with the teachings of the Buddha, as soon as we start to try to meditate we can observe the change in our mind, seeing how the disturbed thoughts calm down and positive thoughts arise more easily. There is a tranquility because we are away from those agitated thoughts that, were we to follow them, would lead to fear, loneliness, depression, and so forth.

To just start on a meditation practice can show us the potential of the mind. When we can hold the mind in meditation for even a short while, we can start to see how we are able to totally transform our mind. Because we are trying to live in the Dharma, living positively, trying to follow a good meditation practice, we are protected from the tsunami of attachment, anger, and all the other delusions that can plague us. We have space to think of others, space to develop love and compassion.

Giving up attachment does not mean we must give up our friends or possessions. Friends and possessions are not the problem; the problem is the dissatisfied mind of attachment, and the only solution to that is through overcoming our grasping onto external things as real happiness. And that can only be achieved with the profound understanding that comes through meditation. By meditating on the shortcomings of desire we can see that we have enough; we don't need more, whether it's more friends, more wealth, more possessions, or whatever. When we come to that conclusion in our meditation, immediately there is contentment, satisfaction, peace of mind.

We need to fully overcome delusions by using many different meditations. First, we must avoid harming others and that means observing our karma. The door to our entire Dharma practice is watching what actions of body, speech, and mind we do and ensuring they are always positive. Unless we are aware of when we are creating negative karma and unless we have the wish to create only positive karma, how can we stop our suffering? We don't have to learn meditation in order to *create* the cause of suffering. We already know how to do that very well.

Every meditation we do should be a tool to transform the mind, to bring ourselves peace and satisfaction. For instance, by meditating on impermanence and death and seeing that there is no guarantee we won't die soon, even tomorrow or today, we can understand that it is absolutely pointless to follow desire. Right there, wherever we are sitting, in the office or at home, the unhappy, dissatisfied mind, the mind weighed down with a mountain of problems, disappears. By remembering the nature of life—which is impermanent and ends in death—on that same seat, at that very moment, our meditation cuts off the dissatisfied mind and we immediately find satisfaction and happiness.

Meditation Is Not Separate from Daily Life

Dharma is not something unrelated to our life. When Western people think about religion, it seems to me that they often don't relate it to their everyday life. Religion can help those who practice it, but it's a specific type of action, and to be happy in daily life you need to do other things. With that kind of thinking, life breaks into religious and secular and sort of becomes split, confused.

This is wrong thinking. Dharma or spiritual activity is something that we must relate to any normal activity. It should be an integral part of our life from the moment we wake up until the moment we go to sleep. Anything that leads us toward a greater inner peace is the Dharma, or spirituality, or whatever name we want to give it. Another way of saying it is that the Dharma is that which has the capability to overcome suffering and the cause of suffering. If our "religious" activity, such as meditation, does not do this, if it just creates the cause for more suffering, it is not Dharma, even if we give it that name. That is like calling poison "medicine."

Dharma is the right action of body, speech, and mind, and that right action does not only mean reciting mantras or saying prayers. It is any action done with the correct motivation, one wishing for happiness of future lives, for liberation, and—the best motivation—for full enlightenment. In that way, whatever we do becomes the path that leads us to inner happiness.

Students tell me that life in the West is so busy that it is difficult to find time to meditate. Even though we might not be able to have a fixed meditation routine, it is important that throughout the day we don't forget the subject of the meditation we are trying to develop. Whatever lifestyle we have, whatever work we do, everything we do—eating, sleeping, sitting, walking—our whole life must become Dharma; it must become a meditation. If that seems a huge goal at present, we can aim to keep a wholly positive attitude for half a day. Then, even if for the rest of the time we are creating more problems for ourselves, at least that half of the day becomes the unmistaken cause of happiness. The time we actually sit in meditation is very short—an hour or two, half an hour, or even less. Therefore, we should try to make the rest of the day as meaningful as possible.

When we keep our mind in the Dharma, nothing is meaningless. When we wander around a city, observing the people and animals there with open eyes, we are being given a great Dharma lesson. Watching television or reading a magazine, what we see is other human beings unable to stop themselves creating more and more suffering—which causes compassion to naturally arise. Clearly seeing that anything other than the Dharma is meaningless, we are inspired to develop our mind on the path even more.

Because meditation is about transforming the mind, it is vital for everybody, not just Buddhists. Those with another religion or none, whether they believe in karma or reincarnation or not, still need to transform their mind. Therefore, anybody at all who wants happiness and does not want suffering needs to meditate. Of course, if they *don't* want happiness and they *do* want suffering, that's totally different! But that's not the case. Everybody—Buddhist or non-Buddhist, believer or non-believer—wants only happiness.

In America, soldiers returning from wars such as in Iraq or Afghanistan, where there is so much violence and death, are often taught meditation to help them. When they return, they often can't make sense of their life, thinking it has no meaning. They can go kind of crazy. So, now the American government has introduced mindfulness meditation to help them cope.

I learned about this from a soldier who came to visit me. He was quite intelligent, working in charge of technology or something. He had been introduced to meditation and found it useful, so when he saw something about Lawudo Retreat Centre[3] in Nepal he went there, which is where I met him. After I asked him some questions, I gave him practice to do for quite a number of years—I don't know if he will live that long!—but the most important thing is that he is learning the Dharma and meditating. In that way he can benefit himself and numberless other sentient beings. Even the athletes training for the Olympic Games practice meditation, finding it very useful to release stress.

The best way we can help others is to introduce them to the Dharma, to teach them meditation. That is the *utmost* need. Just as somebody who has had a heart attack needs medication immediately, all sentient beings need meditation immediately. The meditation center is more important than the emergency ward of a hospital, because without overcoming the deluded mind there is no chance of long-term recovery. Even though the doctors in a hospital might be able to help in an accident or with an illness, making the body temporarily healthy, they cannot ensure us that we will never be sick again. They cannot transform our negative mind and stop us creating more negative karma and therefore having to experience more suffering. Unless we have purified the causes of that illness, it will recur. The only way to stop it is to take care of the mind, which means meditating, practicing the Dharma.

The Power of the Mind

What is mind? It is a phenomenon that is shapeless, colorless, formless, and nonsubstantial, and whose nature is clear and knowing. Mind is able to perceive objects, just as a mirror can give a clear reflection of things in front of it.

Mind exists by depending on causes and conditions. Today's mind exists because of yesterday's mind. Yesterday's mind exists because of the day before yesterday's mind, and so on. Like that, it goes back in a continuous stream. And just as today's mind is the result of yesterday's mind, today's mind is the cause of tomorrow's mind. In that way, this moment's mind is both the result of the previous moment's mind and the cause of the next moment's mind. So, each moment of mind is a dependent arising, arising in dependence on the previous moment.

Any mental experience, such as a thought, also arises in dependence on the object it experiences, which is the condition rather than the substantial cause. There can be no mental experience without an object to be experienced, whether it is a physical object or a mental one, such as a mental image that is the basis of memory. Because there is continuation of thought from one moment to the next, from yesterday to today, we can remember what we did yesterday, what we saw yesterday, what we thought yesterday, and the same for last week and last year and so forth.

Only through analytical meditation can we take this logic back, seeing how this moment of mind arose from the previous moment, and so on, back and back, until we come to the first moment of mind that happened in the fertilized egg. We then need to consider where that first moment of this life's mind came from. Was there a previous continuation of mind or not? Did our mind start in our mother's womb or was there a previous moment that was the cause? By developing our wisdom through such meditations, we can discover from our own experience what the truth is. There is a meditation on the continuity of the consciousness we can do, which you can find in appendix 1.

Even without meditation, because of a very clear mind with fewer obscurations, many students have been able to remember leaving their mother's womb. Others, however, through meditation, have been able to take their mind back to within the womb and to the very first moment of this life, the mind that first associates with the fertilized egg. Some have even had very clear memories of past lives. One student could even plainly remember a Tibetan kitchen. They were able to remember this within their meditation as clearly as we can remember the events of yesterday.

Through developing the mind in meditation, we achieve what is called *shamatha* or calm abiding, remaining focused on any object we place our mind on as long as we wish without any distraction at all, as immovable as a mountain. As we advance through the various levels of shamatha, our capacity to remember increases; highly advanced meditators are able to remember thousands of previous lives.

The Mind That Creates Suffering Must Eliminate Suffering

We have a physical body and a mind that is nonphysical. The body consists of bones, flesh, blood, and so forth. It is born and it dies, and in between there are many problems due to having what are called contaminated aggregates. That means that even though we try to escape from problems, there always seem to be more.

Besides the sufferings of birth, old age, sickness, and death, for most humans the main problems are not getting what we want, getting what we don't want, losing what we have, or not finding satisfaction in it. We are unable to obtain the delicious food we crave; we want a good reputation or to be praised and get just the opposite. Rich or poor, these are sufferings that constantly plague us. In this way, we always suffer from dissatisfaction. While meditation can relieve us of such suffering, that is not its primary aim. As I have said, the goal of our meditation should be much higher.

Soon we will die, and what happens to us after death should be of concern to us now. The body dies but the mind, which came from our previous life, continues on to the next life. What kind of future life we will have depends on our present life—how we act, how we live—just as the life we have now is the result of how we acted in our previous life. The work of our previous life is finished; we are experiencing the results now. What we need to do now, our present life's responsibility, is to make arrangements for our future lives. It is in our hands.

Happiness and suffering don't come from some external source; they haven't been created by God or other people. If we want to be happy and to attain liberation and enlightenment, this is something only we can do. This is work we must do for ourselves. We alone created our own suffering and we alone can overcome it to become truly happy. The essential work we must do is on the mind, through meditation; otherwise our suffering will be endless.

The delusions that bring us all our problems are not an integral part of the mind. They can be removed. That means our mind has infinite potential. As explained by the Buddha and the great teachers of Buddhist philosophy, we have buddha nature or buddha potential, the potential to become fully enlightened. No matter what problems we face now, they are just temporary. By applying the correct meditation techniques, we can slowly overcome all of them, following the path that takes us all the way to buddhahood.

Once we have overcome the obstacles that currently block them, realizations will pour down upon us. The key is correctly following the spiritual teacher who can give us perfect instructions on how to progress. The teacher is like somebody holding a bright light to guide us through the dark night. Our relationship with the teacher can also be compared to a stick and a gong. Although a gong has the potential to make a sound, it will only do that when it is beaten by a stick. Similarly, although we have buddha nature, only through meeting the virtuous teacher and correctly following him or her will that potential start to be actualized.

THE IMPORTANCE OF MOTIVATION

In a text of questions and answers by the First Panchen Lama, Panchen Losang Chökyi Gyaltsen,[4] there is the question, "What is the beginning of meditation?" He replies, "The beginning of meditation is the motivation."[5]

If an action were virtuous simply because it didn't involve harming others through killing and so forth, whenever we meditated there would be no need to generate a virtuous thought; just doing the meditation itself would be virtuous. This is incorrect. Because we must begin with a virtuous motivation, watching the mind and changing it into a virtuous one is strongly emphasized. If we can, we should also try to have a motivation of renunciation for the whole of samsara—and better still, a bodhichitta motivation.

If our motivation is worldly concern, then the action becomes a worldly activity. It cannot be Dharma, even if the action is reciting prayers, meditating, and so forth. It can be *like* Dharma but it is not Dharma. And a person who "practices" Dharma with a motivation of worldly concern is *like* a Dharma practitioner but is not a Dharma practitioner. There is a big difference.

Without understanding the distinction between Dharma and non-Dharma, no matter how many different "spiritual" actions we do, no matter how long we do things such as building monasteries, making prostrations and so forth—even if we do them until we die—there is the real danger that our whole life will become filled with negative actions, binding us to suffering.

Whether any action is Dharma or worldly, whether it is virtuous or nonvirtuous, depends entirely on the motivation. As the *Treasury of Precious Qualities* says,

If the root is medicinal, so are its shoots,
if poisonous, no need to say its shoots will be the same.
What makes an act positive or negative is not how it looks
or its size, but the good or bad intention behind it.[6]

When our motivation is virtuous, our verbal and physical actions will be virtuous, and that will bring happiness. Happiness does not come from outside; it is a state of mind, one we develop through letting go of the clinging to external things as a source of happiness.

Both happiness and suffering depend on what kind of motivation we generate. As the great bodhisattva Shantideva explains in *A Guide to the Bodhisattva's Way of Life*,

In vain [beings] wander through the vast open spaces of the
     universe
seeking to put an end to sorrow and reach happiness—
these beings who do not cultivate
the mysterious mind that contains all Dharmas.[7]

Not knowing the "secret of the mind," which is here called the "mysterious mind," means being unaware of how everything—all happiness and suffering; enlightenment and hell; nirvana and samsara, and so forth—depends on our own mind, on what kind of attitude we have.

Unless we know this "secret" of how our positive and negative motivation produces happiness and suffering, no matter how much we wish to achieve happiness and avoid suffering, we will continue to helplessly wander in samsara.

In the next verse, Shantideva says,

Therefore, I should focus my mind correctly,
and keep a careful watch over it.
What good will it do to keep many vows,
if I neglect the vow of watching over the mind?[8]

When we know this and when we diligently watch our mind, never letting it slip into negativity, then we can be happy no matter what we have or where we are. We can be a penniless beggar, we can even be in a prison, but our mind will remain peaceful and happy.

We need these two understandings: what is the source of happiness and how it can be achieved. This is exactly what Dharma is, what meditation is. Without it, nothing gives satisfaction; with it, we have the ability to be totally happy and satisfied. Even before we learn to completely control the mind, our meditation practice will quell the dissatisfied minds of desire and anger, giving us methods to overcome them, stopping our problems, stopping the harm we do to both ourselves and to others.

We can also do something with a neutral motivation. For example, there is the meditation during which while we are walking we practice mindfulness that we are walking, aware of that and nothing else. Or we are watching the abdomen rising and falling, or just being aware of what sensations we have, whether it is pain or whatever. In this kind of meditation, we just watch with no special emphasis on the motivation.

Perhaps we are doing this meditation solely to have some calmness, to subdue our busy mind for a little while. While that is perfectly okay, it is still just seeking some comfort, the happiness of this life, without discriminating between a virtuous thought and a nonvirtuous one; therefore, as we have seen, it is not Dharma. I would say that even though the meditation might be watching the mind, it still does not actually fulfill the purpose of watching the mind, which is to observe whether the mind is virtuous or nonvirtuous. Is our main goal the happiness of future lives, liberation, or enlightenment, or is it simply relaxation? Understanding our motivation is vital, and so too is always having a positive motivation.

Holy Dharma or Worldly Dharma?

We can meditate or recite mantras thinking we are practicing the holy Dharma, but unless our motivation is free from the attachment to the happiness of this life, the Buddhist practice that we are doing is not holy

Dharma, just worldly dharma. (In the context of worldly dharma, the word "dharma" is used differently, referring to phenomena, specifically actions done with a mundane motive.) No action can be both holy Dharma and worldly dharma; it is either one or the other.

Once, Milarepa's guru, Marpa, gave him this advice,

> Son, don't mix the Dharma and this life's work. If it is mixed you will lose the Dharma. Think on that: you, the son, are suffering in samsara. Even if I try to explain the nature of suffering an infinite number of times, it is unspeakable, it is infinite. Even if I transform hundreds of mouths and tongues to explain it for hundreds of thousands of eons, I would never be finished. So, my instruction to you is don't waste the Dharma. Don't mix this life and Dharma.[9]

If we mix our Dharma practice with worldly concern, if our Dharma is only mouth "Dharma," it cannot bring the result we expect. The texts describe it as like milking the horn of a goat, utterly futile. Nobody can attain both the work of this life and the holy Dharma. However much we desire to do both without losing either, we are only deluding ourselves.

We can do both holy Dharma and worldly dharma, but not at the same time. One action cannot become both holy Dharma *and* worldly dharma because they are complete opposites. The Kadampa *geshé* Potowa[10] said that "a two-pointed needle cannot be used for sewing cloth."

One day, when Dromtönpa[11] came across an old man circumambulating a temple, he asked him what he was doing. The old man replied, "I am practicing Dharma." Dromtönpa replied, "It is good that you are circumambulating the temple, but wouldn't it be better to practice Dharma?" The man thought that maybe he should be studying instead, so he stopped his circumambulations and started to read the scriptures. Again, Dromtönpa saw him and asked what he was doing and again the old man replied he was practicing Dharma, to which Dromtönpa replied. "It is good that you are reading the scriptures, but wouldn't it be better to practice Dharma?" So, the old man stopped that and, deciding that meditating must be practicing Dharma, started doing that. When Dromtönpa saw him meditating, he asked the same question and, getting the same reply, said, "It is good that you are meditating, but wouldn't it be better to practice Dharma?" By now, the old man was very confused and so he asked Dromtönpa, "What do you mean by practicing Dharma?" Dromtönpa just said, "Renounce this life!"

Renouncing this life means subduing the mind. Whether we live in a monastery or a big city, whether we are a monk or nun or a lay person with a family, a job, and a busy life, if what we do helps to subdue our mind, that is practicing Dharma.

Cultivating a Compassionate Motivation

When we come to understand the mind through meditation, we not only see the importance of meditation, we also automatically know how to do everything else skillfully—how to eat, how to wash, how to do our job, even how to sleep. If we don't know this, nothing becomes the Dharma. We might be at the very top of our profession, but if our motivation is a selfish one, our job is of no use at all; it is only the cause of suffering.

The texts, for instance *Liberation in the Palm of Your Hand* by Pabongka Dechen Nyingpo, talk about four people practicing the Dharma with four different motivations. The first person meditates with the motivation to achieve enlightenment for the sake of all other sentient beings; the second to achieve liberation; the third to achieve happiness in future lives; and the fourth only seeking happiness in this life.

The actions of the first three people are all actions of holy Dharma. The fourth person's action, however, is not holy Dharma; it is worldly dharma because it is done with worldly concern, clinging to this life. The motivation is nonvirtuous and the result will be a suffering rebirth. So, even though the activity might be a Dharma one, the person's action does not become holy Dharma.

Here we can clearly see the borderline between Dharma and non-Dharma, between virtue and nonvirtue, between the cause of happiness and the cause of suffering. The fourth person's action of giving money (or meditating, or reciting Tara prayers) does not become the cause of achieving full enlightenment or liberation. It does not even become the cause of happiness in future lives.

With a positive motivation, however, everything we do leads to happiness, the happiness of future lives, of liberation, or of enlightenment, depending on the level of motivation. It is our choice. It's like our mind is a television set and we can choose which channel we want to watch, one showing a peaceful movie or one showing a violent one. Depending on our motivation, we can choose virtue and happiness or nonvirtue and unhappiness. Unless we know that, there is the danger that we can waste our whole life doing many various things, even meditating, that only plant the seeds for unhappiness.

Meditation can transform the dissatisfied mind into one of satisfaction and contentment; it can transform the impatient, angry mind into a patient, loving one; it can transform a selfish mind into one cherishing others. This is at the heart of any Dharma activity we do.

The Buddha says,

> Do not commit any unwholesome actions.
> Engage in perfect, wholesome actions.
> Subdue one's own mind.
> This is the teaching of the Buddha.[12]

Abandoning harm is the very basic practice. Unless we can do that, there is no possibility of developing our mind further. Our motivation must at least be to attain another higher rebirth so we can continue the spiritual path. But it should be more than that. We need to not only not harm others but to help them, to "engage in perfect wholesome actions." In order to best help all sentient beings, we should make the motivation for everything we do the attainment of enlightenment.

So, we need to start each meditation session with a pure motivation, by the loving-compassionate thought of attaining enlightenment. For instance, with a breathing meditation, we should think, "I'm going to practice this breathing meditation in order to attain enlightenment for the benefit of all the sentient beings." When done with this pure motivation, even if we just meditate for a few minutes, besides creating the cause for our own happiness, all the way up to enlightenment, it can benefit all sentient beings. Then, we happily bear whatever hardships our meditation brings—pains in the knees or the backside, getting tired, and so forth—because it is so worthwhile, so meaningful.

COMBINING STUDY, REFLECTION, AND MEDITATION

In Tibetan Buddhism, especially within the Geluk tradition,[13] there is a great emphasis on detailed study of a subject before we meditate on it. Many people fail to see the reason for this, thinking that we should surely just be able to start meditating straight away. But it makes little sense, especially with analytical meditations, to think we can do the meditation before we understand the topic of the meditation.

We might dream we can become a great meditator, but it won't happen. It's like going to a car showroom where super-expensive cars are sold, dreaming we can buy one, when in fact we don't have a penny in our pocket. This is a very childish way to think. When people first attend a meditation course, however, they often think all they have to do is sit there and wait for something magical to happen to their mind. They have no idea about the fundamentals of meditation. Just sitting and hoping something will happen isn't that beneficial.

In *Thirty-Seven Practices of the Bodhisattva*, the highly realized being Thokmé Sangpo says,

> Having gained this rare ship of freedom and fortune,
> Hear, think, and meditate unwaveringly night and day
> In order to free yourself and others
> From the ocean of cyclic existence—
> This is the practice of bodhisattvas.[14]

His teaching shows us the stages we must go through to progress to enlightenment:

- listen to and study the subject matter carefully
- reflect on what we have studied to eliminate doubts
- meditate to make it one with our mind

The first stage is understanding the subject, listening to the teachings by following a perfectly qualified teacher. Even a little understanding of the benefits of listening to the Dharma will give us the conviction that the more we study the richer will be our understanding. We see that even if we cannot understand the subject well now, this not through some fault in the teachings but through our own obscured mind, and that by continuing to listen and study, any doubts will be clarified.

In *The Great Treatise on the Stages of the Path to Enlightenment* (*Lamrim Chenmo*) Lama Tsongkhapa[15] says,

> First *study* with someone what you intend to practice, and come to know it secondhand. Next, use scripture and reasoning to properly *reflect* on the meaning of what you have studied, coming to know it firsthand. Once you determine the meaning of what you originally intended to practice with this kind of study and reflection and you have no doubts, then familiarize yourself with it repeatedly. We call this repeated familiarization "meditation." ... *Meditation* means becoming familiar with what you have ascertained using the wisdom that comes from reflection.[16]

Whereas some other traditions assert that analyzing a subject is not meditation, in the *Lamrim Chenmo*, Lama Tsongkhapa says clearly that analyzing is itself a meditation.

If we go into a solitary place and try to meditate without having studied and reflected, we can make a lot of mistakes. Instead of steadily developing our mind on the path to enlightenment, we can waste a lot of time. Therefore, at the beginning we should extensively listen and study, and, while studying, we need to contemplate the meaning as deeply as we can. Whenever we listen to a teaching or read a Dharma book, we use what we are studying to overcome our delusions and subdue our mind. That becomes a real meditation.

We need these three levels of ever-deepening understanding because the Dharma is a new subject for us, a new path that our mind has not traveled before. Unlike an academic subject we study at university, we need to not only know the subject but also to become thoroughly familiar with it.

Most meditations involve both analytical meditation and fixed meditation, and analysis comes from correct understanding. It is said that the person who meditates without first listening is like an armless rock climber. Therefore, it is necessary to listen and study as much as possible at the beginning. The Buddhist teachings are vast. One meditation is insufficient to solve all the problems in our life and each subject requires deep contemplation.

Study is meditation, meditation is study. Listening to explanations, studying texts, reflecting on the meaning, practicing meditation—these are the elements to actualize the path to enlightenment, and they are not separate. Dromtönpa explains, "While I am listening, I am reflecting. While I am reflecting, I am meditating." According to the Kadampa tradition, these three things are practiced without separation.

GAINING REALIZATIONS

The first reason for extensively studying the Buddhist teachings, with all their reasonings and logic, is to gain the realizations of the path, where we progress from a conceptual understanding of a Dharma subject to a nonconceptual direct experience, our mind and its subject becoming indistinguishable, like pouring water into water, effecting a deep change within us.

The other reason is to make our understanding stable, unshakeable. Unless our understanding is profound, we can easily be misled by those with wrong views. Somebody can tell us something that attracts us, causing us to discard our correct understanding and become confused, developing many wrong concepts.

Attaining realizations depends on having sufficiently ripened our mindstream. Unless we have assembled the right conditions, no matter how hard we try nothing much will happen. Pabongka Dechen Nyingpo compares it to having a boil where, if we are impatient and squeeze it too soon, it will be reinfected, whereas if we do it at the right time, the pus will come out and it will heal. We can also compare it to a piece of fruit; we must wait until it is ripe to enjoy it. Likewise, only when we have sufficiently purified our mindstream and accumulated enough merit will we be able to attain a realization.

This will not happen though meditation alone. This is the advice that Manjushri gave Lama Tsongkhapa, that we must integrate these three practices: purifying our negativities, accumulating merit, and meditating on the path.

Furthermore, Manjushri explained that the quickest way to accumulate merit and purify negativities, and thus attain realizations, is by remembering that the guru is oneness with the deity and praying to him or her. Then, finally there is meditation! That is because without the accumulation of merit and purification that comes from depending on the guru, just putting effort into meditation alone does not bring the complete experience of that meditation. This type of guru practice opens our mind, like a ripening fruit.

Meditating on the stages of the path in order to become enlightened is the biggest trip we will ever take. It is the most fantastic thing we can do, but also the most difficult. It's a huge step, and because of that there are bound to be a lot of hindrances. But once this trip is finished, *everything* is finished.

People who have earnestly followed the advice of the guru with a very sincere heart have seen the advantages, even after meditating for a very short time. Meditation is all about transforming the mind, and sincerely doing a guru practice is the most powerful way to transform the mind.

Some students have this experience when they are in retreat. After a long period of purifying, accumulating merit, and meditating where little seems to be happening, suddenly it feels like there is a big change, and they find incredible meaning in the prayers that they have been reciting for so long. Suddenly, each word seems so precious, so holy, that tears flow from their eyes. This kind of positive emotion is a sign that they have achieved some degree of purification and received some blessing from their guru. Even if it doesn't happen that strongly, we can still suddenly sense our meditations becoming very effective, cutting through delusions like a very sharp knife.

In the beginning, both analytical and fixed meditations are what is called effortful; they both require us putting effort into gaining results. For instance, we meditate on a lamrim topic such as perfect human rebirth using analytical meditations until we have a strong feeling and then we stabilize that with a fixed meditation. Building up a familiarity with a subject through study, reflection, and meditation for a long time in this way requires effort.

Often, meditators try to gain an effortful experience of each of the topics of the path—perfect human rebirth, impermanence, emptiness, and so forth—and then spend more time on one topic until it becomes effortless and they attain a realization. Then they move to the next topic and try to attain a realization of that, and so on. More capable meditators practice all the meditations together, without spending time separately on one. There comes a time when their meditation becomes effortless. In that way they can very quickly gain realizations and progress on the path.

The Five Paths and Ten Bhumis

Although the way they are described and the goals to be attained are slightly different, both the Hinayana and the Mahayana traditions[17] talk about the five paths we must progress through to attain our final goal. They are the following:

- the path of merit
- the path of preparation

- the path of right seeing
- the path of meditation
- the path of no more learning

Within the Mahayana tradition, the first path, the *path of merit*, refers to the period when we accumulate merit by listening to the Dharma, reflecting on the meaning, meditating, and so forth, to fully realize the teachings. With the *path of preparation* we gain a penetrative insight into emptiness, where the conceptual understanding of emptiness is conjoined with a very deep meditative experience, but we have yet to realize it directly, so we are still an ordinary being.

Then, through the continual meditation on emptiness, we enter the *path of right seeing*. Before, our understanding of emptiness was mixed with conceptualizations, but now it is a direct realization. We become an *arya* being. We no longer have to involuntarily go through death and therefore to experience rebirth, old age, sickness, and yet another death again.

With the *path of meditation*, our direct realization of emptiness becomes stabilized and continuous. Because there are still very subtle residual defilements, during the fourth path we work on slowly destroying even these.

From the time of realizing emptiness directly on the third path until the last path we develop through the ten *bhumis* (literally, *grounds*) or stages, and it is when we achieve the tenth *bhumi* while on the fifth path, the *path of no more learning*, that we attain enlightenment.

Even when they achieve the first *bhumi*, a bodhisattva can go to a hundred different buddha pure lands and receive teachings from the buddhas there at the same time. They can manifest in a hundred realms and, with a hundred different bodies at the same time, give teachings to sentient beings. They can abide in that state for a hundred eons. Then, when they achieve the second bodhisattva *bhumi*, they can go to a thousand different buddha pure lands and receive teachings and manifest into a thousand bodies to give teachings to sentient beings. With each succeeding *bhumi* the numbers increase—with the eighth, ninth, and tenth *bhumis* the bodhisattva can go to billions and zillions of pure lands and manifest in billions and zillions of forms, getting ever closer to enlightenment. What a bodhisattva can do to benefit sentient beings is so amazing it doesn't fit our ordinary, limited concepts.

In the Hinayana tradition, the vehicle of individual liberation, once all five paths are complete, suffering is completely overcome and nirvana or liberation is attained. From a Mahayana perspective, although such a state is amazing, there is further we can go; we need to continue to try to free all sentient beings by entering the Mahayana path and actualizing bodhichitta. Then, as a bodhisattva, we go on to practice the bodhisattva's activities, the six perfections or *paramitas* and the four means of drawing disciples to the Dharma.[18] Then, having worked through the five paths and attained the path of no more learning—enlightenment—we can work perfectly for the welfare of all sentient beings.

This is the path according to the Paramitayana, the nontantric aspect of the Mahayana, but it is also possible to attain enlightenment extremely quickly by entering the Vajrayana or tantric path once we have actualized the common path of renouncing samsara, attaining bodhichitta, and realizing emptiness.

Only with highest yoga tantra can we attain enlightenment within one brief lifetime in this degenerate time. Having received an initiation from a qualified vajra master, when our mind is ripened, we can practice the generation stage and the completion stage. When we attain the final stage of the completion stage, called the union of clear light and illusory body, we achieve the unification of no more learning, the fully enlightened state.

FAR-SIGHTEDNESS, DETERMINATION, AND A RELAXED MIND

Generating the realizations of the graduated path to enlightenment is a new experience. Because we have never done this before, we need to put as much effort as possible into developing our mind. We should not have a little mind.

We need three things to best progress on the path:

- far-sightedness
- strong determination
- a relaxed mind

We need to be very far-sighted, seeing that it will take a long time and much effort to achieve our goal of enlightenment. To achieve all the realizations, we must follow the path step by step.

For that, we need to generate a very strong and vast mind, which means the determination to never give up, even if it takes three countless great eons to purify our negativities and accumulate the merit we need to achieve enlightenment.

There is so much to study and meditate on that we can get stressed, thinking our goal is impossible and can never be achieved. This becomes a hindrance to continuing our meditations. We need to move forward slowly and determinedly, but in a relaxed way, because our goal, attaining enlightenment for all beings, is so vast.

Guru Shakyamuni Buddha[19] and numberless sentient beings who have become enlightened were the same as us in having all the delusions, all the problems that we now have, and yet they continuously put effort into developing their minds life after life, for eons and eons. We should think in the same way and make plans that span eons, instead of thinking that if we do some meditation now we will achieve enlightenment within a few years.

His Holiness the Dalai Lama often advises us not to be shortsighted; don't assume enlightenment will come in a very short time, but instead plan for many hundreds of lifetimes. If we plan to practice Dharma for a long time and put much effort into our practice with that goal, it is possible we might actually be able to achieve enlightenment in a short time. But if we don't have a plan like that, if we are shortsighted, we can very easily become disillusioned and give up when it doesn't happen.

As Shantideva says in *A Guide to the Bodhisattva's Way of Life*,

There is nothing that will remain difficult after practice,
therefore, if one first practices
with less severe afflictions,
even the greatest torments will become bearable.[20]

If we train our mind, it becomes easier and easier. That is the nature of the mind. Because it is a dependent arising, arising in dependence on causes and conditions, the mind can be changed. Our mind did not begin from this birth; it has no beginning. Because it has been habituated with delusions from beginningless rebirths, of course it is not easy to change. Therefore, we must expect that transforming it into a virtuous mind, habituating it to positive attitudes, is going to take a very long time. Certainly, to realize our full potential and attain enlightenment may well take hundreds of lifetimes, maybe even eons.

Just doing one retreat, such as the one-month group retreat we hold in Kopan Monastery[21] in Nepal every year, and expecting huge changes is unrealistic. Of course, how quickly we realize the meditations differs with each person. It depends on our level of intelligence, on our practice and understanding, and on how much purification we do. But a month of intensive meditation cannot bring us ultimate happiness; it's not that easy. Countless lifetimes of delusions cannot be wiped away within a week or a month, just as putting drops of honey each day on an acidic plant growing in the garden cannot make it sweet. It's not like putting a few coins in an automatic vending machine, pressing a button, and watching a packet of food pop out!

Unless we have a long-term plan, it will be very difficult to bear the many hardships we will encounter as we purify our negativities and accumulate merit. But once we have a plan and start implementing it, it is not like a worldly action, which we must continuously do again and again. Eating something does not satisfy our hunger forever. In a short while, we are hungry again and have to eat something else. Like this, our need for food never finishes. This is true of all worldly activities; there is no end to the effort we must continuously put into attaining worldly ends.

Dharma work is completely different. Once we complete Dharma work, it is finished. When we attain a realization, we don't have to start again and re-attain it. Therefore, it is worth our while to make a long-term plan, thinking, "Even if it takes many lifetimes, even if it takes one hundred lifetimes, a billion lifetimes, I have to cut off all the wrong conceptions and attain enlightenment to benefit other sentient beings."

When we couple such a long view with great determination, having the will and patience to endure many difficulties, it is possible to achieve enlightenment in this life or within three lifetimes or within sixteen lifetimes.

The final attribute we need is having a relaxed attitude. We cannot progress if we have a tight mind. Even people in worldly life with big projects, such as those who build huge factories, must be relaxed as well as determined, or their projects collapse. They make so many plans and go through such hardships before the project even starts, and then they work with great determination, no matter how long it takes. Getting uptight because things are not happening quickly enough only causes stress and maybe failure, so they move ahead slowly but determinedly. Likewise, we need to move forward slowly and determinedly in our Dharma practice, but in a relaxed way.

These three things—being far-sighted, determined, and having a relaxed mind—are vital. Without them, it is very difficult to generate the realizations of the path and achieve enlightenment. With them, enlightenment is definitely possible—within a very short time, if the conditions come together. Because we have this perfect human rebirth, we have this amazing potential.

We have everything we need, unlike Milarepa, the great Tibetan meditator. Other than a place to meditate and a pot to cook with, he had nothing, absolutely no money, and not even any clothes other than a scrap to cover himself. And what he ate was nettle soup, day after day after day. Because of that, he was of course very skinny, but also his skin turned a bluish color from the diet. There was no salt, no chili, no oil—only nettles.

One day a thief came to Milarepa's cave and, when he could find nothing to steal, Milarepa cooked him nettle soup. When the thief asked for some salt and chili to spice the soup, Milarepa put a few more nettles in the pot and said, "This is the salt," and then a few more and said, "This is the chili." There was nothing else, just nettles, and yet Milarepa was totally satisfied. With no material possessions at all, living a life so austere we can't even imagine, he was still able to achieve enlightenment in one short lifetime. If he managed that, why is it impossible for us?

2. TYPES OF MEDITATION

THERE ARE TWO TYPES of meditation:

- analytical or checking meditation (*vicarabhavana, ché gom*)
- fixed or single-pointed meditation (*sthapyabhavana, jok gom*)

Both are vital if we wish to attain enlightenment. Analytical or checking meditation is so called because we analyze a subject to attain a deeper understanding. Analytical meditation is most helpful at the beginning of our practice. This kind of meditation expands the knowledge of our mind, clarifies the nature of the object we are meditating on, and enables us to gain correct understanding and realizations. Unless we carefully analyze our subject, the possibility of wrong understanding is great.

In fixed or single-pointed meditation, the mind stays single-pointedly on the object it is focusing on. Once our concentration is strengthened to the point where we can maintain this for a long time, free from distraction and wandering, our mind becomes very powerful.

ANALYTICAL MEDITATION

Except for shamatha, calm abiding meditation, which is intense concentration on one object, most of the meditations we do—on renunciation, bodhichitta, emptiness, and so forth—are principally analytical meditations: checking and reasoning with quotations and logic.

Within our analytical meditation, however, there should also be fixed meditation. For example, when we become distracted while meditating on a subject like the precious human rebirth, it is easy to lose any concentration we have, but if we can firmly hold on to the subject we are meditating on, then this is a kind of fixed meditation. Within the analysis we are doing, there is a stable concentration even though it is not an actual fixed meditation practice. If we are doing a tantric practice, from the beginning when we take the refuge until we finish, while going through the various prayers and visualizations, if we hold our concentration and don't allow the mind to wander off, this too is a kind of fixed meditation.

Gaining realizations requires both types of meditation, but only through sharp analysis can we reach a degree of familiarity that allows the realization to happen. For instance, if we are meditating on refuge, we need to see how the Buddha is completely trustworthy, how his teachings are utterly infallible, and how countless practitioners have gained enlightenment by relying on his teachings. We need a strong and sharp analytical practice on points such as this to move the mind toward a realization.

The analysis we do within a meditation is different from a Western scientist's analysis, which is principally to gain knowledge. This analysis is to subdue the mind, to get out of the oceans of samsaric suffering and to become free from the causes of suffering—ignorance, anger, attachment, and all the other suffering minds. Not only that, we should also be doing it to liberate others. Whatever meditation we do, analytical or fixed, that is its purpose.

Analysis is vital if we want to understand our mind and why we suffer, if we want to see how things are impermanent and free ourselves from the false sense of permanence that brings so many problems, and if we want to understand the nature of reality, how all things including our sense of self are empty of any inherent existence. Because misunderstanding this emptiness is the root of all suffering and because emptiness is a very subtle object to be understood, the analytical meditation required for this is very profound and difficult.

We cannot just accept; we must check for ourselves and see how these subjects are profound truths, and then take that understanding deeper. Even in our daily life, we don't buy something without checking it—where it was made, what it is made from, whether it will work, whether it is worth it, and so forth. We always check the freshness and the value of the food we buy. Before we part with *any* money at all, we check very carefully!

Analyzing a Dharma subject is infinitely more important than checking items we buy in a shop. We might get sick from eating something past its use-by date or waste our money on a product that doesn't work, but our inattention doesn't make us create negative karma. Unless we clearly know why we are meditating, we can presume it is worthwhile but we could be actually increasing our ignorance. Therefore, checking through analysis is vital.

Seeing analysis as a hindrance to meditation rather than actually *being* meditation is cheating ourselves, moving us further from wisdom and closer to ignorance. Thinking that analysis is a hindrance to our meditation is an extremely foolish way of thinking.

Within Tibetan Buddhism, we have a wealth of subjects to analyze and realize, most of which fit into the framework of the lamrim, the graduated path to enlightenment. If we want to transform our mind through meditation, the wisest choice we can make is to meditate on the lamrim subjects, which bring many benefits, the greatest one undoubtedly being that they lead us directly to enlightenment.

The lamrim is a comprehensive explanation of the entire eighty-four thousand teachings of the Buddha. The subjects that lead us to individual liberation come from the earlier teachings of the Buddha within the Pali canon, named after the language that was used. In the Mahayana, this is called the Hinayana tradition and contains the vital teaching on the four noble truths as well as the noble eightfold path.[22] Following the teachings of this vehicle, or *yana*, we can free ourselves from the whole of samsara and its causes: karma and delusions.

Then, there is the Mahayana or Great Vehicle, which focuses on bodhichitta, the altruistic mind that wants to attain full enlightenment for the sake of all sentient beings. This has two divisions: the Paramitayana or Perfection Vehicle, and the Vajrayana, where, within highest tantra practices, we can attain enlightenment in one lifetime.

All levels of teachings contained in the lamrim are summarized in the Buddha's fundamental advice to not commit unwholesome actions, to engage only in wholesome ones, and to thoroughly subdue the mind.

To not commit any unwholesome actions and therefore refrain from harming others is the core of the Hinayana teachings. In the lamrim, this fits into subjects that come within the graduated path of a lower capable being and the graduated path of a middle capable being, where the motivation is to attain a higher rebirth and liberation from samsara respectively. To engage in perfect, wholesome actions and therefore to benefit others fits into the graduated path of a higher capable being, where the motivation is bodhichitta, wishing to attain enlightenment to free all beings from suffering and lead them to enlightenment. The whole path to enlightenment is there. The words are incredibly simple, but within the teaching there are so many levels, so much to study, so much to meditate on, so much to actualize.

FIXED MEDITATION

Fixed meditation can be defined as holding the mind single-pointedly on an object, unobscured by either sinking thoughts or scattering thoughts. The essential way of accomplishing this single-pointedness is to bring the mind to the object of meditation, such as the breath, and hold it there, and to be able to return it to the object whenever it wanders. The aim is to not forget the object of meditation, to continually remember it as long as we want. At first, this can happen only for a short period before the mind gets distracted and wanders off to another object, but, if we continue, we will be able to hold the object for longer and longer periods. When we can single-pointedly concentrate on a chosen object, thoughts of past, present, or future do not arise, freeing us from all fears or excitement. There is just the experience of the object of meditation.

The vital tools we need to achieve stronger and stronger concentration are *mindfulness* and *awareness*, where with mindfulness we are conscious we are still concentrating, and with awareness we are watching to see what is happening. If the mind moves off the object, awareness sees this, and we can bring the mind back. Developing these two minds is the very root of what we call *shamatha*, or calm abiding.

For us beginners, holding the object is difficult. For that reason, at first we should keep our meditation sessions quite short, maybe only for ten or fifteen minutes initially. Lama Tsongkhapa recommends something like sixteen short sessions a day. Perhaps that is not necessary, but we need to do whatever length best suits our level of concentration. Although they should be short, during those sessions we must try to keep the concentration on the object as much as possible.

Initially, holding the object of meditation *clearly* is not that important. Say we are meditating on the visualization of a deity, if only half the deity appears to us, we should be satisfied with that, otherwise it might take days to even find a place to focus the mind. It is a great mistake to expect too much. If we put too much effort into trying to see the object clearly, it might work for a short time, but we will be unable to hold it and we will lose the meditation altogether, making it more difficult to develop our focus in future sessions. Putting too much effort into it early on becomes a cause for the mind to be distracted later.

The whole point is that from the very beginning we should be very skillful, kind of relaxed but not completely relaxed. If we are completely relaxed, we might meditate for many hours until somebody comes to wake us up! Or we might travel the whole world by sitting on the meditation cushion. It must be balanced, being both relaxed and effortful, the mind putting just the right degree of effort into focusing on the object.

COMBINING THE TWO

When we analyze the objects of our meditation, we are able to develop a full understanding of them in order to realize them. We are an inner scientist, probing the nature of reality, discovering the truths on the path to enlightenment. It is when we can combine the two types of meditation, analytical and fixed, that we effectively transform our mind into that path. Developing an ever-deeper understanding of the causes of the delusions that plague us, we can gradually remove them, leading to liberation from all suffering. Furthermore, by perfecting our analytical and fixed meditations on all the subjects of the graduated path to enlightenment, we can go on to full enlightenment and lead other sentient beings to the peerless happiness of enlightenment. This is a mind-blowing achievement!

Our aim is to realize on every level what we have discovered through reasoning within our analytical meditations. For example, having studied and meditated on the perfect human rebirth, we might logically understand we have this precious opportunity, but we still don't really feel it. However, as we continue to meditate on the various characteristics of the perfect human rebirth, we become increasingly convinced of the points covered within the subject. If we are meditating on the freedom of not being a hell being, say, we really come to understand just how awful such a state would be. A strong sense arises of how we are unbelievably fortunate to be free from it, how only with this precious life we now have can we develop our true potential. We then stop the analysis and hold that sense of gratitude. This is the fixed meditation that enhances the analytical one.

In this way, we alternate the analytical meditation on these points with the fixed meditation on the feeling that arises at the conclusion, doing this again and again, until we generate a realization of the point, a stable, irrefutable awareness that goes beyond logical understanding.

This is how we should proceed with all our meditations. Our analytical meditation on guru devotion concludes with a deep sense that the guru and the Buddha are indivisible, causing strong guru devotion to arise. Meditating on the nature of samsara leads us to the unwavering conviction that it is nothing but suffering and the strong determination to be free from it. And after meditating on bodhichitta, when the thought to become enlightened to help all sentient beings comes up very strongly in our meditation, we should try to hold that altruistic mind, living the rest of our day with that experience.

Although we might have quite a good intellectual understanding of something like the perfect human rebirth, having a realization of it could seem very far away. We have no need to worry. As long as we continue deepening our understanding within our meditation, the feeling will come. Each time we meditate, we get closer to the realization.

Sometimes, somebody without much knowledge of a subject gains a realization of it, maybe from just hearing the subject once or twice and then doing a bit of meditation. This is certainly because they have meditated on this subject in previous lifetimes and their mind was well trained then. For most of us, however, without much understanding of or conviction in the Dharma, we must work hard at it. Repeating a meditation over and over can become tiresome. That is mainly due to ignorance. The more we are convinced of how beneficial the Dharma is, the more inspired we will be and the more energy we will have to meditate. If we persevere, slowly our intellectual understanding will grow and our meditations will become deeper. One will feed the other.

The Glance Meditation

A very important thing we should do every day is to read a short meditation prayer called a *glance meditation* (also called a *direct meditation*), which contains the essence of the whole graduated path to enlightenment. There are many different types. It is called a glance meditation because we read the words without taking time to check on specific points. This allows us to get an overview of the whole path by going straight through the outlines, taking in the essence of the meditations. After reading the glance meditation prayer, if there is time, we can do an analytical meditation, concentrating on one aspect of one particular subject, such as impermanence.

Doing a glance meditation leaves an impression on the mind each day, making it easier to do a more detailed meditation later based on the outline that is in our mind from the glance meditation. In that way, we can more easily gain a deeper understanding of the meditation. If we don't have the chance to do a specific lamrim meditation within our daily practice, at least we are planting the seeds to later understand and realize the subjects.

I say we just read the words of the glance meditation prayer, but we must read them mindfully, not just say them without concentrating. Done mindfully, it becomes a direct meditation on the whole path to enlightenment—both sutra and tantra. Because it leaves an imprint and makes the rest of our day meaningful, I would say that doing a glance meditation on the lamrim mindfully is one of the *most* important practices we can do. Just as there is the expression "an apple a day keeps the doctor away," we can perhaps say that a lamrim meditation a day keeps the lower realms away.

The more of an imprint we can leave, the easier and quicker it will be to actualize the graduated path to enlightenment. Either in this life or in future lives, as soon as we hear the teachings, we will experience the path. For instance, as soon as we hear the teachings on emptiness, we will immediately be able to experience it. Many meditators have had this experience.

Pabongka Dechen Nyingpo explains that even just doing a glance meditation on the lamrim is much more meaningful than reciting hundreds of millions of mantras or even seeing the buddhas. Why? Because even if we actually meet a buddha, we still have to meditate on and actualize renunciation, bodhichitta, and emptiness, as well as the two stages of highest tantra. Just seeing a buddha will not give us these realizations.

Kadampa geshé Chen Ngawa[23] was asked by one of his disciples, Puchungwa,[24] which he would prefer if he had the choice between meditating on the lamrim or having single-pointed concentration that could last for eons, so focused that even a big drum beaten in front of him could not disturb him. Chen Ngawa said that just inquiring about the nature of the lamrim is preferable to having the five types of clairvoyance. We have achieved all those psychic powers in the past, but we have not achieved the graduated path to enlightenment; this is a completely new experience. Therefore, it is essential.

VISUALIZATION

Using Analytical and Fixed Meditation in Visualization

When we try to visualize a deity in a tantric practice, we are either trying to see ourselves as the deity, which is called "self-generation," or to see the buddha in front of us, which is called "front generation." For both, we need to use both types of meditation: analytical meditation, where we try to go over the various aspects of the deity's appearance, and fixed meditation, where we hold on to one aspect or the whole.

A fixed meditation on ourselves as the deity has two aspects. One is *pure appearance* (*sel nang*), where we imagine ourselves as the deity, and the other is *divine pride* (*lhayi ngagyal*), where, by holding that appearance, we dispel the sense of ourselves as an ordinary deluded being. With analytical meditation we achieve pure appearance and with fixed meditation we achieve divine pride.

Many people feel discouraged because they feel their visualizations are not good. It often happens that we might achieve quite good visualizations in the beginning, but after a few days they seem to degenerate and we get fed up. We should not feel discouraged, especially when we are trying to visualize a deity in a tantric practice. Even if we can't make the visualization clear, with each aspect of the deity perfect, we should just concentrate on the general feeling as much as we can. Feeling we are in the presence of the Buddha is more important than how clearly we see him.

It is like somebody who writes wonderful letters but whose handwriting is terrible. What they write is more important than their handwriting. Similarly, while trying to make the visualization as clear as possible, because it is the most powerful and positive object there is, whatever we can manage will be incredibly beneficial.

For instance, when we are supposed to imagine rays of light entering us from the Buddha and purifying us, even when we can hardly visualize the Buddha at all, if we feel that this is what is happening, it makes our meditation very meaningful. We receive incredible blessings, no matter how imperfect our visualization of the Buddha is. The strength of our purification comes from our devotion to the Buddha and to the guru, not from our ability to visualize well. So, we should not be discouraged but just continue with whatever visualization we can manage and concentrate as much as we can.

Lama Tsongkhapa advises that, because it is the more important, we first try to establish some degree of calm abiding without being bothered too much by lack of clarity in our visualization. The main thing is to establish our concentration and then, when that is quite good, we try to establish clear appearance. By doing that, all the aspects of the visualization—the head, arms, and so forth—come very easily. It is like when a sculptor makes a statue. First, the shape is very crude; maybe we can hardly tell which deity it is going to be. But then, as the sculptor continues, the very detailed, very beautiful image of the deity emerges.

Trying to evoke all the details of a deity such as Shakyamuni Buddha or Chenrezig in a visualization involves analytical meditation on each detail one by one, from the head down to feet, until we have the whole aspect as it is explained in whatever *sadhana*[25] (meditation manual) we use. Even a simple deity like Tara is a complex visualization, so we will almost certainly be unable to see every detail vividly. Concentrating single-pointedly on whatever we can manage, we can then slowly expand that to the rest of body: the limbs, the hands, the ornaments, and so forth. Then, when all *that* is clear, we move to the mandala—the divine abode of the deity—and the other deities in the mandala if there are any, until even the small details appear vividly. Finally, we are able to concentrate single-pointedly on the whole mandala.

When our visualization becomes unclear, we can repeat an analytical meditation on the various features of the deity and then focus on the general aspect, on whatever comes up in our mind. We carry on like this until the visualization becomes as clear as possible.

If we try to make our visualization clear by tightly concentrating, we will be unable to sustain it; we will lose our concentration very quickly and scattering thoughts will certainly arise. But if our concentration is too loose, if we are too relaxed, sinking thoughts will arise; there will be little energy to hold the object of meditation. More than sinking thoughts, fogginess can happen. Then a very comfortable sleep comes! His Holiness Zong Rinpoché[26] says that this kind of sleep in meditation is much more pleasant than the sleep we have at bedtime.

The skill is not being too tight. A little bit of clarity can come when we squeeze a little bit, but although it looks beneficial, it doesn't help the development of our concentration because it doesn't last. Rather, it becomes a cause of further distractions. At the beginning, it is actually a hindrance to try to get every detail of the deity perfect. This will come in time. As the commentaries explain, as we develop our skill at concentrating and the mind gets more relaxed, our visualization will become clearer and clearer. Then, after some time, it becomes unbelievably clear, even clearer than the eye can see.

The main point to understand is that at the beginning what we are trying to do is lengthen the period we are able to concentrate. Whenever the mind becomes distracted, we bring it back to the object, the general aspect of the deity. That is the very first step.

The Importance of Visualizing the Buddha

Buddhas appear in many aspects. They can emanate in a *sambhogakaya* (enjoyment body) aspect, which is how many of the tantric deities are depicted in *thangkas*,[27] or in a *nirmanakaya* (emanation body) aspect, one that we humans can see and relate to, such as the way the Buddha is depicted in pictures: sitting in meditation posture, dressed as a monk. In the twenty-first century, we don't have the karma to see Guru Shakyamuni Buddha in his *sambhogakaya* aspect, or even his *nirmanakaya* aspect, but that does not mean that we don't see the Buddha. When we see a statue or picture of the historical Buddha or one of the many buddhas depicted in Tibetan Buddhism, we are seeing the Buddha.

Just seeing an image of the Buddha, just being in the presence of one, we automatically become calmer and more peaceful. We find we can concentrate better, and negative thoughts drop away. Even though we can't articulate it, we get a good feeling from being near a statue or thangka. This is the power of a Buddha image. We feel the peace radiating from the statue and we think that we too would like to have that peace.

This power works on a very deep level. Although we can study the symbolism of all the different aspects of the Buddha's body, we don't need to know that to receive the benefits. Just seeing the crown protrusion, the long ears, the long, gentle eyes, we are comforted, whether we know how they work at a subconscious level or not. When we have an idea of all the incredible qualities of the Buddha that these represent, we are naturally inspired to direct our actions so that we too can acquire these qualities. Just the sight of a Buddha image can be the trigger to start the whole road to enlightenment.

Some people think that visualization meditations are just playing games with images and that real meditation is pure concentration. They somehow feel that visualizing the Buddha is a kind of distraction to the real business of meditation, which is to control the mind. This is completely wrong. By visualizing Guru Shakyamuni Buddha or another deity, we control the mind in the most positive way.

We are always doing visualizations anyway. Our mind is always full of images, as we think about what we want to do later in the day or remember a dinner we had with a friend. The difference with these worldly visualizations, however, is that they almost always involve objects of attachment or aversion. We think of our dear friend, or that delicious dinner, and attachment naturally arises; we remember the argument we had at work with our boss and aversion naturally arises. Therefore, our normal visualizations only increase our ignorance.

It is entirely the opposite when we visualize the Buddha. By holding the mind on an image of the Buddha, we diminish the dualistic mind, we transcend our attachment and aversion, and we plant the seeds for becoming like that visualization—in other words, a buddha ourselves. It is the power of the holy image that just by visualizing it, no matter how inexpertly, it purifies eons of negativities. It becomes the remedy for the deluded mind and the cause of a very quick enlightenment.

Lama Tsongkhapa made prostrations while visualizing thirty-five aspects of Guru Shakyamuni, and as a result, he saw the Buddha on the walls of his cave. In the same cave, which still exists in Tibet, Khedrup Jé, one of his two main disciples, saw the manifestation of Lama Tsongkhapa and letters such as Manjushri's seed syllable,[28] which appeared spontaneously due to the power of Lama Tsongkhapa's purification practice. If our minds are purified and we have devotion, it is certain that we will be able to see the different aspects of Buddha.

This doesn't mean that the Buddha, the person who lived 2,500 years ago, was exactly like the depiction in the thangkas. Actually, the shape of the Buddha's holy body is beyond all that. What we see is just an approximation created so we sentient beings can purify our negativities and create merit. Even a symbolic representation of the Buddha or any of the other deities has so much power to affect the mind.

Although we can use any image to develop shamatha, for a Buddhist there is no more powerful object of meditation than the image of the Buddha or of the meditational deity we normally practice. Visualizing the aspect of any enlightened being can never cause the negative mind to arise. Each time we see a thangka or statue of the Buddha, it purifies our negative karma. This is not due to what it is made from, whether it is gold or some other valuable material, but to the power of the Buddha's holy omniscient mind, his great compassion and love, his bodhichitta. The impression it leaves on our mind can not only close the door to the lower realms—meaning we will never have to be reborn there in the future—but each time we look at a representation of the Buddha, it creates the karma to meet his teachings and see him directly in future lifetimes.

In the usual Guru Shakyamuni Buddha practice, after visualizing the Buddha and saying the mantra, when the Buddha absorbs into us, all our delusions and wrong views become completely empty, and our mind becomes one with Guru Shakyamuni Buddha's blissful omniscient mind. This very profound technique can be found in the *Daily Meditation on Shakyamuni Buddha*.[29]

The Need for Analytical Meditation

As we have seen, some people think that there is no need to study in order to meditate. They feel we should just be able to sit down and start meditating right away, without need for any understanding. Rejecting analytical meditation, not seeing it as meditation, is faulty thinking.

Other people believe that any thought that appears in a meditation is a distraction. They even reject the fact that with single-pointed meditation there must be an object of meditation. For them, meditation means making the mind blank. A person trying to meditate like this can easily believe that nothing exists. If they tried to meditate on how fire does not exist while they were sitting in the middle of a burning house, that would not make the fire nonexistent; they would still be burned. In the same way, meditating on nothing is the biggest hindrance to realizing how things actually exist.

How can meditating on nothing, trying to hold our mind blank, help in any way to relieve our suffering? None of our delusions are diminished at all by stopping our thoughts in meditation. If the purpose of our meditation is freedom from suffering rather than just simple relaxation, we need to not only understand the mind but also understand and realize the nature of the self, and that can happen only through rigorous analysis.

Even in our daily life, we are never free from conceptual thoughts. We are always engaged in some form of rational analysis. To make lunch we need to discern what we need and assess how to best go about it. To have a cup of tea, we must determine what is tea, what is sugar, what is water, and so forth, and rationally follow a step-by-step procedure.

There is no way to live without thoughts, so when people think meditation requires us to empty our mind, they are deluded. When people say they have no thoughts while they are working, they probably mean they are in a sort of semi-conscious state, like sleeping, mindlessly doing the actions of working, eating, and so forth.

Whatever we do must become an antidote to our disturbing, obscuring thoughts. Even if we live in a solitary place like a cave for many years and bear so many hardships—not eating, not talking, not seeing anyone—if our meditation practice does not become the antidote to our delusions but instead becomes a support for them, particularly the attachment clinging to this life, it does not become Dharma; it just becomes another cause of suffering and the lower realms.

Just meditating does not mean that much unless we know *how* to meditate. Meditation must transform the mind. Otherwise, we might spend decades meditating for hours each day but still burst with excitement from a little bit of praise or become utterly depressed from a mild criticism. There is something wrong with our practice when our mind is unduly upset by external factors. Real Dharma protects the mind. Unless that happens, there is no real progress.

Mindfulness Is Not Enough

When we watch the breath in a breathing meditation, we naturally attain a degree of calmness and peace. This is excellent. It can immediately bring some peace to an agitated mind, like stopping to take a rest after working very hard or going into the shade to cool down when we are overheated from being in the sun. Our noisy mind becomes quiet. If that is the sole purpose of the meditation, it is still very worthwhile, but just watching the breath can do nothing to ultimately overcome our delusions. For that we need a range of meditations.

Merely practicing mindfulness, which in itself is neither positive nor negative, is not the most skillful way to live our life. We can be mindful and still create nonvirtuous actions mindfully. A bank robber needs to be extremely mindful, knowing when and where to break in and what to take, always watching to see if they have been spotted. If we wanted to steal something from our boss, for instance, we would have to watch carefully for a long time, knowing just the right time to break in to get the object, whether it was a hamburger or a precious jewel. And, after we had grabbed it, we would need to know how to make our escape. There's a lot to be mindful of!

We can be mindful of anything. "Now I'm eating, now I'm putting my spoon on the plate, now the food is going in the mouth, now it's being chewed, now it's being swallowed, now it's reaching the stomach." "Now I'm working." "Now the thorn has gone inside in my flesh." "Now attachment has arisen for that object and I am stealing it." Mindfulness alone is not enough. We might feel the action is nonvirtuous, but that doesn't stop us doing it. We can be aware that a sense of pride has arisen and simply continue to follow that nonvirtuous mind of pride, even though we are practicing mindfulness.

We not only have to be aware of what is happening in the mind but also watch to see whether our mind is virtuous or not. Checking for this is the best kind of mindfulness. For example, if we are doing a tantric meditation practice, although we may have begun with a genuine bodhichitta motivation, we still need to be mindful. Throughout the practice we should recheck our motivation, ensuring it is still one of bodhichitta. We might find that somehow it has slipped and self-cherishing has crept back in; we are now doing the meditation primarily for our own happiness. Mindfulness is a vital tool, but we need other methods to transform our mind.

Perfect Concentration Is Not Enough

Shamatha is not just a Buddhist practice. Hindu meditators can achieve perfect concentration with shamatha meditations, allowing them to attain the higher realms. Samsara has three realms: the desire realm, the form realm, and the formless realm. Relying on the external sense objects to experience pleasure is the defining feature of the desire realm, the realm we are in. When a meditator has seen the shortcomings of the desire realm—looking at the short lifespan, the many problems, the dissatisfaction, and so forth—they are attracted to the great peace of the form realm, which arises from the serenity gained through concentration. With that motivation, they overcome all attachment to the desire realm and attain the form realm. The attachment of the form realm is not to sense pleasure but to mental peace, but it is still attachment.

Then, for the form realm being, even the happiness of the form realm starts to seem gross, still in the nature of suffering, and they look at the formless realm, where they no longer have a corporeal form, as having superior peace and happiness. Feeling aversion for the comparative grossness of the form realm, they aspire to be reborn in the formless realm. It is like buying a car, but then, after a few years, thinking that it is so old and that the new model advertised on television is so much better, and so developing aversion to the old one and attachment to the idea of having the new one.

As their concentration increases, they are able to attain the formless realm and progress through its four states: *limitless sky, limitless consciousness, nothingness,* and *neither-existence-nor-nonexistence,* also called *the tip of samsara.* By thinking on the shortcomings of their current state and the advantages of the next, higher state, they finally reach the highest state in samsara, the tip of samsara. Having reached there, there is no higher state in samsara to aspire to. They have developed renunciation for the desire and form realms and the first three levels of the formless realms, but with no sense that there is anything beyond samsara, they cannot renounce the tip of samsara, and so they are unable to enter the path to liberation.

We too have attained the form and formless realms numberless times in our previous lives, and it has not helped us. It's nothing special. What we haven't attained in the past are the total renunciation of samsara, the realization of emptiness, and the attainment of bodhichitta, which are the three principal aspects of the path. Now, *that* is something very special.

With very advanced concentration come many psychic powers as a side effect. They are wonderful, but they too are nothing special. Meditators can attain powers such as flying, walking on water, and seeing the past and the future. But there is nothing wondrous about flying. Birds and even insects like flies and mosquitoes fly, and they are beings of the animal realm, not human beings. The ability to fly or walk on water, and so forth, is not the meaning of our human life. Somebody with the clairvoyance who can tell the past and predict the future cannot show the path to liberation and enlightenment. They might seem more charismatic than a qualified virtuous teacher, but the power to predict the future is not the meaning of our human life. It is nothing exceptional.

Clairvoyance is not new to us; it is a power we have all had countless times in our countless lives. It is not even some special human quality; there are some hungry ghosts[30] that can see very distant things and samsaric gods who can see where they were born before and what their future life will be. This power just happens through karma, it has not been attained through meditation.

We will look at how to develop shamatha later, but while attaining unshakable single-pointed concentration is a wonderful thing, that alone is not enough. It is not the meaning of our human life. We could have reached the stage of concentration where hundreds of planes flying overhead would be unable to disturb our meditation in the slightest, but that is nothing special; that is nothing new. We have experienced this level of concentration numberless times in our previous lives. It does not mean we have any degree of wisdom. Without realizing emptiness, nothing becomes a remedy to samsara. It is like our mind is sleeping.

The core of our practice must be the meditations that have the power to overcome our ignorance. Not even a powerful tantric practice, such as one where we concentrate on the *chakras* and vital energy channels[31] that run through our body, is enough. Without incorporating the three principal aspects of the path into such a practice, it cannot even become the cause of liberation, let alone a shortcut to enlightenment. The key is bodhichitta. We easily travel from one country to another in a plane, which is constructed of a fuselage, wings, an engine, and so forth, but the vital thing, the one that makes it move, is the fuel. In the same way, a tantric practice is an incredibly skillful means of progressing quickly toward enlightenment, but without the fuel of bodhichitta it is useless. Trying to attain bodhichitta is far more important than trying to understand and control the winds and chakras.

The job of meditation is to eliminate the very root of suffering, ignorance. For that we need to become skillful in knowing which meditations are needed at which point in our spiritual journey. Just as a doctor prescribes a specific medicine for a specific disease, choosing from the many medicines available, we need to cure our various mental diseases with the various meditations there are.

Physical disease can be cured with the right medicine, but it is not so easy with inner disease, the ignorance that brings us all our problems and all its incumbent delusions. We need to study the teachings of the Buddha to discover the benefits of overcoming these mental diseases, and then we need to apply the right medicine, the meditations that are the antidotes.

3. OBJECTS OF MEDITATION

....

To MEDITATE, we must meditate on something; there must be an object. To meditate on nothing is not meditation, just spacing out. His Holiness Zong Rinpoché explains that those who meditate on nothingness are creating the cause for the mind to become dull, losing its sharpness and memory. Because of that, we are either reborn as an animal or in the third level of the formless realm: nothingness.

When we try to meditate on nothingness, it is impossible to develop any wisdom at all. Wisdom realizes *something*, some subtle object that appears to exist but doesn't. Meditating on nothingness, on the other hand, can never make mind less negative; it can never diminish greed or hatred or help to destroy the ignorance that is the root of all delusions.

It is therefore important to be aware of the various objects of meditation and to choose which is the most suitable for us at our particular level of development. The breath is possibly the most common meditation object. There are also the various analytical objects and the objects used in shamatha meditations, as well as the various visualization meditations we can do, such as visualizing the Buddha or one of the deities in a tantric practice.

THE BREATH

Breathing Meditation Brings the Mind into a Neutral State

The breathing meditation, simply watching the breath, is said to be the simplest meditation. It is an ideal way to calm and focus the mind, especially when our mind is distracted and unable to settle. Because of this, we often start a meditation session with a breathing meditation, stilling the distractions, making it easier to move to the main object of meditation. It is also a key object when we are trying to develop single-pointed concentration, although there are many other objects we can use for that, such as the conventional nature of the mind.

Whether we are doing an analytical or fixed meditation, many of us find that trying to remain focused and undistracted for even a minute can be extremely difficult. Every time we try to bring the mind to the object of meditation it immediately wants to wander off somewhere else. Sometimes it drifts off gently; sometimes it can be quite violent, like being blown about by a strong wind. We can spend almost the entire session, say an hour or so, just trying to calm the mind, maybe just getting a minute or two of concentration at the very end.

Most of the time, especially as beginners, we are plagued by an uncontrolled mind that is constantly wandering, making any concentration at all very difficult. This is where the breathing meditation is especially useful. Because breathing is a natural activity that is happening all the time, it is much simpler to focus on than most other objects of meditation.

Through watching the breath, we can calm and settle the mind, bringing it into a neutral state. If it is agitated because of delusions such as anger or jealousy, even one or two minutes' breathing meditation can transform it from a nonvirtuous mind to a neutral one. From there, it is very easy to transform it into a positive state.

The analogy is given of the dirty cloth that we want to dye. Although the cloth is white, we won't be able to dye it a beautiful red or blue while it is very dirty and greasy. First, we must wash it to clean it thoroughly. Only when all the dirt is removed will the dye take and cover the cloth evenly. Similarly, only when we have calmed the mind thoroughly and removed the dirt of the disturbing thoughts through a practice such as a breathing meditation can we begin a meditation that will lead the mind without distractions into a virtuous state, such as meditating on compassion.

A meditative mind is opposite to a worldly one, which generally boils with attachment and anger. Because living with a negative mind is normal, it is difficult to generate a positive one, so we need a skillful method—we might even need to trick it into becoming positive! Just as two people cannot sit on the same chair, virtuous and nonvirtuous thoughts cannot coexist. Say, we really want to sit on our favorite chair, but a friend is occupying it. Just yelling "Get up!" won't work, so we must trick them to leave by saying there is a delicious cake or a great party in the next room. We need the same sort of strategy to get our negative mind to budge. This is where we use the breathing meditation to clear the space for our subsequent meditations. Although the object of our meditation, the actual breath, is not important in itself, what we are really trying to do is prepare the mind by bringing it into a neutral state.

How to Do a Simple Breathing Meditation

There are various types of breathing meditation. You can just watch the breath or you can count each separate breath. All are very helpful, especially when the mind is full of distractions, unable to concentrate for even a few seconds. But while just watching the breath can be beneficial, I strongly recommend that you take time to generate a good motivation before you start. Then the meditation becomes pure; it become Dharma. The simple act of breathing is turned into a weapon to destroy the delusions. And if the breathing meditation is done with a bodhichitta motivation, even just one single in-breath or outbreath becomes the cause of enlightenment.

One type of breathing meditation is counting the breath, which is often explained as the eighth element of the seven-point Vairochana posture, which we will look at below. Counting the breath is just that. You start with a positive motivation, ensuring your mind is not possessed with attachment or anger, and then, breathing normally, you count "one" as you breathe out and then breathe in normally. Then, you count "two" as you breathe out again, and so forth up to ten or twenty-one, and then you start the counting again. When you lose your concentration and realize you are no longer counting, you simply return to "one" and start again.

Although generally with any breathing meditation you are encouraged to breathe normally, it is useful to take three deep breaths at the beginning, to bring more air into your lungs. Then, when you settle into your normal breathing pattern, you will be able to put more effort into your concentration; it will be stronger and last longer.

Another breathing meditation is the nine-round breathing meditation, which consists of three rounds of three breaths. For the first three rounds, you close the left nostril and breathe in through the right. Then close your right nostril and breathe out through the left. For the next three rounds, you close the right nostril and breathe in through the left and close the left nostril and breathe out through the right. Then, for the last three rounds, you breathe in through both nostrils and out through both nostrils. A very effective way to do this uses a visualization where you imagine white light entering with the in-breath, filling you with merit, and black smoke leaving with the outbreath, completely purifying you. This meditation has many variations, one of which you can see in appendix 2.

Analytical Objects

In contrast to fixed meditations, every other meditation involves analysis in some form or other, using analytical objects. In Buddhism, whatever object we analyze, the aim is always to overcome delusions and lead us to liberation and enlightenment. We can analyze how things exist with meditations on emptiness, where the object analyzed is the thing that appears to exist from its own side but does not. The object can be the suffering of others when we meditate on compassion, or on the imminence of our death when we meditate on impermanence. We can also meditate on objects in order to overcome specific afflictions, such as analyzing the shortcomings of anger to overcome it and develop patience. There are also important visualizations within tantra and within the thought-transformation meditation of taking and giving, where we take others' suffering on ourselves and give them all our happiness and good qualities.

The Conventional Nature of the Mind

One very important object of analysis is the mind itself. A simple way to start to understand the mind is to just watch it, observing its conventional nature.[32]

You start with a breathing meditation. As you breathe out strongly from both nostrils, you purify, and as you breathe in, you visualize you are receiving the knowledge of the buddhas and bodhisattvas. Then, you keep the mind inside, not letting it wander. In this way, you start to become aware that you are thinking. You then concentrate on your thoughts.

Whatever thoughts you have, be aware, "I'm thinking this" and watch that thought. Question yourself, "What I am thinking?" When you catch the thought, recognize it and then just watch it, without becoming involved with it in any way. For instance, if an angry thought arises, that is very good because it gives you a chance to just observe it, without judging or becoming entangled in the emotion. If the thought of attachment arises, you don't go with the desire but just see it as it is, the deluded mind of attachment, and be happy you have recognized it, just as an observant police officer will be vigilant and recognize the thief in order to catch them. In that way, you can analyze the nature of anger and the nature of attachment.

When you watch a thought of attachment, you can examine its nature. You can ask what the feeling of attachment is like, whether it has things like color or shape. Ask yourself questions like, "What is its color? What is its shape?" If it seems to have color and shape, then examine this to see whether the mind's color and shape is real or just your visualization. You can do the same thing with anger, pride, jealousy, and so forth, whenever they arise.

Check where these negative minds come from. Do they seem to arise from the head, the chest, the feet? Does your experience of anger or attachment come from the brain? Is it oneness with the brain? Is there any difference between the intellectual conception of your thoughts and your emotional experience? In that way, try to recognize your real experience, without being influenced by your emotions or your intellectual conceptions.

Emptiness

Understanding how everything comes from the mind is a vital part of transforming the way we look at the world and our relationship to it. We need to ask deeper questions. What makes these external things— the climate, the place, the diet, and so forth—become conditions for our suffering? The deeper we see the causes affecting our life, the more skillful we will be in resolving those problems. We suffer because we have mind. Trees and stones don't suffer; the elements don't have pain. This physical body of ours has problems because we have mind.

Everything we experience comes from the mind: all the pleasant and unpleasant events and objects, all the attractive and nasty people, all the desirable and undesirable objects. When somebody gets angry at us, who is harming us? That apparent harmer comes completely from our own mind; it is a creation of our ignorance. If we were not clouded by fundamental ignorance, there would be no experience of being harmed and there would be no appearance of a person who harms us.

Even though things appear to us as inherently beautiful or ugly, good or bad, they are nothing more than creations of our own mind. Our mind has the potential to be completely free from all defilements. The nature of the mind is clear light; all the delusions that currently plague us are not an intrinsic part of the mind but just like the dust that smears an essentially clean mirror. We can clean that mirror; we can purify our mind and remove the very cause of all our suffering.

How everything comes from mind is a very important meditation, helping us overcome negative emotions and developing positive qualities like patience. Meditating on seeing things as creations of the mind becomes like watching a movie on television, showing us nothing we see, hear, smell, taste, and touch comes from outside, existing in its own right. This movie we are watching becomes very interesting.

To begin the meditation, you first look at how things appear to exist— whether the sound, smell, and so forth appears to be merely labeled by the mind or not. Recognizing that, without analyzing, things automatically appear to exist independently, from their own side, you can then understand that this appearance is the exact opposite of how things really exist. Nothing exists from its own side; anything that appears to be independent, not merely labeled by the mind, is a hallucination.

You should practice this mindfulness of recognizing these hallucinations as hallucinations not just during a sitting meditation session but at any time, while you are eating, walking, working. Although this I (the subject), what you do (the action), and the object of your action all appear to exist from their own side, train yourself to see them as hallucinations. The people you see appear to exist from their own side, not merely labeled by mind, but that is also a hallucination. Form, sound, smell, taste—the way everything appears is a hallucination. Constantly practice the mindfulness that this is a hallucination.

Seeing all these as hallucinations naturally reinforces your understanding of how they are all empty of existing inherently, how the I is empty, the action is empty, everything is empty. This way of practicing mindfulness makes the mind very peaceful because it cuts off all the superstitions.[33] It becomes a very enjoyable practice, as well as the most powerful way to purify heavy negative karma.

A good way to observe how the I exists is to first focus on the conventional nature of the mind. When the mind is not obscured by scattering or sinking thoughts, you can start to recognize that it is clear, colorless, shapeless, empty of form, like a mirror that can reflect back anything. If you stir water in a pond with a stick, the sand and the water mix together so the water cannot give a reflection, but when it becomes calm it can reflect the trees, clouds, and whatever things are around. When the nature of the mind is clear and calm, any appearance can arise in it.

For this meditation, while single-pointedly concentrating on the conventional nature of the mind while it is calm and clear, use a very subtle part of the mind to also skillfully watch the I at the same time. Look at what is watching. See how the I appears to you and how ignorance believes that appearance of a real I, how it holds on to it as real.

This I that appears real, existing from its own side, is the object that needs to be investigated and rejected, and thus it is called the object of refutation, one of the most important meditation objects within

Tibetan Buddhism. Only though recognizing and refuting this object that appears to exist truly can you free yourself from suffering. It is the key point in the four-point analysis that is a vital meditation on emptiness.[34] By discovering this "real" I is empty, you find the infallible right view. This is a quick method to realize emptiness.

OBJECTS FOR PURIFYING AFFLICTIONS

The unknowing mind, ignorance, gives rise to all the other mistaken thoughts, such as anger, attachment, jealousy, and pride. By exaggerating the object, by putting a positive or negative label on it, our ignorance is like a magician who deceives the audience into seeing all sorts of illusions—jewel palaces, beautiful men and women, and so forth. There is a projection, a hallucination, and we believe that to be true. Then, because of a positive or negative label, we decide that the thing is good or bad, beautiful or ugly, and then attachment or aversion arise. No such beautiful, good object or ugly, bad object exists, but we believe it does. We are the audience that has been "illusioned" by the magician, our ignorance, into totally believing the hallucination.

To fully realize this—to realize emptiness—would mean we overcome all our negative emotions at once, because they are all based on that false assumption. However, realizing emptiness is extremely difficult, and so, until we do, we need many antidotes to overcome these negative thoughts, such as looking at the shortcomings of desirable objects as an antidote to attachment or meditating on patience and loving-kindness as an antidote to anger.

Overcoming Attachment

We generally have attachment for things we find attractive and aversion for things we find ugly or repulsive. When we encounter a desirable object, the object itself is neither beautiful nor ugly, it is our mind that determines this. A good way to overcome attachment to the object is to change the aspect of the object, the way the mind views it.

So, just as our attachment has decided the object is beautiful, we can train our mind to decide it is not. This is not tricking the mind. Attachment sees the object as truly beautiful and attractive, which it is not, so by reversing our attitude toward the object we are destroying that wrong conception. Although the most effective way of dealing with attachment is realizing how the object of attachment is empty of inherent existence, unless we were to profoundly explore the emptiness of the object, just thinking that way is not strong enough to bring about a change in our attitude. However, by actually confronting our attachment with an image of ugliness we can break through this wrong view.

If you desire somebody, the object of your attachment is probably their body. One way to overcome that attachment is to see their body as physically harmful by visualizing it as made of red-hot burning iron, instead of soft flesh. Of course, it is not made of red-hot iron and would not burn you, but your attachment certainly burns, in that it destroys your happiness, and so this visualization is no more a fantasy than the fantasy that the body can bring you true happiness.

When you meditate on the nature of your own body, you see that its nature is both unclean and a cause of dissatisfaction. Caused by the mind of ignorance, through craving and grasping, because the cause is contaminated, there is not a moment when the body is free from gross or subtle suffering. If you had not created the karma for this present body, there would be no ageing, sickness, death, not getting what you want, and so forth. Without this suffering body, how could this body age? How could this body get sick? You wouldn't need food to feed it or clothes to cover it, nor would you need a house to protect it and make it comfortable.

Think of how much time and energy you put into this samsaric body. Not just food to sustain it, but sweet things to satisfy its cravings, drinks to make it feel happy, fashionable clothes to make it look beautiful and be envied. You take it to a gym to give it muscles. You paint it and groom its hair; when it gets wrinkled with age you have a surgeon pull it tight again. And yet, still it lets you down by getting sick and old and then dying.

The meditations where you explore the body in this way come into the first of the four foundations of mindfulness,[35] the mindfulness of the body. It is very good to check your own body in meditation, to be aware of the sensations of the body and the aspects of the body that are not apparent from the outside. Usually, you ignore the internal working of your body unless there is some discomfort or disease, but when you explore what the body is and how it works, it can be quite awkward, because it becomes apparent that the body is not the pleasant thing you assume it to be. This is a very effective way to break your attachment to the body.

Many of us are too attached to food. One way you can deal with that attachment is to change the way you see the food. When you no longer see it as something utterly desirable but as something harmful and repulsive, your attachment bursts like a pricked balloon.

The problem isn't with the food, but with the mind. A human being eating food should be different from the dog eating food. A dog sees the food and just gobbles it, expecting happiness. Your motivation for eating food should be higher than this. You should find a method of eating that brings peace and not more suffering through attachment. In this way it becomes worthwhile, it becomes wise eating.

Say somebody has offered you a delicious cake. Normally, you accept it and eat it greedily, and you see that person as your good friend because they have offered you something you like. Thus, that one gift of cake increases your attachment to food and to the giver and causes you to discriminate, preferring them to all those who have not given you cake. All in one little slice of cake!

You can overcome your attachment to food by seeing it as red-hot iron or coals, as with the body, or even as kaka! You can go to the most expensive restaurant in the world, where the food looks so attractive, and in a few hours it will be kaka going down a toilet bowl. A thousand-dollar dish or a plate of rice and dal, the result is the same.

Another way to cut your attachment is to consider what it has taken to get that food onto your plate, and especially all the other beings that have been killed and injured in order for you to enjoy it. Obviously, if you are eating meat, that meat was once a sentient being, treasuring its life as much as you do yours. It went through such pain and suffering for you. If you could really see the conditions that animal had to go through, not only would your attachment vanish but tears of compassion would well in your eyes.

But even if the food on your plate is vegetarian, that does not mean you can attack it with attachment. Even for a plate of rice with a few vegetables, countless sentient beings have suffered, dying when the rice or vegetables were sprayed or when the machines harvested the crops. And just as the beings have suffered, the farmer who harvested that food, by causing that pain and death, will suffer in the future. Understanding that, how can you thoughtlessly enjoy it, overwhelmed by attachment?

That is not to say you should never eat again, but there is a way of eating not motivated by attachment but rather by concern and compassion for all who have suffered. You eat to maintain a healthy body in order to be able to best progress on the path to enlightenment. *That* is the way you can be happy eating the food.

You can employ the same sorts of meditations to destroy your attachment to each of the eight worldly dharmas (cravings for possessions and gifts, happiness, praise, and a good reputation; and aversion to being without possessions, being unhappy, being criticized, and having a bad reputation).[36] There is nothing wrong with having or receiving material possessions; what causes problems is your attachment. Similarly, it is your attachment to being praised or having a good reputation that brings you problems, not the praise or reputation itself. This is what you need to meditate on.

The pleasure you might derive from that object of attachment never lasts, whereas the suffering you experience as a result of that attachment keeps you continually circling in samsara. Therefore, you need to use every method available to free yourself from your attachment.

Like the body and food, when you encounter any of the eight worldly dharmas, you can see them as red-hot iron or coals or as molten lava, and so, rather than being drawn to them, you can recoil away from them. You can see a gift as a gift-wrapped lump of red-hot iron that will burn away your hands completely if you were to even go near it. When somebody praises you, you should see the words coming from their mouth like sparks shooting out and burning your body, causing you terrible pain. There should not be the slightest attraction for words of praise.

Your attachment to such things has been causing you problems since beginningless lives and will continue to do so. It has stopped you from gaining any realizations at all; it has constantly interrupted your peace and forced you into suffering rebirth after suffering rebirth.

Therefore, you should guard your mind like a police officer with a dangerous criminal, ready for the mind to try to escape into negativity at any moment. Always watching the mind becomes your safeguard; it is a meditation you can do at any moment in any place. Whenever you have problems, you can see how it is the mind of attachment that lies at the root of them, and you can develop even stronger aversion to it.

For beginners like us, who have no clear understanding of emptiness, meditations like these can cut our attachment, and, as such, are very effective ways to deal with our worldly problems.

Overcoming Anger and Other Afflictions

You can apply the same meditation technique to all the afflictions, reversing your usual deluded view of the object of that affliction. When you are angry at somebody, your anger causes you to see the person as undesirable, as ugly. Therefore, you try to meditate on love by seeing the person in beauty. This has nothing to do with the beauty of the body. This love is not like giving your pet dog a pat on the head; it is not like saying things like "my dear, my darling." You can use those words even when full of anger for that person. It means looking below the surface cause of your anger, the thing that person did that has harmed your ego in some way, to the essential goodness of that person, their buddha nature, and how they just want happiness and to avoid suffering in exactly the same way you do.

To control ignorance, you should meditate on the dependent nature of objects, how they arise in dependence on causes and conditions and are not the permanent, independent things your deluded mind sees them as. To control pride, you should meditate on just how little you know, that there is no reason at all to feel superior to others. You can also reflect on the shortcomings of pride and the advantages of humility.

The most powerful meditation that covers so many of these unsubdued minds is the meditation on impermanence and death, showing clearly the preciousness and fragility of this life and the suffering that pervades the whole of samsara. We will look at this below.

PART II
DEVELOPING A
MEDITATION PRACTICE

4. THE SIX PRELIMINARY PRACTICES

W HEN WE ARE SERIOUS in wanting to meditate every day, it is important to know what to do in both the actual meditation session time and when we are living the rest of our life, the time between sessions. Why? When we are able to make our life meaningful not only in the session time but also in between sessions, all the twenty-four hours of a day become highly meaningful. In this way, our whole year—our whole life—becomes highly meaningful.

In that way, our whole life is divided into these two. Then the actual meditation session is further divided into three:

- the preparatory practices
- the actual body of the meditation
- the completion

The preparatory practices are what we do before the meditation actually begins. As an analogy, unless we make the necessary preparations before making a cake—buying the right ingredients rather than just going to the fridge and finding the eggs are off—the cake will turn out disgusting, and our friends will realize the complete renunciation of the cake. Therefore, before we even begin the cake, we need to make careful preparations, buying all the ingredients, ensuring they are the best quality, having a good recipe, and so forth. Similarly, how rich our meditation is depends on how well we have prepared for it. Therefore, we should never skip or rush the preliminary practices, thinking they are not important.

There are generally said to be six preparatory practices:

1. cleaning the meditation room
2. making offerings
3. sitting in a suitable posture
4. visualizing the merit field
5. reciting the seven-limb prayer and offering a mandala
6. requesting the lineage lamas[37]

When we have a regular meditation practice, it is very helpful to have a particular place dedicated to our meditations.[38] It can be a separate room or a corner of a room; it can be simple or ornate, but it should be a welcoming place, one we want to be in. It is good to have an altar where we can make offerings before we start to meditate.

The altar is where we place the holy objects. A Buddha statue or picture should be in the center, with a Dharma text, symbolizing the enlightened holy speech, to the left of the Buddha (as we face the altar), and a stupa, symbolizing the enlightened holy mind, to the right. Thangkas of any deities we have can be hung on the wall above the altar or on either side of it.

After the first preparation, cleaning the meditation place, we make offerings, such as a row of water bowls. Both cleaning the place and performing offerings are extremely useful methods to collect merit and purify delusions.

The third preparation is sitting in a suitable posture, which traditionally is the seven-point posture of Vairochana,[39] but it could also be just sitting comfortably on a chair. After that, we clearly visualize the object of refuge, the merit field. This is the object we rely on in order to be saved from the sufferings of both the lower realms and the whole of samsara. This can either be Guru Shakyamuni Buddha or an elaborate visualization of all the buddhas and lineage lamas.

The fifth one is accumulating merit and purifying our delusions by doing the seven-limb practice and the mandala offering. Then, finally with the sixth practice, from the depth of our heart we make requests to the lineage lamas of the lamrim teachings, in order to quickly generate the realizations of the steps of the path to enlightenment.

Each of these preliminary practices has a profound meaning. We really need to understand the whole path to be able to understand their significance. The deeper our understanding, the deeper the feeling we get from these six preparatory practices and the more essential they seem. This is not just a custom we are being asked to follow; each practice has great significance, but that might be clouded until we can understand many other aspects of the path, such as the full significance of relying on the Buddha, Dharma, and Sangha, and what karma is.

Cleaning the Meditation Room

Even if the altar and meditation room are not particularly dirty, you should still clean them. You should think that this is Guru Shakyamuni Buddha's room and clean it out of great respect for the Buddha. This is his mandala, his palace, and cleaning it is offering service to him, rather than becoming a service to your negative mind. You should therefore check your motivation carefully as you are cleaning the room.

You can recite this prayer while cleaning:

Abandon dust; abandon stains.

"Abandon dust" refers to abandoning the inner dust, the dust of anger, the dust of attachment, and the dust of ignorance, and all the disturbing-thought obscurations (*nyöndrip*). "Abandon stains" refers to the subtle defilements, the obscurations to knowledge (*shedrip*) that block you from attaining enlightenment. When you say this prayer, you can relate the "dust" to your own delusions that prevent you from achieving liberation and the "stains" to the subtle obscurations that prevent you from achieving enlightenment for sentient beings.

Although cleaning is the first of the preparatory practices, that does not mean you can do this cleaning meditation only when you are in your meditation place about to meditate. Whenever you clean anything—your home, your car, your work—it is very worthwhile to meditate in this way. It transforms what you are doing into holy

Dharma, and with a bodhichitta motivation, it becomes the cause of enlightenment.

Making Offerings

If you have an altar in your home and you offer incense and lights to the statues on that altar with the mind of bodhichitta, the effect is so powerful. You can also have a "mental altar" just by visualizing the Buddha, but a physical altar can become the focus of your meditations. Once your altar is set up, every time you see the altar you see the Buddha. This is not some projection from your own side. The Buddha *is* there. To think this is just in your imagination disturbs your practice.

If the effect on the mind of just seeing a statue or picture of the Buddha is inconceivable, then the effect of making offerings to a Buddha image is utterly inconceivable. In *The Sutra of the Mudra Developing the Power of Devotion*, it says,

> The minute you see a holy object you create infinite merit,
> so without question, if you actually make prostrations,
> offerings, and so forth, you create far greater merit.

You make offerings, prostrate to the enlightened beings, and clean holy places to purify your negativities. The power of these actions comes not only from the action itself but from the power born out of the limitless wisdom and compassion of the Buddha. As you perform these actions, if you are aware of the great qualities of the Buddha, this increases your devotion and therefore the effectiveness of the action. Even if you don't have so much as a stick of incense to offer, just visualizing a buddha image and offering mentally created offerings creates such unbelievable merit.

This is such an easy thing to do. Whenever you see something beautiful you can offer it to the Buddha, Dharma, and Sangha. If you have a garden, you can enjoy it yourself, but you can also use it as a wonderful ever-present offering to them. Every time you go out into it or see it from the window, you can offer to them, the Three Rare Sublime Ones.

Every time you do some work on it, you can feel you are working for them. Then, working to make one flower beautiful is working for Guru Shakyamuni Buddha.

When you make offerings, you should do it without deceit, which means without any nonvirtuous motivation at all, such as seeking worldly gain, which would poison the offering. What makes an offering pure is having a pure motivation.

There is a story of the great yogi Geshé Ben Gungyal that exemplifies this.[40] One day, because a benefactor was visiting his hermitage, he cleaned his room thoroughly, but when he sat down and examined his motivation, he saw he had done it in order to impress the benefactor: the motivation was a worldly one. Realizing this, he suddenly stood up, took a handful of ash from the fireplace and scattered it over the altar, making a real mess. He had recognized that although what he did had the form of a Dharma action, it wasn't. And so, to immediately practice the antidote and let go of the attachment, he threw the ash over the altar.

Because you are making an offering to a holy being, it is important not only to be mindful and respectful, but also to make the action of offering as beneficial as possible. Don't be lazy or sloppy. Make sure the bowls, the water, and any other offerings you have are clean. If a dear friend came to see you, you wouldn't offer them dirty water from a dirty glass, would you? From the side of the buddhas, cleanliness is not important. Even if you offered them kaka, for them it would be the purest nectar, but it is so important from your side to make everything to do with the offering as clean and nice as possible. To offer something dirty pollutes your mind and blocks realizations.

Traditionally, there are seven or eight bowls. The bowls don't have to be big, but they shouldn't be tiny, like a child's plaything. They can be very simple, but it is very good to make them as beautiful as possible. Crystal or gold bowls make the altar look so much nicer and the mind feels so much happier than if cheap, ugly ones are used.

The custom is to always have the bowls upside down on the altar when they are empty, otherwise it's like you are offering nothing to the

Buddha. When you are ready to make the offering, first you symbolically clean the bowls by taking the upturned bowl in one hand and purifying it by swirling the smoke from an incense stick in it, making sure you say "OM AH HUM" at the same time.

Pour some water into the first bowl and place it on the altar. Then turn the next bowl over and pour a little of the water from the first bowl into it, again saying "OM AH HUM." In that way, transfer the water from the second to the third bowl, until you have all the bowls upright on the altar with just a little water in each. Then, you fill up each bowl with water, to just below the rim, again saying "OM AH HUM." The bowls should be neatly in a line and almost touching but not quite—about the space of a rice grain between each.

The reason for saying "OM AH HUM" is to protect yourself from interference from spirits who can steal the essence of the offerings. For instance, it is said that if you don't say these three sacred syllables as you are offering light, it can become the cause to be very dull and distracted. Even when you turn on a light in a room, especially one with holy objects in it, this is very good to do.

Another way of laying out the offerings is with actual substances instead of water. So, there will be incense, a candle, food, and flowers. This makes a very attractive offering. This corresponds to the offerings you see in prayers and sadhanas:

argham:	water for drinking
padyam:	water for cleaning the feet
pushpe:	flowers
dhupe:	incense
aloke:	light
ghande:	perfume
naividya:	food
shapta:	music

For instance, for the nonwater offerings, you can place some rice in the bowl and the offering on top of that, a small flower, a stick of incense, a tea light, and so forth. You can have water in the perfume bowl and add some fragrance you really like. For the music offering, you can have a bell or even a recording of beautiful music. For the nonwater offerings, you don't have to turn the bowls over when clearing away the offerings at the end of the day.

Whatever you use, mentally transform it into divine nectar for the Buddha; it's no longer a bowl of water or a chocolate biscuit. Physically, what you have in the bowls is just mundane substances—water, rice, incense, and so forth—but by saying "OM AH HUM" and visualizing the offerings as divine offerings you transform them into what you are actually offering the Buddha. This practice brings continuous benefits. This is why we call the Buddha a "field of merit." He is the field from which we harvest all good qualities.

It is traditional that before sitting on your meditation cushion, you make three prostrations. See the section on the seven-limb prayer, below, for this.

Sitting in a Suitable Posture

Having cleaned the room, made offerings to the Buddha, Dharma, and Sangha, and prostrated, you then sit down in a proper meditation posture. Sitting as correctly as you can helps make the mind stable. The texts say this should be Vairochana's seven-point meditation posture:

1. legs in vajra (full lotus) position or crossed
2. hands in meditation mudra
3. back straight
4. head tilted forward
5. eyes slightly open, gaze directed downward
6. jaw relaxed, tongue against palate
7. shoulders level and relaxed

The full vajra position is where your legs are crossed with each foot, sole upward, placed on the opposite thigh. This is difficult for many

Westerners, so a half vajra (with just a foot on the opposite thigh) or with the legs just crossed is also acceptable. You can also sit like Tara, with the right leg stretched out slightly. Having a cushion to raise your buttocks slightly enables you to easily keep your back straight for an extended period. If sitting on the floor is too uncomfortable, you can also sit on a chair.

The meditation mudra[41] is holding your hands on your lap, just below the navel, palms upward with the right hand on top of the left and thumbs touching, forming a triangle. Arms and shoulders should be relaxed, the two shoulder blades slightly stretched, like wings, neither hunched nor rigidly locked. Holding your arms out slightly from your body allows the circulation of air.

Your back should be straight but relaxed. It helps to imagine your spine as a pile of coins rising straight up. A straight back helps to keep the channels straight, which in turn helps the psychic wind flow easily, making it functional. The wind is the vehicle of mind, so when wind becomes functional, the mind becomes functional, meaning you are able to direct the mind as you want. Otherwise, it is difficult to direct the mind on to the object of the meditation.

Your gaze should be slightly down, keeping the middle way—not raised too much (which would lead to scattering thoughts) or lowered too much (which would lead to sinking thoughts). Your eyes should be half open. This is often difficult for new meditators, so having them closed is acceptable. However, this can lead to drowsiness, just as having them fully open can lead to distractions.

Your jaw should be relaxed, with your tongue lightly touching the roof of your mouth, just behind the teeth, which helps control the saliva that can form in your mouth. Your teeth should be slightly apart and your lips lightly together.

VISUALIZING THE MERIT FIELD

The visualization of the merit field is a very important part of the practice within not just the Geluk tradition but the other Tibetan traditions as well. The objects you go to for refuge—the guru, Guru Shakyamuni Buddha, and all the buddhas and bodhisattvas—are called the "merit field." This is a literal translation of the Tibetan *tsokshing*, *tsok* meaning "merit" and *shing* meaning "field." It is called a "field" because this is the source of all happiness, just as farmers' fields are the source of the crops that give them their livelihood. With this field of holy objects visualized in front of you, you make offerings, do prostrations, say prayers, and so forth, planting virtuous seeds, ensuring crops of future happiness.

Although the analogy with an ordinary field is often used, it breaks down quickly. When farmers plant seeds, they might be able to receive two crops a year, if they are lucky, and the harvest is limited. With the merit field, you have the freedom to plant as many seeds as you like as often as you like, day and night, and because of the power of the objects you are offering to, the merit accumulated is infinite.

In texts such as the *Lama Tsongkhapa Guru Yoga*, you are asked to visualize the merit field either in a simple way—the "many into one," where all the Buddha, Dharma, and Sangha are visualized in the one aspect of Shakyamuni Buddha—or in a more elaborate way, the "one into many," where you visualize the essence of your root guru in the manifold aspects of all the buddhas, bodhisattvas, and so forth.

You will find many different descriptions of the merit field, depending on the lineage and the practice. You can imagine the gurus, buddhas, and bodhisattvas on lotuses resting in the branches of a tree or on thrones. An example is such a visualization described in the *Lama Chöpa Jorchö*.[42] In it, you visualize your root guru, in the aspect of a monk, sitting on a lion throne on the crown of a wish-granting tree. At his heart is Vajradhara[43] and surrounding him are the direct and lineage gurus, *yidams*, buddhas, bodhisattvas, *dakas*, and *dakinis*, all encircled by an ocean of Dharma protectors.[44]

Lama Tsongkhapa's disciple Gyaltsap Jé explains that when you visualize the merit field, it should not be like the physical eye seeing a physical object. With the mind already transformed into the path by the previous practices, the visualization should be like placing a clear crystal in front of a color, where the crystal takes on the aspect of that color.

So, from the hearts of those you have visualized, you imagine light—the essence of all their enlightened qualities: patience, loving-kindness, compassion, wisdom, and so forth—radiating out and into you, filling you with those qualities.

RECITING THE SEVEN-LIMB PRAYER

The seven-limb prayer is essential to purify negative karma and to accumulate merit. The limbs are these seven important practices:

1. prostrating
2. offering
3. confessing
4. rejoicing
5. requesting the teacher to turn the wheel of Dharma
6. requesting the teacher to remain for a long time[45]
7. dedicating

Because the seven-limb practice is an essential means to create the causes and conditions to develop the mind on the path to enlightenment, it is extremely important to do this practice as many times as possible every day. That is why it is always a part of a Mahayana practice and why any deity practice has it as a preliminary.

The seven factors of the seven-limb practice are like seven vital parts of a plane that enable it to function and to take passengers to the places they wish to go. It might not be immediately apparent how doing this practice is vital for the success of your Dharma practice, but when you study karma in some depth, especially the four aspects,[46] you will see how profound this practice is.

There is a Kadampa saying:

A practice without the accumulation of merit is like a seed without wetness.

> A practice without the accumulation of merit is nothing more
> than the drawing of a flame, not the flame itself.

A painting of a flame on a wall cannot function as a flame; it can't give light to dispel the darkness. Similarly, if you don't do practices to accumulate merit, you can't effectively eliminate the darkness of ignorance. Only meditating without accumulating merit is like a seed without any moisture, the condition it needs to make it sprout and become a plant and bear fruit. Therefore, it is wrong to think of the seven-limb practice and the mandala as just some ritual or custom that has nothing to do with real life. It is a vital part of accumulating merit.

Each of the seven limbs is an antidote to a particular delusion. It's important when you recite the seven-limb prayer to take your time over it, contemplating each limb and remembering which delusion it is a remedy for. Seeing the incredible benefit each limb brings, you can never be bored with this practice.

That is why I usually do the seven-limb practice and the mandala offering very slowly. If you just chant it nicely, it might become an offering, but without meditating on the meaning, just saying words alone, like a parrot reciting it, it will be difficult to transform your mind quickly. You should read one line, then stop to meditate, then read the next line and stop to meditate, and so forth. If you really meditate while saying the prayer, without your mind wandering, you collect infinite merit, even in the short time it takes you to say the prayer.

Generally, in a normal meditation session, before the seven-limb prayer, you recite the refuge and bodhichitta prayers and the four immeasurables prayer[47] as a means of increasing your bodhichitta motivation. Then, there is the seven-limb prayer. A commonly used prayer is this:

I *prostrate* reverently with my body, speech, and mind.
I present clouds of every type of *offering*, both actual arranged
   and mentally emanated.

I *confess* all my negative actions and downfalls collected from
   beginningless time.
I *rejoice* in the virtues of ordinary beings and aryas.
Please *remain* until the end of cyclic existence
And *turn* the wheel of Dharma for transmigratory beings.
I *dedicate* my own and others' virtues to great enlightenment.[48]

Prostrating

Prostrating is a very strong antidote to pride, which is a huge hindrance
to progressing on the path. It is one of the most effective methods to
both eliminate the obscurations collected from beginningless rebirths
as well as to accumulate extensive merit, the necessary condition for
attaining realizations. This is reflected in the Tibetan term *chagtsel*.
Chag is "to clean," as in cleaning away all the garbage with a broom, but
here you are cleaning away all your defilements. *Tsel* means "to seek":
here, seeking to attain all the realizations from guru devotion up to full
enlightenment.

The line in the usual seven-limb prayer is "I prostrate reverently with
my body, speech, and mind." This is often expressed in a more elaborate
way, such as in *The King of Prayers*:

You lions among humans,
Gone to freedom in the present, past, and future
In the worlds of ten directions,[49]
To all of you, with body, speech, and sincere mind, I bow
   down.[50]

Very often, when you do the limb of prostration with the seven-limb
practice, you simply recite the line and put your palms together in the
prostration mudra. Even if you don't do a full-length or a five-limb
(half) prostration, you must at least do that, otherwise it is such a waste.

The prostration mudra is a very simple action that can take less than
a second, but it is incredibly powerful. Each aspect of the mudra has

significance. You place your hands at your chest, palms together and fingers straight and facing upward, much like a Christian prayer mudra. The thumbs are slightly tucked in, signifying offering a jewel. The hollow between the palms signifies the *dharmakaya* and the two thumbs inside the hollow signify the *rupakaya*, the dharmakaya and rupakaya being the two buddha bodies that result from completing the two paths of wisdom and method.

The full-length prostration is according to the tradition of Naropa. When you prostrate, standing with your feet together, first place your hands in the prostration mudra on *your crown*, which causes you to create the merit to achieve a crown pinnacle, one of a buddha's thirty-two holy signs and eighty holy exemplifications.[51] Then, touch them to *the forehead*, which purifies the negative karmas collected with the body from beginningless rebirths and creates the cause to achieve the vajra holy body. Next, touch them to *the throat*, which purifies the negative karmas collected with the speech from beginningless rebirths and creates the cause to achieve the vajra holy speech. Then, touch them to *the heart*, which purifies the negative karmas collected with the mind from beginningless rebirths and creates the cause to achieve the vajra holy mind.

When you go down, either with a full or half prostration, you must touch the ground with your forehead, otherwise it doesn't become a complete prostration. But then, you should get up quickly, signifying a quick release from samsara. To lie there without immediately getting up creates the karma to be reborn as a worm or snake—a creature who slides along the ground!

You should also be careful to hold your hands in the correct fashion when you are on the ground, with the fingers straight out. If you splay them you create the karma to be reborn as a duck or a creature with webbed feet, and if you bunch them up you create the karma to be reborn as a horse or a creature with hooves. Doing prostrations correctly brings the most amazing benefits, but because you are prostrating to the Buddha, Dharma, and Sangha, a sloppy prostration can bring great suffering results.

With the full-length prostration, you then lie flat on the floor, stretching your arms in front of you and touching your head to the floor. The more you spread your body, the more atoms touch the ground. In the *Compendium of Trainings* Shantideva quotes from a scripture:

> If a fully ordained monk prostates with extended limbs and a clear mind to a stupa of hair and nail relics, he will come to enjoy as many thousands of universal monarch kingdoms as there are particles of dust that cover the ground all the way down to the golden foundation.[52]

The sutra says "particles of dust" but we can read that as "atoms," so that means that, when you do a full-length prostration with your hands fully extended, you create the merit to be born a wheel-turning king many thousands of times over for each atom of the floor your body covers, and that is not just the atoms on the surface, but from the surface right down to "the golden foundation," meaning the center of the earth. It is unimaginable.

A five-limb or half prostration is when you simply go down on your knees and touch your head to the floor.

Offering

The practice of offering is a specific antidote to miserliness. If you are miserly, you should practice charity and make offerings as much as possible. From making offerings, you receive the inexhaustible perfect enjoyments of a buddha.

The verses for this limb in *The King of Prayers* are this:

> Beautiful flowers and regal garlands,
> Sweet music, scented oils, and parasols,
> Sparkling lights and sublime incense,
> I offer to you victorious ones.

Fine dress and fragrant perfumes,
Sandalwood powder heaped high as Mount Meru,
All wondrous offerings in spectacular array,
I offer to you victorious ones.

With transcendent offerings peerless and vast,
With profound admiration for all the buddhas,
With strength of conviction in the bodhisattva way,
I offer and bow down to all victorious ones.

The line in the short prayer is "I present clouds of every type of offering, actually arranged and mentally emanated." As you recite this, imagine clouds of offering going from your heart and being offered to the entire merit field.

I often mention you can make offerings of all the extensive offerings in FPMT centers. Wherever there is an FPMT center *gompa*,[53] there are extensive offerings, so you can imagine all those and offer them. At Aptos, my house in the United States, there are many hundreds of water bowl offerings in two rooms, and, because the water bowls are huge, it makes a very large water offering. There are also thousands of light offerings throughout the house, as well as flower and food offerings inside and outside.

Making offerings like this to the holy objects definitely creates the cause for enlightenment, so naturally it creates the cause for liberation, the happiness of future lives, and even the happiness of this life. Offering even one tiny tea light or one light from a string of fairy lights creates all those causes. If you offer ten thousand fairy lights, you create ten thousand causes for enlightenment. It's so easy. Within a minute, you collect limitless skies of merit so many times. The more merit you collect the easier to achieve realizations, and the easier to achieve enlightenment.

There are different benefits from doing this practice of offerings, depending on what you offer. For example, offering incense creates the cause to live in pure morality, while offering light helps to develop Dharma wisdom and clairvoyance as well as creating the cause for long life. There are many other kinds of benefits.

Confessing

Next is the limb of confession, which is an antidote to the three poisonous minds of attachment, anger, and ignorance. It is also said to be a remedy to all obscurations, enabling you to eliminate all delusions and achieve the dharmakaya.

The verse for this limb in *The King of Prayers* is this:

> Every harmful action I have done
> With my body, speech, and mind
> Overwhelmed by attachment, anger, and confusion,
> All these I openly lay bare before you.

The line in the short prayer says, "I confess all my negative actions and downfalls collected from beginningless time." As you recite, think that, by confessing, not even the slightest negativity exists any more in your mental continuum, that everything that is an obstacle for realizations has been completely purified.

For example, if you examine the actions you do within one day, from morning until going to bed, almost everything is done with attachment, clinging to this life. Getting up, dressing, eating breakfast, going to work—it's all done with attachment. Similarly, the hours of work you do each day, if you are honest, are mainly done for the comfort of this life, so it all becomes negative karma. It's normal to think that such activities are perfectly okay, that there is nothing negative in them, but you have to remember the definition of nonvirtue, then you will see all these things are done only for your own interest.

This is what you need to confess and to purify. You and all the sentient beings you visualize surrounding you confess with regret, repenting all the negative karmas and downfalls accumulated in the past.

When you confess your past negative karmas, it actually means that from now on you are going to try to practice virtue.

The stronger your regret, the thinner your negative karma becomes. You should feel strong regret, as if you had swallowed deadly poison. Unable to live with your negative karmas for even a second longer, you see the need to purify them right this second, making the determination never to commit them again, even if it endangers your life. Then, as you recite the line from the seven-limb practice, you think that all your obscurations become nonexistent and your mind becomes completely pure.

You can also think of the emptiness of the negative karma. As you do the confession limb, when you think of the delusions, it looks as if they are real. However, none of the delusions are as they appear; they are all empty. They don't exist even in name. Thinking of the emptiness of the negative karmas in this way becomes a powerful purification.

Rejoicing

The fourth of the seven limbs is rejoicing, which is a specific antidote to jealousy. We all know how difficult it is to feel happy in the good fortune of somebody when we are jealous of them, but that is exactly when you should rejoice by remembering their good qualities. The result of rejoicing is that you achieve a buddha's holy body, which is sublimely beautiful, without a trace of ugliness.

King Prasenajit once asked the Buddha for advice, explaining that he was too busy with his duties as a king to go to an isolated place to retreat and therefore didn't know how to make his life meaningful. The Buddha told him that there were three ways he could make his life most meaningful: to rejoice, to practice bodhichitta, and to dedicate his positive actions. This shows how fundamental rejoicing is in developing our potential.

The verse for this limb in *The King of Prayers* is this:

> I lift up my heart and rejoice in all positive potential
> Of the buddhas and bodhisattvas in ten directions,

Of solitary realizers, hearers still training, and those beyond,
And of all ordinary beings.

The line in the short prayer says, "I rejoice in the virtues of ordinary beings and aryas."

You create so much good merit by doing the seven-limb and the various other practices, but rejoicing is the best and easiest method. This is quite logical when you think about it. If you don't rejoice in the positive qualities or good fortune of others, you make yourself jealous or angry and are therefore unhappy; if you rejoice, you naturally have a light, happy mind. Rejoicing also makes whatever merit you have increase greatly, like constantly getting interest on a hundred dollars you have invested so that it quickly becomes tens of thousands of dollars, or even hundreds of thousands or millions of dollars.

Simply saying the rejoicing line of the seven-limb prayer without contemplating the meaning doesn't really become the practice of rejoicing. As with all the practices within the seven-limb practice, it is extremely important to remember to meditate on the meaning of the prayer and to not let your mind wander.

If you rejoice in your own merit from doing a virtuous action, you accumulate more merit than actually doing the action. When you rejoice in the merit of other sentient beings, if their level of mind is lower than yours, you accumulate more merit than they do—some texts say double—but if their level of mind is higher than yours, you get half of that merit. As Pabongka Dechen Nyingpo explains in *Liberation in the Palm of Your Hand*, if you do nothing but virtuous actions your whole life, you would still not attain anywhere near the merit a new bodhisattva attains in one day, whereas just by rejoicing in their root virtues, you get half that amount of merit.[54]

Even if you are very busy, this virtue can be created in a second. It simply involves your mind thinking in a particular way, and the merit you accumulate is as infinite as space. Because you can practice rejoicing while you are eating, walking, working, lying down, it is something you should do as many times as possible every day.

You should rejoice whenever you see good things happening to other people. When other people develop their Dharma practice and have realizations, or have education, wealth, a happy family life, or many friends, you should always think, "How wonderful it is!" When somebody succeeds in a business venture or a project, you should always rejoice, thinking, "How wonderful it is!" It then becomes the best business for you. Why? Because by rejoicing you are creating the cause for your own success, success in your Dharma practice, in benefiting sentient beings, and success in even the ordinary works of this life. But if you feel jealous of other people's success, which is the opposite of rejoicing, you are creating obstacles to your own success.

With this awareness, you should first rejoice in your own merits of the three times: past, present, and future. You can then rejoice in the merits of the three times of all ordinary sentient beings, and then the buddhas and bodhisattvas of the ten directions.

A good way to practice is by thinking like this: "Without good karma, without merit, there is no way at all for me to experience happiness. I have accumulated merit numberless times in the past, I am accumulating it now, and I will accumulate it in the future. This will result in so much temporary and ultimate happiness, including enlightenment."

From the very depths of your heart feel, "How wonderful it is that I have accumulated so much merit in the past, am collecting it now, and will collect it in the future." You can repeat "How wonderful it is!" many times, maybe counting the repetitions on a *mala*.[55]

Then rejoice in all the merits of the three times of all ordinary sentient beings, with the awareness that those merits result in so much happiness, temporary and ultimate, up to enlightenment. Being more specific makes it even easier to rejoice, because you relate to particular people in each country. Many people, lay and ordained, are accumulating incredible merit day and night by living in the Dharma, bringing their lives into the path. Thinking of the countries you have been where you have seen this happening makes it seem more real. Again, think, "How wonderful it is!"

Then, rejoice in all the merits of all the buddhas and bodhisattvas of the three times, who are uncountable in number and who create so much merit in every second. Again think, "How wonderful it is! How wonderful it is! How wonderful it is!" Count your repetitions. If you are short of time, you can think of all the ordinary sentient beings, bodhisattvas, and buddhas in all the ten directions and rejoice in their merits together.

You can vary your practice, such as rejoicing in your own merit in one session and in the merits of others in the next, or rejoicing in your own merit at the beginning of the session and in others' at the end, or you can turn that all around. You can do it in different ways.

Requesting the Teacher to Turn the Wheel of Dharma

The limb of requesting the teacher to turn the wheel of Dharma[56] is an antidote to ignorance. In particular, it purifies the heavy negative karmas created by avoiding the holy Dharma, such as by disrespecting Buddhist scriptures or criticizing the different types of Buddhadharma. This happens, for example, when a practitioner of one of the Tibetan traditions—Nyingma, Sakya, Kagyü, or Geluk—is critical of another tradition, or a Mahayana practitioner criticizes the Hinayana or vice versa.

The verse for this limb in *The King of Prayers* is this:

> You who are the bright lights of worlds in ten directions,
> Who have attained a buddha's omniscience through the stages of
>   awakening,
> All you who are my guides,
> Please turn the supreme wheel of Dharma.

The line in the short prayer says, "[Please] turn the wheel of Dharma for transmigratory beings."

Requesting to turn the wheel of Dharma creates the cause to achieve a buddha's holy speech in the future, as well as being able to turn the Dharma wheel for other sentient beings. Others will ask you to give teachings and you will skillfully teach them.

When asking the merit field to turn the Dharma wheel, you visualize offering a thousand-spoked golden *dharmachakra* (literally, "Dharma wheel") to your guru in the aspect of Guru Shakyamuni Buddha or whatever deity you are practicing, as well as to the direct and indirect gurus and all the rest of the merit field. Think that the *dharmachakra* is large and radiant. Visualize that you are not just one but numberless, and every one of your replicas is holding a *dharmachakra*. You then ask the merit field to turn the wheel of Dharma. The more you can visualize, the more merit you collect.

Requesting the Teacher to Remain for a Long Time

With this limb, you request the guru and the entire merit field to not pass into *parinirvana*[57] but to stay until samsara ends. This purifies the heavy negative karmas of having criticized or given up the guru or having disturbed his or her holy mind. It also naturally becomes a cause for your own long life, even if that is not your intention. The final result of this practice is that you achieve the indestructible vajra holy body of a buddha.

The verse for this limb in *The King of Prayers* is this:

> With palms together I earnestly request:
> You who may actualize parinirvana,
> Please stay with us for eons numberless as atoms of the world,
> For the happiness and well-being of all wanderers in samsara.

The line in the short prayer says, "Please remain until the end of cyclic existence."

You visualize that you are holding and offering a golden throne decorated with jewels to the guru deity and all the merit field. The throne has a variegated double vajra in front and is raised up by four or eight snow lions, like Shakyamuni Buddha's throne. Visualize numberless replicas of yourself offering a throne. This golden throne then absorbs into the thrones of the guru and the merit field. You then think that they have accepted the request to live long in order to turn the Dharma wheel.

Dedicating

With the final limb, you dedicate all the merit you have accumulated to achieving enlightenment for the sake of all sentient beings. Dedication is a particular antidote to heresy.[58] Its specific result is to achieve the qualities of a buddha's holy body, holy speech, and holy mind.

The verse for this limb in *The King of Prayers* is this:

> Whatever slight positive potential I may have created,
> By paying homage, offering, and acknowledging my faults,
> Rejoicing, and requesting that the buddhas stay and teach,
> I now dedicate all this for full awakening.

The line in the short prayer says, "I dedicate my own and others' virtues to great enlightenment."

You dedicate all the merits you have just accumulated by doing prostrations, making offerings, confessing, and so forth, as well as all the merits of the three times. You can strengthen this by thinking that the merely labeled I is dedicating the merely labeled merit to attain the merely labeled enlightenment for the sake of the merely labeled sentient beings.

OFFERING A MANDALA

Offering a mandala[59] is one of the most powerful methods to collect merit. Besides purifying all other delusions, the specific delusion it purifies is miserliness.

Although there are four ways of making a mandala offering—the outer, inner, secret, and suchness offerings—unless you make a mandala offering in the context of highest yoga tantra, you will really only come across the first two.

The outer mandala is an offering to the guru and merit field of everything beautiful and precious you can think of. There are long mandalas where these are listed extensively, but it is common, especially at the beginning of a meditation session or a teaching, to recite the short mandala:

> This ground, anointed with perfume, strewn with flowers,
> Adorned with Mount Meru, the four continents, the sun, and
>   the moon,
> I imagine it as a buddha land and offer it.
> May all transmigratory beings enjoy this pure land.[60]

Visualizing the mandala offering as beautiful as possible, as a pure realm with the highest quality enjoyments, is a wonderful antidote to miserliness. Psychologically, it helps break strong attachment to material possessions. You can think of all the things you most covet, your most desirable and expensive possessions, and offer them. Rather than grasping onto them, you completely, from the depths of your heart, let go and offer them to the buddhas and bodhisattvas, thinking they are no longer yours.

You can offer as much as you can imagine, not just your possessions and your own body, but all the incredible wealth and enjoyments of this world and of all the other realms. It is said that just one earring of the king of the long-life gods is more valuable than all the wealth in this world, and the god realms are filled with unimaginable treasures. You can offer all that.

Offering like this is so beneficial. Imagine, now, if you were to give somebody something you are incredibly attached to. You would feel miserable. It would feel like a thorn going in your flesh. If you could do it without any sense of clinging, on the other hand, you would feel so calm, so happy, free from the unsubdued, sticky mind that bound you to that object. Doing a mandala offering is a powerful method to purify this unsubdued grasping mind.

The drawn mandalas you see are round and flat, with Mount Meru represented in the center, and the continents surrounding in different colors. However, when you visualize the mandala, you shouldn't just think of it in two dimensions like that, but as a three-dimensional universe. As the prayer says, what you offer is, first, the base, scented with incense and covered in beautiful flowers, then, in the center, Mount Meru, the center of the Buddhist universe. It is surrounded by the four continents and sun and moon.

When you offer the mandala, you visualize that the east is in front of you, whether that is actually so or not. You can also imagine the mandala in front of the merit field, in which case the east will face them and be away from you. One way is for purification, the other to receive realizations. Generally, however, you have the east in front of you.

Each side of Mount Meru is formed of different jewels or precious metals, which reflect to create the skies of the world systems that face that side. The east of Mount Meru, the side facing you, is silver and therefore the color of the sky and ocean of the eastern continent, Tall Body Land (Videha; Lüphakpo), is white, not blue as ours is—a reflection of that side of the mountain. We humans live in the southern continent, Rose Apple Land (Jambudvipa; Dzambuling), the one that faces the south face of the mountain, which is lapis lazuli; its blueness makes our sky and sea blue. The western side is made of rubies, so the sky and ocean of the western continent, Cattle Gift Land (Godaniya; Balangchö), is red, and the northern side is made of gold, so the northern continent, Unpleasant Sound (Kuru; Draminyän), has a yellow sky and ocean. When you offer a long mandala, you recite the names of these four continents or world systems. Then you offer the intermediate lands and other offerings such the wish-granting tree, the precious wheel, the eight goddesses, the sun and moon, and so forth. This varies depending on the mandala, some having thirty-seven "heaps," some twenty-three.[61]

You can also visualize all the realms where sentient beings abide as pure lands, filled with great enjoyment. Rather than horrible environments such as deserts or thorny, rocky places, places of extreme heat or cold, you transform them into extremely beautiful places that the beings living there enjoy.

For the mandala practice, you can just offer with the mandala mudra, but for a long mandala it is best to use a mandala set of base and three rings, which you fill with grain. Any material can be used for the offering, even sand if you cannot find grain. (Many people also like to add precious things to the grain, such as jewels, beads, and the like.)

For the mandala base, although you can even just use a flat stone, like ascetic monks do, a metal one, such as from brass, is better. If you can afford to buy a good mandala set, you should, as the more beautiful it is the more merit you create when you use it.

Since you should not hold the mandala with an empty hand, you take some grain in your hand, then hold the base. You put a little grain on the base, then wipe it off outward three times, thinking that you are purifying your negative karmas of body, speech, and mind and your obscurations, as well as those of all sentient beings. You then add a little grain again and wipe it off in the opposite direction three times, thinking that you and all sentient beings are receiving the blessings of the holy body, holy speech, and holy mind of the guru and of the merit field.

The rings should not be put on an empty base, so first you need to put some grain in the middle of the plate, and then place the largest ring on the base. As you recite the prayer you place a small heap of grain in the various parts of the base, one for each offering, adding the rings as you finish each section.

When you have completed filling the mandala with grain visualized as all these precious things, you place the umbrella and banner on top, lift the mandala up, and offer it at your heart. You can then recite the short mandala and finish with IDAM GURU RATNA MANDALAKAM NIRYATAYAMI, dissolving the mandala by spilling the grain back into the cloth it came from.

In order to multiply the number of the mandala offerings, recite the multiplying mantras[62] three times to bless and increase the offerings, and think that this causes the guru and the merit field to receive clouds of mandala offerings. Visualize that the whole of space is filled with mandalas, just like looking down on a city from a mountain or an airplane at night and seeing all the city lights.

There is also the inner mandala. The prayer says,

> The objects of my attachment, anger, and ignorance—
> Friends, enemies, strangers, body, and enjoyments—
> Without any sense of loss I offer them. Please kindly accept
>   them,
> And bless me to pacify the three poisons in dependence on their
>   own objects.

Your attachment, anger, and ignorance, and the objects of those disturbing thoughts—friends, enemies, and strangers—as well as your own body and your possessions and even the merit you have accumulated: these are things you need to renounce. As long as you hold on to these things, and particularly the three poisonous minds, you will still create negative karma and still have to experience suffering.

The prayer says you offer everything without any sense of loss. Say, you were about to eat a delicious ice cream when a starving beggar comes up to you and asks for it. You might feel you *should* give it to them but in your heart you don't want to. You spent so long in the shop buying it and it cost so much and it's such a hot day. And it's *your* ice cream! You need it for your happiness! So, even if you do give it to the beggar, it is very difficult. That is what "without any sense of loss" means. There should be great joy in giving, not loss.

You normally don't say this inner mandala during teachings, just the outer mandala, but it is there in many of the daily prayers. It is very good to visualize the outer mandala and say the prayer and then continue with this mandala prayer, imagining your entire body absorbing and transforming into the mandala.

REQUESTING THE LINEAGE LAMAS

The last limb is requesting the lineage lamas, although sometimes this is considered to be separate from the seven-limb practice. It is an important preliminary prayer to do after the other limbs and the mandala offering and before the main body of the meditation.

Because the lineage lamas are the spiritual teachers who form a direct line from the founder of the teachings up to the present day, single-pointedly making requests to them is a very powerful way to receive blessings. There is a simple prayer called *Special Requests for the Three Great Purposes* that encapsulates all wishes. This is excellent to recite.

> I prostrate and go for refuge to the Guru and the Three Rare Sublime Ones. Please bless my mind.
>
> Please bless me and all mother sentient beings to immediately cease all the wrong concepts from disrespect to the virtuous friend up to the subtle dual appearances of white appearance, red increase, and dark near attainment.
>
> Please bless us to immediately generate all the right realizations from respect for the virtuous friend up to the unification of no more learning.
>
> Please bless us to immediately pacify all outer and inner obstacles.[63]

The first request asks the Guru[64] and the Three Rare Sublime Ones (and therefore all the lineage lamas) to enable you to cease all the wrong views that you currently hold, from the fundamental wrong view at the very beginning of the lamrim, disrespecting the guru, all the way up to the most subtle wrong view, the final one you must abandon to attain enlightenment, the three dualistic appearances just before attaining the clear light: the white, red, and dark appearances.[65]

The second request is to generate all the right realizations, again from the very fundamental one, guru devotion, up to the very final one, the unification of no more learning, which is the state of buddhahood.

Finally, you request that all your outer and inner obstacles are pacified. There are different interpretations of this line. One way of explaining it is that "outer" means others who block you from practicing Dharma, such as being under the control of kings or outside powers. Inner obstacles include your sicknesses and delusions. You request that all these outer and inner obstacles are pacified immediately.

Everything you need is contained here. I find this request is very effective for the mind, especially in that you purify your broken *samaya* vows, the particular negative karma accumulated in relation with the virtuous friend.[66] Then, by meditating that you and all sentient beings are under the protection of the guru, you receive incredible blessings.

There are also extensive prayers to the lineage lamas, such as the one to the lamrim lineage lamas within the *Lama Chöpa Jorchö* practice, that are very inspiring. In that prayer, there are the names and accomplishments of the masters of the various lineages, such as Maitreya and Asanga as masters of the Method lineage, Manjushri and Nagarjuna as masters of the Wisdom lineage, and the various masters of the Kadam lineages,[67] as well as prayers to the more recent gurus, such as His Holiness Zong Rinpoché and His Holiness the Dalai Lama. It concludes like this:

> Eyes viewing all the infinite scriptures,
> Supreme gateway for the fortunate traveling to liberation,
> Engaging with skillful means moved by love:
> To the illuminating spiritual friends, I make requests.
> May I not give rise to heresy for even a second
> In regard to the actions of the glorious guru.
> May I see whatever actions are done as the stainless [actions of a
>   buddha].
> With this devotion, may I receive the guru's blessings in my
>   heart.[68]

The Completion

After the preliminary practices, there is the main body of the meditation session, whether that is a lamrim meditation, a calm abiding practice, a tantric deity practice, or whatever. When that is concluded, you must finish the session with dedication prayers, dedicating the merits that you have created during the session.

The dedication prayers are absolutely vital. It is so rare to create merit, much rarer than finding the most precious jewel. Normally, nonvirtuous thoughts abound, never allowing even the slightest virtuous ones to arise. As Shantideva says in *A Guide to the Bodhisattva's Way of Life*:

> Only through the inspiration of the awakened ones,
> occasionally arises in a human being, for one instant,
> a thought directed toward the good,
> as lightning flashes for only an instant in clouded night skies.[69]

Therefore, when you do something virtuous, even if it is just a few minutes' breathing meditation, it is crucial you dedicate it at the end of your meditation session so the energy will not be lost. Unless you do, there is the strong possibility that whatever merit you have accumulated by doing the meditation will be destroyed by some powerful negative emotion arising, such as anger or wrong view. The positive imprints you have placed on your mindstream are burned and unable to bring a result, like how grain that has been burned in a fire cannot grow into a plant.

Anger can so easily arise. Even something small, like a friend insulting you or just giving you a strange look, can cause anger to flare up. A small thing, but with the potential to do great damage. Likewise, heresy, holding a wrong view about the teachings of the Buddha or disrespecting the guru, can so easily arise, completely destroying any undedicated merits.

Because it is so important, the dedication practice is not something to do only at the end of a meditation session, but whenever you have done something virtuous and accumulated even a little merit. If you have given a handful of food to a dog with a bodhichitta motivation, you must dedicate the merit right away, thus sealing the merit in your mindstream.

It is useless to dedicate your merits for worldly happiness. You have been experiencing worldly happiness from beginningless lifetimes until now, but you are still not free from delusions. You should also not dedicate your merits solely for your own liberation. Instead, you should dedicate to attain enlightenment for the benefit of other sentient beings.

5. ESTABLISHING A PRACTICE

MAINTAINING A REGULAR MEDITATION practice is the most positive habit we can develop, allowing us to deepen any understanding we have of the Dharma subjects we are studying. It makes us more aware of what we do throughout the day and ensures that everything we do is as virtuous as possible. Whatever we meditate on in the morning should stay with us, coloring our actions and making them pure Dharma. It means there is much less confusion and worry in our life, because we understand the nature of any problem we encounter and can do something to alleviate it. When something goes wrong, we are more relaxed, happier, and more able to solve the problem.

As we deepen our practice, our mind becomes less clouded with negativity. Somehow, something unblocks, the mind opens. We understand things on a more profound level, mainly because of the purification that occurs naturally as we meditate.

Because meditation is familiarizing ourselves with a virtuous object, we should *continuously* meditate, going over one subject again and again. It is very difficult to make the meditation effective unless it is repeated. And by repetition, we are building a very positive habit. At first, we will be unable to hold our object of meditation for more than a few seconds, but repeatedly returning to the object time after time—and day after day—our ability to focus will improve and we will gain a deeper and deeper understanding.

The main thing is to take care of the mind, to try to be aware of its different states and keep it pure. City authorities take great care to keep the water supply of a city pure to stop people being poisoned by a polluted source. Similarly, we must take care of the mind, which is the source of all the positive or negative actions, the actions that brings happiness or confusion. Through having a regular meditation practice, if we constantly watch our mind and use what we learn in our meditations, we can diminish and eliminate the unsubdued minds such as anger, ignorance, or pride, and develop all our positive qualities.

PURIFICATION, ACCUMULATING MERIT, AND GURU YOGA

When Lama Tsongkhapa asked Manjushri what should be done in order to quickly generate the realizations of the path, Manjushri advised three things:

- purification (*sansargi, jangwa*)
- accumulating merit (*punya, sönam*)
- guru yoga (*lama naljor*)

If we conscientiously do these three practices, realizations come like rainfall, without many hardships, without the need to wait many lifetimes. On the other hand, if we don't include these three practices in whatever meditation practice we do, our meditation will be dry and our progress will be slow, with hindrances arising all the time.

At the moment, our mind is like a desert, very hot and arid. Without fertilizing it and making it wet with the twin practices of purifying and accumulating merit, accompanied by a guru yoga practice, no matter how many seeds we plant, nothing much can grow.

Attaining realizations depends on many factors. First, we must *refrain from committing negative actions*, but that is so difficult because we have been habituated to nonvirtue for countless lifetimes. Second, we must *destroy the seeds of the negative actions* that remain on our mindstream so that they can never ripen into suffering. And third, we also need to *accumulate merit*.

Attaining any realization depends on perfecting all the conditions. This is often compared to growing a flower. Besides the seed not being rotten or burned, for it to become the flower depends on having all the right conditions: the perfect soil, water, heat, and so forth.

Usually, when we try to meditate, we start by placing the mind on the chosen object of meditation, such as the breath or the image of the Buddha, and within a few seconds it is somewhere else entirely, our concentration disappearing like a cloud on a hot day.

Mostly what arises in the mind is some material thing or person we are attached to. We can spend hours constructing a long story, like watching a movie. The mind moves around so much, like being blown by a very strong wind, jumping from desirable object to desirable object. Even if we manage to do five minutes' meditation at the beginning, for the rest of the hour we are making a big trip! Sometimes we are busy in the West, sometimes we are traveling in Nepal or India or Indonesia. Attachment to external sense pleasures is the main cause of scattering thoughts, one of the two main hindrances to our meditation.

The blocks to our meditation practice come from the negative karmic seeds we have built up over countless lifetimes. Pabongka Rinpoché explains that in all our countless rebirths we have built up a store of the seeds of each negativity equaling the number of precious objects in a wheel-turning king's treasure house—in other words, incalculable. They are all on our mental continuum just waiting to ripen.

Since our mind is very weak and our delusions are very powerful, almost every single action we do is motivated by worldly concern, the wish for the happiness of this life, which means that it is all nonvirtue. Worldly concern keeps us in bed on a cold day, rather than doing that hour's meditation before work. We say we can't find time to meditate, but we seem to have plenty of time to eat and drink, plenty of time to talk, plenty of time to sleep. And even if we have plenty of time to meditate, our agitated mind won't let us.

Whereas accumulating virtue is like rolling a huge rock to the top of a mountain, creating nonvirtue is unbelievably easy; it happens uncontrollably, like the rock tumbling back down the mountain. Creating nonvirtue is also often compared to a waterfall, the forceful way our negativities pour down on us. In *A Guide to the Bodhisattva's Way of Life* Shantideva says,

For the sin of one instant
one falls into the avici hell for one cosmic age;
but if it is about sin accumulated since beginningless time,
how can you speak of good destinies?[70]

Because it is so important to avoid even the smallest negative action and strive to do even the smallest positive one, we need to watch our mind at all times, looking out for even the slightest disturbing thought to arise and, if one does arise, immediately averting it.

We need to not only refrain from committing nonvirtuous actions but also purify the imprints of previous ones that sit in our mindstream, ready to ripen at any moment. Both are vital. Unless we stop creating nonvirtue, no matter how much we purify, it will be futile. We purify, but then there is always something new to purify. Like an elephant who cleans off all the dirt by washing in the river and then immediately rolls in the dirt again when it comes out, our need to purify will have no end! There will be no end to the prostrations we need to make or the Vajrasattva retreats we need to do.

On the other hand, purifying our previous negative karma while not creating new negative karma is the infallible method to free our mind from the obscurations that rob us from happiness now and in future and block us from all realizations. And the most powerful mind to have while purifying is bodhichitta. If we can recite even one Vajrasattva mantra with bodhichitta, we receive the same benefit as having recited it one hundred thousand times.

How to Purify

When we do a powerful purification practice, we can destroy the imprints of even very heavy negative karma. When our purification is less powerful, the heavy negative karma is weakened rather than completely destroyed. This means, for instance, instead of experiencing rebirth in a lower realm in the next life, the karma will be exhausted through experiencing a disease or some other problem in this life.

Of the many ways to purify, the lamrim texts usually list six:

- prostrating and reciting the holy names of the buddhas, such as the Thirty-Five Buddhas
- reciting purifying mantras such as the Vajrasattva mantra
- making holy objects such as thangkas, statues, and *tsatsas*[71]
- reciting *Prajnaparamita* (*Perfection of Wisdom*) texts such as the *Heart of Wisdom Sutra* or the *Diamond Cutter Sutra*
- meditating on emptiness and bodhichitta and similar subjects
- making offerings to the Buddha, Dharma, and Sangha

There are specific meditation practices designed to purify our mindstream quickly, such as the Vajrasattva practice, but other methods are also very effective. Purification and accumulating merit form part of all deity practices, implicitly or explicitly, such as in the simple Shakyamuni Buddha meditation. A much more extensive purification practice is the incredibly powerful two-day fasting *nyungné* retreat, based on prayers and prostrations to Chenrezig, the compassion buddha. By fasting and focusing on the suffering of others, our mind is cleansed of self-cherishing.

Another extremely effective purification method is the practice of the Thirty-Five Buddhas, where we visualize the Thirty-Five Buddhas and prostate to each one as we say his name. It is very good to do this every day either in the evening before we go to bed or whenever we can. This purifies any negative karma we have created during that day.

Because Vajrasattva is the specific deity for purification, reciting the Vajrasattva mantra daily or in a long retreat—usually three months with a hundred thousand mantras—is considered the supreme method of purification. The practice has the ability to not only purify our general nonvirtues but even the very heavy negativities such as breaking the bodhisattva or tantric vows.

It is recommended that each day we recite either the long hundred-syllable mantra twenty-one times or the short one twenty-eight times[72] in order to stop the increase of any negative karma we have accumulated during that day as well as purifying the negative karma accumulated during this life and beginningless previous lives. Of course, reciting a full mala of the long mantra is more powerful than just twenty-one recitations, but even if we cannot do that before going to bed each day, a shorter recitation will still purify our negativities.

To be able to do a three-month Vajrasattva retreat is truly wonderful. It is stated that the Vajrasattva mantra is so powerful that reciting it a hundred thousand times purifies any infraction of the root tantric vows, and even the five heavy negative karmas without break and the five nearing heavy negative karmas without break[73] are purified. Therefore, what more worthwhile thing is there to do in life than this?

Another way to purify is by making holy objects, but we can also purify by having them in our home—as many as possible—and prostrating to them by placing our palms together whenever we enter a room they are in.

Reciting texts is an incredibly powerful way of purifying negativities, especially the holy sutras like the *Arya Sanghata Sutra*, the *Diamond Cutter Sutra,* and the *Heart of Wisdom Sutra*, as is meditating on emptiness or bodhichitta, and making offerings to the Three Rare Sublime Ones.

The Four Opponent Powers

Purification does not depend solely on the number of mantras recited. As Pabongka Dechen Nyingpo explains, how effective the purification is depends on both strong regret and strong determination not to commit the negative action again.

With these two factors, the purification becomes extremely powerful, especially when done within the practice known as the four opponent powers. Lama Tsongkhapa says that by cherishing the practice of the four opponent powers, we not only purify the stains of the negative actions we have done in the past but also turn away from doing them again in the future. The four opponent powers are these:

- the power of the object
- the power of regret
- the power of resolve
- the power of the remedy[74]

Based on strong refuge in the Buddha, Dharma, and Sangha, the *object*, we look at the negativities we have committed and have a genuine feeling of *regret*, reflecting on the shortcomings of creating negative karma. The more regret we are able to feel, the more powerful our purification becomes, and the more negative karma and obscurations we purify. This naturally leads us to determine not to do such actions again—the third power of *resolve*. Based on this, we do a purification practice such as reciting Vajrasattva mantras or prostrations. This is the power of the *remedy*. Any virtuous practice that we do is the remedy to our negative karma, and therefore this fourth power can be reading a text that explains emptiness, meditating on bodhichitta, or any virtuous action of body, speech, or mind.

When we do a particular purification practice such as Vajrasattva, we often reverse the last two powers, doing the visualization of the purification deity and reciting the mantras—the remedy—and then, before the deity dissolves into us, we make the resolve never to do the action again.

It is very good to do this practice three times in the morning, then three times later in the day, perhaps after lunch, and then once at night before falling asleep. Alternatively, we can do the practice three times in the evening. Powerfully and continually purifying our negativities in this way helps to ensure any negative karma we have committed does not manifest as suffering. Even though the effects of a negative action we did today might not be completely purified by that one purification practice, it will certainly be lessened, and thus it is incredibly worthwhile to make purification with the four powers a regular part of our Dharma practice. Purification is like a fire and negativities are the grain burned in that fire.

Accumulating Merit

Merit refers to the positive imprints left on our mind by virtuous actions. There are two types of merit: the *merit of wisdom* and the *merit of virtue*. The merit of wisdom (*jnanasambhara, yeshé kyitsok*) develops the wisdom side of the path by meditating on emptiness in order to achieve the buddha's holy mind, the dharmakaya; and the *merit of virtue* or the *merit of fortune* (*punyasambhara, sönam kyitsok*) develops the method side of the path by practicing patience, ethics, compassion, and so forth, in order to achieve the buddha's holy body, the rupakaya.

Tibetan Buddhism places great emphasis on collecting merit because without merit there can be no happiness. Happiness doesn't arise from nonvirtue, only from virtue, so without merit nothing positive can be achieved.

As soon as the work of accumulating extensive merit and purifying all obscurations is completed, we are a buddha. In Tibetan, "buddha" is *sangyé*, which means one who has totally eliminated (*sang*) all obscurations veiling the mind and has fully developed (*gye*) all good qualities to perfection. As long as there are some merits still to be created and some defilements still to be purified, there is no omniscient mind. Even the arhats, who have achieved freedom from samsara and have incredible psychic powers, cannot do perfect work for others because they have not completed the two accumulations of wisdom and virtue.

We need to create as much positive potential on our mindstream as we can and guard it well. As I have said, the only way to stop the results of a virtuous action from getting lost is by dedicating the merits that we have created. As soon as we do something positive, we should dedicate that it will be the cause for us to become enlightened for the sake of all sentient beings. That is like locking it into our mindstream. Otherwise, it is incredibly easy for a negative mind to destroy our merit. It is mentioned in the teachings that dedicating our merit in this way is like putting one drop of water into the ocean. As long as the ocean exists, that drop of water exists. Therefore, we should take every opportunity to collect merit.

Guru Yoga

Along with purification and the accumulation of merit, Manjushri's third advice to best gain realizations is practicing guru yoga. Correctly following the virtuous friend, the essence of guru yoga, is actually the integration of the other two. When we have correct guru devotion, all else follows easily. As the Fifth Dalai Lama says,

When the perfect guru and perfect receptacle—the
   disciple—meet,
enlightenment comes like molding dough in the hand.

With a lump of dough, we can easily make many things with our
hands—*momos*,[75] bread, or cakes. Likewise, with guru devotion, we
can easily create an enlightened mind as if shaping it by hand. For that,
we must be the perfect disciple, somebody able to practice the advice of
the guru and bear any hardships that occur.

Among everything, the guru is the most powerful. In the *Samputa
Tantra* it is said,

> Making offerings to one pore of the guru surpasses making
> offerings to all the buddhas of the three times.[76]

"One pore of the guru" can mean a disciple, a husband or wife, a child, a
friend, a neighbor, or even the guru's animal. Even giving a cup of water
or a spoonful of food to a dog or bird that belongs to the guru accumu-
lates the most extensive merit. And tantric texts explain that following
the guru's advice perfectly creates much more merit than doing all the
preliminary practices for many, many years, even for eons.

In the *Foundation of All Good Qualities*, Lama Tsongkhapa says,

> The foundation of all good qualities is the kind and perfect guru;
> Correctly following the guru is the root of the path.
> By my clearly seeing this and applying great effort,
> Please bless me to rely upon the guru with great respect.[77]

Correctly devoting to the virtuous friend is the beginning of the road to
enlightenment. On the path we will undoubtedly encounter obstacles,
and the most skillful means to overcome these is practicing guru yoga,
correctly following the guru.

There are many stories that show us this. Milarepa was able to become
enlightened in one lifetime by perfectly following his guru, Marpa.

Tilopa, the guru of the great yogi Naropa, had him undertake twelve great and twelve lesser hardships before he was willing to initiate him into a highest tantric deity and give him instructions. Therefore, when we show devotion to the guru and follow the guru's advice, we should really rejoice that we are doing the best preliminary practice, just as Milarepa and Naropa did.

Sakya Pandita[78] says,

> Even though sunbeams are very hot,
> without a magnifying glass, they cannot ignite a fire.
> It is the same with the blessings of the buddhas:
> without the guru, they cannot enter the disciple.[79]

In the same way we need a magnifying glass to use the sun's rays to ignite wood, we need the guru. Even though the buddhas have wonderful qualities such as unbelievable compassion, without the guru we cannot receive their blessings.

Because Lama Tsongkhapa founded the Geluk tradition of Tibetan Buddhism, within our lineage many of the guru yoga practices take him as the root guru, such as the entire *Guru Puja* (*Lama Chöpa*) or the *Lama Tsongkhapa Guru Yoga* (*Ganden Lha Gyama*). There are also the extended and short versions of *Six-Session Guru Yoga*[80] and prayers like *Calling the Guru from Afar*.

When we practice *Lama Tsongkhapa Guru Yoga*, Guru Lama Tsongkhapa enters our heart, and we try to remember him in our heart for the rest of the day. In the same way, we should constantly keep our own guru in our heart and do our work for him or her. Then, everything we do from morning until night becomes guru yoga practice.

The first retreat I did in Tibet just before escaping was on *Lama Tsongkhapa Guru Yoga*, but I had no idea what I was doing. The monk who took care of me, Losang Gyatso, gave me the text but gave no explanation, and at the time I didn't have the capacity to understand it. I believe that I finished reciting a hundred thousand *Migtsemas* and then did a tsok offering.[81] On the same night we escaped from Tibet.

A Map for the Complete Day

Developing a regular meditation practice is vital, and there are many ways you can do this, depending on your individual aspirations and on how much time you have.

A skillful way to practice is to start your morning meditation with a purification practice, such as doing prostrations while reciting the names of the Thirty-Five Buddhas. After that, before beginning a lamrim or another meditation, you should do a practice on guru devotion.

It is important to begin every day by developing the mind in guru devotion by doing some form of guru yoga practice, continuing until you achieve a stable realization. For a length of time, even ten or fifteen minutes, you should train in seeing the guru and the Buddha as inseparable until you feel from the very bottom of your heart, without a single doubt, that there is no separation between them, like pouring water into water.

Following that, you then do whatever meditation you want to develop, such as a lamrim meditation on a particular subject, a shamatha meditation, or a tantric practice. If you are doing a regular lamrim meditation, you can slowly work through the three levels of the lower, middle, and higher capable beings to train your mind in the whole path.

Don't remain fixed on one subject. Pabongka Dechen Nyingpo warns that if you meditate on only one meditation during your whole life, you may not achieve even that realization and then you have nothing. For instance, although of course meditating on impermanence and death is considered vital because it cuts the strong desire of clinging to this life, it is not sufficient to spend your whole life on it, no matter how beneficial the meditation is. If you just stay on that one meditation, you can't remove the root of samsara and realize emptiness. You need to progress to the next stage. Therefore, he advises that a quick way to attain lamrim realizations is to do a range of meditations.

Developing shamatha is also very important, taking your mind from its habituation to external objects to the mind itself, allowing you to discover things about yourself that you don't normally see. When you achieve a degree of concentration, the mind becomes extremely powerful, which helps in all the other practices you do.

This is my suggestion for you if you really want to transform your mind and make your life most meaningful. Starting each day with a purification practice, a glance meditation, a meditation on guru devotion and one other lamrim topic, with diligence, you may achieve a realization of guru devotion, which makes all the other realizations come easily. If you are fortunate enough—if you have enough merit—then you may be able to achieve all three principal aspects of the path and even the two stages of tantra in one lifetime.

You should always remember the meditation you did in the morning when you go about your daily life. Especially, when there is a danger of an angry or dissatisfied mind arising, that is the real time to practice Dharma. The meditation session should have created the very positive energy that carries over into everything else you do, allowing you to deal with problems and avert any potentially negative action of body, speech, or mind.

Having generated a bodhichitta motivation in your session, you must then try to live your life for others, to do everything you can for others. With a bodhichitta motivation, every action is transformed into the cause of enlightenment. In that way, every second of your life is highly meaningful.

Besides the morning lamrim meditations, I also recommend that each evening you do a meditation on emptiness, gradually familiarizing yourself with the subject. And before going to bed, you should purify whatever negativities have been acquired during the day by doing a Vajrasattva practice, even if it just saying the long Vajrasattva mantra twenty-one times or the short one twenty-eight times. This will purify any negative actions you did during that day.

Finally, just as each meditation session should end with a perfect dedication, at the end of the day you should dedicate all the merits you have accumulated during the day. There are many standard dedication prayers, such as in the FPMT prayer books. *The King of Prayers*[82] is wonderful but quite long. But even if you cannot do this, there are dedication prayers of just a few verses, and it is very good to do these. What you are mainly doing is praying that your life is the most productive, the most beneficial it can be, for other sentient beings.

Planning for the Year

Just as it is good to have a daily schedule of meditation planned, you can make a general plan for a whole year or more. For instance, you can plan to focus mainly on the meditations of the graduated path of the lower capable being for the first year, spending a year meditating step-by-step from perfect human rebirth up to karma. Then, for the next year, you can focus mainly on the graduated path of the middle capable being, basically to develop some feeling of the renunciation of the whole of samsara. The following year your primary focus can be the meditations on bodhichitta, and then, for the next year, you can spend time meditating on emptiness.

That does not mean you never touch the other meditations at all during this time. As I have said, every day it is good to begin with guru devotion as well as a meditation on emptiness sometime during the day. But this multi-year plan is one way to meditate on the lamrim in order to achieve the realizations of the three principal aspects of the path. Of course you can meditate on bodhichitta while you are meditating on the lower path, but my suggestion is that you mainly focus on one subject at a time.

I mentioned spending one year on each path, but actually how long you take is not the main point. The main point is that when you achieve one level of realization, you then go on to the next level.

6. DEVELOPING SHAMATHA

SHAMATHA WITHIN TIBETAN BUDDHISM

You will hear many names for meditating single-pointedly on an object. The Sanskrit is *shamatha*.[83] The Tibetan term, *shiné*, consists of *shi*, which means "calm" or "peace" and *né*, which means to "abide" or "stay." From that we have the common English term "calm abiding," referring to the state where the mind is able to rest in utter concentration, completely undisturbed by scattering thoughts or sinking thoughts (often called "excitement" and "laxity" or "dullness").

In *A Hymn of Experience* (*Lamrim nyamgur*) Lama Tsongkhapa says,

> Concentration is a king ruling the mind:
> When placed, it is as immovable as Mount Meru;
> When sent forth, it engages all virtuous objects.
> It induces the great bliss of a serviceable body and mind.
> Having understood this, the lords of yogis rely continuously
> On the meditative stabilization that destroys the enemy,
>   distraction.
> You, the perfect guru, practiced in this way.
> I, who am seeking liberation, will also practice in this way.[84]

Until we have attained a good degree of concentration through the practice of shamatha, it is extremely difficult to stop our mind from going wherever it wants, running toward nonvirtuous thoughts and away from virtuous ones. After achieving shamatha, it easily, naturally, and continuously follows virtue. With shamatha the mind is stable, like an immovable great mountain.

When he visited Lama Yeshe and me, our dear friend and great meditator Gen Jampa Wangdu sometimes used to say, "Until you achieve shamatha, what you call meditation is not meditation." To emphasize the point, he would wave his hands around when he said this. I think this was because he himself had had this realization. Through great perseverance, he was able to stay in meditation as long as he wanted, keeping his mind virtuous even outside of meditation sessions.

Generally, when we have some mental clarity it is easier to remember things, whereas we remember less when the mind is foggier, more disturbed. There are times when we can't even remember things closest to us, such as the names of our friends! However, through practice and when certain conditions come together—when we can break free from the usual preoccupation with attachment, anger, and so forth—remembering things becomes easier, developing compassion becomes easier, understanding the nature of reality becomes easier. This is due to having let the mind settle, like a stirred-up glass of murky water becomes clear when we just let the sediment in it settle to the bottom.

Many people are born with special mental aptitudes, such as the ability to remember past lives, while others develop it during their life through particular practices, such as meditating on certain deities. This is an ordinary form of clairvoyance. The most reliable clairvoyance, however, is that which comes through attaining shamatha. Shamatha has nine stages, and as we progress through these, the obstacles to clarity are slowly overcome; the gross scattering and sinking thoughts become subtler, diminishing until they are completely eliminated.

Only after the subtle sinking thought and subtle scattering thought are completely stopped, *only then*, do we have perfect single-pointed concentration, perfect shamatha, without any obstacles. When this happens on the ninth stage, we experience the extremely refined rapturous ecstasy of body and mind. They say that LSD has no comparison to it! I'm joking, but there is certainly no comparison to any ordinary experiences we call "happiness."

For Tibetan Buddhists, shamatha is developed through either a deity practice within Vajrayana or by using the image of the Buddha or a meditational deity as the object of meditation. While any object can be used, the advantages of single-pointedly concentrating on a virtuous object like this are enormous. Not only do we attain shamatha but, by constantly remembering the Buddha, we purify so much and create such unbelievable merit.

At first we cannot hold a complete visualization of the Buddha clearly, or even one aspect of his holy body. Not only that, we need to make the image quite large. But over time our visualization becomes clearer and we can reduce its size, thus increasing the intensity.[85]

When we can make the object clear by intensively holding it, then we try to abide continuously on the object of concentration. When we can abide *continuously* on the meditational object, *intensively* and *clearly* holding it, then we have accomplished stainless single-pointed concentration.

With shamatha, our mind naturally follows virtuous objects. Although it is not ultimate liberation, it is as if we have experienced liberation because there is an unbelievable freedom. Virtuous activities come effortlessly, and the body feels extremely light, like cotton.

The most important function of shamatha, however, is the support it gives to our realization of emptiness, and emptiness is vital for complete liberation from suffering. Without shamatha, realizing emptiness is impossible. In his *Lamp for the Path to Enlightenment* Lama Atisha explains,

> When the practitioner has gained calm abiding,
> Higher perception will also be gained,
> But without the practice of the perfection of wisdom,
> The obstructions will not come to an end.[86]

With shamatha and emptiness we attain liberation. And when shamatha and emptiness are combined with bodhichitta, then enlightenment is assured.

THE PREREQUISITES FOR SHAMATHA

At the very end of the *Three Principal Aspects of the Path*, Lama Tsongkhapa says,

> In this way you realize exactly
> The vital points of the three principal aspects of the path.
> Resort to seeking solitude, generate the power of effort,
> And quickly accomplish your final goal, my child.[87]

If we wish to attain shamatha, we need the best possible conditions, and that means, if we are able to, going into retreat in a quiet, conducive place. I think it is very good for people who are serious about developing their meditations to retreat as much as possible. To develop shamatha well we need five prerequisites:

- dwelling in a conducive place
- having few desires
- being content
- having pure morality
- giving up the worldly life and abandoning distractions

Dwelling in a Conducive Place

A tantric commentary[88] says the retreat place should be isolated but very special. There should be water close by, and the surroundings should be very beautiful, such as being near a wood with lots of flowers, and so forth. In the forest there should be animals singing songs and dancing—maybe at nighttime when we are trying to sleep. I'm joking. But anyway it should be a very beautiful, very peaceful place where we really want to be.

When I wanted to look for really quiet place—not a place where there is no sound, I don't think you could find that—I heard of a very famous area in California, Big Sur, where people who were unhappy or depressed went to get relief for a short time. It is near the ocean and as you drive down the mountain to it there are many flowers. We managed to obtain some land, which we called Land of Calm Abiding. Actually, it is not a normal Tibetan situation for a retreat place, which is generally high up so there is a vast view that is pleasant for the mind and conducive to becoming happy. Land of Calm Abiding is at the bottom of the mountain. You have to go all the way down and through the forest. But I think for Western people it's different. Everybody who has done a retreat there likes it so much and they have had great experiences.

It's not that there is no sound. There is a military base nearby and so you hear jets and maybe sometimes a bomb! Bears have also been coming to the land. Once, while a meditator who has done very long retreats there, Roger Munro, was out, a bear broke down the door to his retreat hut, trying to take the food from the refrigerator. But although Land of Calm Abiding has some problems, it is not a place where there are very dangerous elements such as robbers, thieves, poisonous snakes, and so forth—which is a condition stated in the text.

It should not be a place that has been used by kings, ministers, and so forth, people who are *marungpa*, which means evil beings who are engaged in heavy negative karma. Nor should it be a place inhabited by worldly gods and spirits who dislike the Dharma and Dharma practitioners and wish to harm them. If we practice in such a place, especially as a beginner before we have the realizations of bodhichitta, renunciation, or emptiness, we will be unable to pacify these spirits and will be harmed. We will certainly have difficulty practicing there.

The text says it should be a place where the sun rises quite early, meaning it should not be where there is no sunlight until late, such as mountainous places where the peaks block the sun until mid-morning, giving little time to do things. Living in a place where the sun rises early, it is easier for virtues to increase.

It should be a place less frequented by people, but it should also be easy to obtain what we need, which I guess means food and other essentials, such as firewood, gas, or kerosene. The place should be free from elements that are unhealthy—earth, water, and so forth—things that cause diseases. It is important to find this out before the retreat, because it often happens that people get sick from contaminated water and have to stop their retreat. This doesn't happen so much due to fire or earth, but we need good water.

Having Few Desires and Being Content

We should have few desires. That is another way of saying we should be satisfied with whatever we have—with whatever quality or quantity of materials we have, such as the place, our clothes, the food, and so forth. Just having a few things should be enough. As His Holiness the Dalai Lama often says, even if we are living in a grass hut with only water to drink and ragged clothes to wear, if we have a good heart, a contented mind, there is so much peace and happiness in the heart, so much enjoyment in life.

However we live, the most important thing is the mind living in solitude. Our mind lives in the cave of the mind whether our body lives in isolation or not. We can live in the middle of a city like New York and lead a busy life, but if we have renounced worldly concerns, our mind is in retreat. Conversely, we can be in a cave in the Himalayas but with a mind full of desire, physically in retreat but not mentally. Only when we have renounced all the meaningless worldly affairs can we complete the attainments of the path.

The real isolation is when we have cut off the clinging to this life. Generally, we also have to be isolated from the self-cherishing thought and from self-grasping—the ignorance that believes the I is truly existent. If that is so, wherever we are living—even at the beach, in the busiest city, in the most luxurious hotel—we are living in an isolated place. That place is our hermitage.

Gen Jampa Wangdu used to encourage me when I slept too much, because I was so lazy. In Dharamsala, he lived in a cave which was not so much within a rock wall as under a big stone. Further up the mountain, at Tushita Retreat Center, I lived in comparative luxury, with everything there to help practice the eight worldly dharmas, to cherish them and make them more powerful, which is why my room had so many decorations. His cave was a Kadampa geshé's cave, for somebody who had renounced this life, with no decorations, just bare rock, and so low you couldn't even stand up or stretch your body. To sleep, there was no bed with springs; he simply put leaves on the floor and sat on them. In that place, he was completely content.

Having Pure Morality

Living in morality is vital. Without it there is no foundation for realizations, for liberation or enlightenment. How well we are able to concentrate without obstacles directly depends on how moral our life is.

This is especially true when we are trying to attain shamatha, which depends on having gathered the causes by protecting our morality well. If we are going to do a long shamatha retreat, whether we succeed and how long it takes depends entirely on how pure our morality is.

From his own experience, Geshé Lamrimpa[89] explains that when we practice shamatha we are very sensitive to changes in the weather and in our own aggregates. Being too hot or cold can affect how well we can concentrate, so we must take care of our health, making sure the four elements of our body[90] are balanced. He also emphasized we must avoid those who have degenerated their samaya, the pledges made in front of the guru. That heavy negative karma pollutes everything around them, including anybody they meet. Even staying in a place where somebody has broken their samaya with their guru, their mental pollution can affect us, making it difficult to practice. His Holiness Zong Rinpoché said that even the drinking water becomes polluted.

Giving Up the Worldly Life and Abandoning Distractions

The next one is also called "avoiding the opposite of calm abiding," which implies not just avoiding the distractions of worldly life, which seems a bit limited, but also avoiding all distorted concepts. Because of our clinging to the view of the changeable aggregates—seeing the body and mind (and all phenomena) as permanent and unchanging whereas they are the complete opposite—we become attached to the I and what is "mine," to people and things—which block us from focusing our mind. By seeing the shortcomings of clinging to the eight worldly dharmas, we can generate renunciation, which will mean being in isolation is much easier and we develop strong concentration much more quickly.

In *A Guide to the Bodhisattva's Way of Life*, Shantideva says,

> Distraction is not possible in one
> whose body and mind are withdrawn.
> Therefore, one should renounce the world
> and abandon the inner discourse of desire.[91]

Associating too much with relatives and friends is a great distraction when we are trying to meditate. Talking and doing things with them can easily trigger various delusions. What worldly people mostly talk about is anything other than the Dharma, things to do with objects of attachment or anger. It then becomes so easy for what we talked about with them to take over our meditation session, blocking us from any degree of concentration.

Isolating ourselves from objects of desire is another method to avoid distraction. If we have particular things we are attached to, we should make sure we keep away from them during the retreat to avoid our attachment to them interfering with our meditation.

Worldly concern means clinging to *my* body, *my* possessions, *my* family, *my* relatives, *my* this and that. Because the attachment we have for both other sentient beings and external objects blocks us from forsaking this worldly life, we should do everything possible to abandon this clinging. Similarly, with anger, because it destroys so much merit and makes concentration impossible, we must do everything we can to overcome our anger and develop our patience. If our mind is occupied with such things, how can we possibly gain concentration?

Lama Tsongkhapa's *Foundation of All Good Qualities* says,

> Please bless me to pacify completely
> The collections of outer and inner obstacles.[92]

Outer obstacles are those external things that stop us from practicing the

Dharma. Even though from our side we might have the wish to do so, we cannot because we are under the power of other people, politicians or bosses, or we have to go into the army to avoid being imprisoned and punished—things like this. These are gross external hindrances, but it could also be something as simple as a dog barking outside or a sudden flea bite, causing us to lose our concentration. Of course, if we had not created the cause for it to happen, then there would be no such obstacle, but the conditions are external.

Inner obstacles are states of mind or body that disturb our concentration, things such as sickness, anger, and the like. Therefore, to experience fewer distractions in our retreat, we must look after ourselves. In his tantric commentary, Gyaltsap Jé explains how, although it also depends on the weather and other external conditions, to concentrate well we must take care of our diet, our health, and so forth, making sure we don't get sick or too tired. We all know from daily life how tiredness can affect our concentration.

When we have actualized shamatha, our mind will be able to concentrate single-pointedly on the absolute nature of reality without any distractions. Until that time, there will be obstacles, and our job in retreat and in our daily life is to lessen and then eliminate those obstacles. The prime preparation for achieving shamatha is living in morality. In that way, we protect our body, speech, and mind, keeping them away from creating negative actions, thus making our mind conducive to concentration.

The Five Hindrances and the Eight Antidotes

There are five hindrances to the development of shamatha:

- laziness
- forgetting the object
- sinking and scattering thought
- not applying the appropriate antidote
- applying an antidote when it is not needed

These five hindrances are counteracted by the eight antidotes:

- confidence or faith—opposes laziness
- determination—opposes laziness
- perseverance—opposes laziness
- pliancy or tranquility—opposes laziness
- mindfulness—opposes forgetting the object
- awareness—opposes sinking and scattering thought
- application of the appropriate antidote—opposes any of the above
- equanimity—opposes overapplying an antidote

Asanga explains that to achieve shamatha we need to overcome the five hindrances by practicing the appropriate antidote. The fourth hindrance is when we fail to do that. Sometimes we unnecessarily apply an antidote, such as bringing awareness to investigate whether we are still fully concentrating and hence breaking our concentration. This is applying an antidote when it is not needed and is itself a hindrance.

These hindrances and antidotes are explained in the lamrim commentaries such as Kamalashila's *Stages of Meditation* (*Bhavanakrama; Gomrim*)[93] and the shamatha sections of Pabongka Dechen Nyingpo's *Liberation in the Palm of Your Hand*.[94] If we could practice shamatha according to these teachings, we would be able to generate perfect shamatha, but many people just read a few pages of advice and seem satisfied with that. Even if we were to try to generate faultless concentration for our whole life, unless we learned how to recognize the faults and apply the antidotes, perfect concentration would be impossible.

Laziness and Its Antidotes: Confidence, Determination, Perseverance, and Pliancy

What mainly prevents us from attaining shamatha is laziness. When we feel lazy, we become discouraged and lose interest in trying to develop concentration. Therefore we need to apply the antidotes of confidence, determination, perseverance, and pliancy or tranquility.

There are three types of laziness:

- the laziness of procrastination
- the laziness of attraction to samsaric activities
- the laziness of discouragement

Having no energy to practice virtue, we put it off, thinking that relaxing is a pleasure whereas practicing the Dharma is not. This can refer to any virtuous action or a specific Dharma action such as, in this instance, the intention to develop shamatha. We keep delaying our meditation because it seems such hard work—relaxing is much more enjoyable—and we actually develop an aversion to trying to meditate. This becomes a habit. This is what stops the mind and body from becoming functional, blocking us from progressing along the path.

The second laziness is attraction to samsaric activities. It could be keeping ourselves very busy with worldly activities such as work, parties, holidays, and so forth, or indulging in things like alcohol, cigarettes, or drugs. We can be working incredibly hard to obtain what we want, but it is considered a laziness because it keeps us from practicing the Dharma. Being attracted to any of the ten nonvirtues[95] agitates our mind and makes us unable to concentrate and therefore is considered a laziness.

The third laziness is discouragement. Because of our low sense of self-worth, we feel we are unable to meditate. Maybe we would like to do a retreat but never get around to it because we convince ourselves we would be hopeless at it. Putting ourselves down like that stops our ability to develop our meditation practice.

To remedy laziness, we need to practice the first four of the eight antidotes: confidence or faith, determination, perseverance, and pliancy. Thinking of the many advantages of developing single-pointed concentration and how so many others have achieved it using the same methods we have been advised to use, we become firmly convinced we too can achieve shamatha, causing us to have great joy and determination that we will succeed. From *that* arises the perseverance needed to completely develop our concentration. Then, as a result, pliancy of the mind arises, producing an extremely refined bliss. This all seems a long way off for us beginners, but through confidence, determination, and perseverance it will certainly happen.

Forgetting the Object and Its Antidote: Mindfulness

When we are trying to develop shamatha, forgetting the object of meditation is a persistent problem. This can also be called "forgetting the advice" or "forgetting the instruction." We try to hold the object of meditation, but we so easily slip off it, "forgetting" it.

Because this hindrance is the exact opposite of mindfulness, mindfulness (*smrti, drenpa*), also called "remembering" or "recollection," is the vital factor in ensuring we can remain focused, stopping sinking and scattering thoughts from arising. Forgetting the object means just that: placing our mind on the object of meditation and then, due to lack of mindfulness, allowing the mind to wander, losing the object. As a beginner, we need to very quickly learn the skill of seeing when our mind has slipped from its object by using our awareness, and then bringing it back to the object. This is something we will have to do repeatedly, again and again and again and again.

When discussing this hindrance and its antidote, Pabongka Dechen Nyingpo uses the example of visualizing the Buddha.[96] He explains not only how to build a vivid image of the Buddha in our mind, but also the problems that we can experience.

For beginners, it is very difficult to have a clear appearance of the whole aspect of the Buddha, but by building an overall picture and scanning the visualization several times, back and forth, we can find our object of meditation, whether it is one detail, such as the head or a hand, or the entire body that appears to the mind. We should not expect much clarity but rather be satisfied just with whatever clarity there is. Then we should hold the object of meditation intensely, with mindfulness.

If the visualization of the Buddha's holy body becomes unclear, we can again do the analytical meditation on the details from the head down to the feet. Then we again concentrate on the general aspect, whatever comes. We just carry on like this as much as possible so that the visualization of that aspect of the Buddha becomes clear. After some time, after many sessions, we can slowly incorporate the other aspects and build a complete visualization of the Buddha, seeing even the small details. We will finally be able to visualize the holy body extremely clearly, clearer than we could physically see it were the Buddha actually sitting there.

Scattering and Sinking Thoughts and Their Antidote: Awareness

We need a balanced mind when we are concentrating single-pointedly on an object, taking the middle road between having scattering thoughts or excitement and sinking thoughts, also called laxity or dullness.

With shamatha, we are trying not only to hold the object clearly but also to hold it for as long as we can. Because stability means being able to hold the object without wandering, the chief obstacle to stability is having scattering thoughts, the mind that runs to other objects, whereas the chief obstacle to clarity, seeing the object clearly or intensely, is having sinking thoughts, which cause the mind to become dull. If we hold the object of meditation too tightly, the mind easily gets distracted, whereas if we hold the object too loosely, the mind lets go of the concentration and sinks into a dull state. Only when we have reached the ninth level of calm abiding will we be free from the very subtle levels of these two obstacles and have perfect meditation.

Our concentration is a fine balance between excitement and dullness, between scattering thoughts and sinking thoughts. It's like we are trying to drive a car at exactly the right speed—too fast and we'll be pulled over by the police; too slow and we won't get to work on time. Not getting booked and not getting fired takes great skill!

The common English term for *shamatha* is calm abiding, abiding in calm. In what way is it calm? It is the calmness or peace that comes from being free from the disturbances to concentration, namely scattering and sinking thoughts. Single-pointed concentration is a blissfully peaceful mind. Experiencing any *un*peaceful mind at all is due to one of these two hindrances.

Even if we have been meditating for a long time, unpeaceful minds can easily arise, like weeds choking a crop unless they are carefully watched. We might have the name "meditator," having meditated for many years in a solitary place, but we find we still face hindrances. Just as a farmer must attack the weeds at the roots—just pulling off the stems will have little effect—we must remove the root of our hindrances, the mind's propensity to either follow other objects or to fall into dullness. Unless we do, they will always interfere with our meditations.

There are two types of scattering thoughts, a gross type and a subtle type. First, there is the gross kind, what I usually call "attachment scattering thoughts" (*auddhatya, göpa*), which is where the mind loses the object of meditation through attachment. This is the most common type. Generally, when we try to focus the mind, it will quickly move from the object of meditation to an object of attachment, such as a delicious chocolate cake.

The other type of scattering thought, the subtle type, is sometimes just called "scattering" (*visarana, trowa*). This refers to any mind wandering from the object of meditation through force of habit. This is a more general description, and in fact attachment scattering thoughts fall within this category. Besides moving to objects of attachment, this hindrance can also include when our mind moves to an object of aversion, such as an angry colleague, or from the intended object of meditation, which is a virtuous object, to another virtuous object, but one that is not what we are supposed to be focused on. For instance, our object of meditation might be a visualization of Shakyamuni Buddha, but somehow we find our mind now has an image of another virtuous object, such as Tara, or even some thoughts on bodhichitta. Even though we might still have a focused, virtuous mind, because we have lost our object of meditation, this is a hindrance. When we meditate on one subject and our mind slips to other things, it is necessary to bring it back. Any thoughts other than the object of meditation become a distraction.

For good concentration we need not only to hold the object of meditation for a long period but also to hold it clearly and intensely. Otherwise it is very easy for the mind to become lax. That dull and heavy mind is sinking thought (*laya, jingwa*). Of the two types of sinking thought, gross and subtle, this is gross, although it is not as gross as the mind that slides into sleepiness, maybe even fully falling asleep. This is called "fogginess" or "lethargy" (*styana, mukpa*). With the body and mind exhausted, every time we try to bring the object of meditation into our mind, we nod off, utterly unable to hold the object for even a few seconds. Then we can have a *very* comfortable sleep. His Holiness Zong Rinpoché said that sleeping like this is much more pleasant than normal sleeping!

With gross sinking thoughts, we may be able to hold the object of our meditation, but it is very unclear. When our concentration is more developed and there is more stability, there is the danger of subtle sinking thoughts. The definition of the subtle sinking thought is that, although the object is very clear, the mind doesn't have the energy to intensely hold it. The object is held clearly but weakly.

Unless we can recognize the mistake of having subtle sinking thoughts, we might believe we are doing a perfect meditation because there is little distraction and our concentration can last for many hours, but there is no energy. Because subtle sinking thoughts are very difficult to recognize, we can actually feel we have achieved shamatha while being blocked from the final stages by this subtle hindrance. Not trying to overcome an obstacle we don't recognize, we will never achieve perfect shamatha, which means there is no way to even achieve liberation from samsara, let alone enlightenment.

The remedy for both scattering and sinking thoughts is awareness or introspection (*samprajanya, sheshin*). As soon as either hindrance occurs, we should try to be aware of it and bring the mind back to the object. The goal is to hold the object with stability, clarity, and intensity, so when one of those factors is missing, we need to address it. Awareness is the part of the mind that watches what is happening in our meditation and, seeing we have slipped to one of these hindrances, refocuses the mind.

You can say that awareness is almost like an analytical meditation within our main meditation, like one corner of our mind is always checking on what the rest of our mind is doing, kind of like a spy, observing whether we are meditating or distracted. Say we are visualizing a deity.

While we are focusing on the image, we should retain the awareness that we are meditating on the deity. Then, if the mind starts to become distracted, we can be aware of it and bring the mind back.

Awareness can catch the distraction right as it is happening. Something starts to creep into our mind—the thought of a delicious cake, the conversation we had with a friend—but we are immediately aware that this is a distraction, threatening to move us from the object of concentration, and we address that distraction.

For awareness, Yongzin Yeshé Gyaltsen[97] gives the analogy of walking down the road with somebody we are a little afraid of. While mostly concentrating on the road to be safe from tripping over, we must still keep watch from the corner of our eye in case they cause us any trouble.

We should train ourselves to apply mindfulness and awareness from the beginning. They are the most important tools we can have to guard our mind and make sure we never create nonvirtue. The two work together. We need mindfulness—the antidote to forgetfulness—to keep the mind focused, and awareness to be constantly vigilant in case scattering and sinking thoughts creep in, like a thief trying to sneak into our house to steal all our valuables.

At first we learn to catch our gross scattering and sinking thoughts and then, as we progress, the subtle ones. Once we are free from them, our mind will be able to stay on the object of meditation as firm as a mountain for however long we like: hours, weeks, months, or even years.

If our distracted or dull mind is just too gross and using the tool of awareness doesn't work, there are other techniques we can try. When the mind scatters and refuses to return to the object of concentration, we can revert to an analytical meditation on the object. Then when some clarity returns due to the analytical meditation, we can revert to the fixed meditation.

We can also break off the meditation and do a few rounds of breathing, such as the nine-round breathing meditation, until the mind has settled, and then try again. A more advanced method is to visualize our mind enclosed in a seed, the size of a mustard seed, made of light, resting at our navel chakra. This helps free us from distracted thoughts.

For sinking thoughts, we can apply the same method, but this time raise the mind up. This makes sense—for scattered thoughts we bring the mind down, and for sinking thoughts we lift it up. With gross sinking thoughts, Phadampa Sangyé[98] advises visualizing sparkling light the size of a sesame seed on the tip of our nose. Similarly, Pabongka Dechen Nyingpo advises visualizing a small white light or a small Tara on the tip of the nose. When the sinking thought goes, we can place the mind back on the object of meditation.

Phadampa Sangyé also advises placing the mind at the navel and then, as meditators do when performing *phowa*,[99] shooting it up the central channel through the crown of the head into the sky, where it becomes oneness with the sky. Keeping it there for some time helps greatly with the clarity of the mind.

If gross sinking thoughts completely disrupt our concentration, we don't need to give up the session but rather just let go of the concentration for a while. Gross sinking thoughts can arise because the mind is discouraged, so we can lift the mind higher. Instead of thinking we are hopeless and unable to meditate, we should feel joy by thinking how we have attained this perfect human rebirth through great morality and great generosity, and therefore we have all the attributes needed for attaining perfect concentration.

We can also remember the particular qualities of the objects of refuge and think of the benefits of bodhichitta, and how perfect concentration is vital to attain bodhichitta. Once we achieve shamatha, every good quality comes to us easily, pouring down on us like monsoon rain. When we have energized our mind with such thoughts, we can return to trying to develop our concentration.

I think, as beginners, we might be able to recognize gross scattering or sinking thoughts when they happen, but it is quite difficult to recognize the subtle ones. Actually, subtle sinking thoughts come from the development of the concentration, particularly clarity. To stop subtle sinking thoughts, while we are focusing on our object of meditation, we tighten the way the mind holds the object a little. If making it a little tighter doesn't stop the sinking thoughts, then they are gross ones.

When our distractions are extremely gross and nothing else helps, we should give up the session for a while and go outside to refresh ourselves. We can walk around a little bit, especially if the meditation place is on a high mountain where there is plenty of space and sky. It may be a little bit dark inside the room, so we can go and look at the mountains or look at something bright inside. Walking around a bit is an excellent way to get rid of those very heavy sinking thoughts. Then we can go back to the session.

Nonapplication and Overapplication of the Antidote

When we know that scattering thoughts or sinking thoughts are occurring, but we fail to remedy the situation by applying the antidote, that is considered another of the five hindrances to concentration: nonapplication of the antidote that is needed.

However, it can also happen that, having attained a degree of single-pointed concentration, we then still use awareness to check on the mind. That itself will disturb the mind. Using an antidote when it is not needed is considered the fifth hindrance to concentration.

THE NINE STAGES OF SHAMATHA[100]

The mind progresses through nine stages before attaining shamatha:

1. placing the mind (*chittasthapana*)
2. continual placement (*samathapana*)
3. repeated placement (*avasthapana*)
4. close placement (*upasthapana*)
5. taming (*damana*)
6. pacifying (*shamana*)
7. thoroughly pacifying (*vyupashamana*)
8. making single-pointed (*ekotikarana*)
9. placement in equanimity (*samadhana*)

Maitreya lists these nine stages in the *Adornment of Mahayana Sutras*, saying,

> Having directed the mind to the object of observation [*placing the mind*], do not allow its continuum to be distracted [*continual placement*]. Having noticed distraction, quickly return [the mind] to that [object] [*repeated placement*]. The aware also withdraw the mind inwardly more and more [*close placement*].
>
> Then, seeing the good benefits of concentration, tame the mind in concentration [*taming*]. By seeing the faults of distraction, pacify dislike for [concentration] [*pacifying*]. Desire and so forth as well as discomfort and so forth likewise should be pacified [immediately] upon arising [*thoroughly pacifying*].
>
> Then, those who make effort at restraint [of faults need only] make [a little] effort to [concentrate] the mind [*making single-pointed*]. Natural arising is attained. Aside from familiarizing with that, one desists from activity [*placement in equanimity*].[101]

The first stage, called *placing the mind*, consists of listening to the teaching and learning about the objects of concentration. Desiring to experience shamatha, we try to not allow our mind to stray to external objects. When our concentration begins to have some stability, we have reached the first stage.

Although the mind can hold the object of concentration, it cannot focus on it for a prolonged period. Like a cascade of water from a waterfall, it seems like our mind is suddenly flooded with thoughts, but the truth is that it has always been in this state; we have just never been aware of it before. Now that the mind is turned inward, these scattered thoughts become very apparent. This should not be regarded as a fault of the practice but a natural experience for anyone beginning to take up concentration.

From the first stage, we move to the second, *continual placement*, where we repeatedly place the mind back on the object of concentration, meaning we can sustain our attention on the object for increasing periods of time. At this stage, thoughts sometimes arise and disturb the mind before naturally dying away, giving us the first experience of being able to stop the thoughts. There are still the faults of scattering and sinking thoughts, causing us to lose intensity and clarity. When this occurs, we need to fix the mind again unwaveringly upon the object.

Because the mind is still being pulled from the object of concentration by distractions, as we develop, we still need to continually reestablish the object. This returning again and again to the object is the third stage, *repeated placement.*

By this stage our power of concentration is strong—we can hold the object well—but with this more powerful mind comes strong scattered and sinking thoughts that need to be dealt with. This fourth stage is called *close placement.*

Continuing to develop the mind, the grosser forms of scattering and sinking thoughts decrease, but there are still the subtler forms to deal with. At this point we are on the fifth stage, *taming.*

Seeing how even these subtle disturbances need to be overcome, with a very strong mind and great awareness, we detect and avert them whenever they start to arise, bringing about a very stable and peaceful meditation. This is the sixth stage, *pacifying.*

Through such awareness, the subtle scattering and sinking thoughts are suppressed, but that does not mean they have been eliminated. Seeing the way even these subtle thoughts can disturb our meditation, we use effort and diligence to overcome them. This is the seventh stage, *thoroughly pacifying.*

By the eighth stage, *single-pointed attention*, we no longer need to put effort into recognizing and averting subtle scattered and sinking thoughts, therefore the mental factor of awareness, which has been a key tool in the earlier stages, is no longer needed. The practice of focusing on the object single-pointedly proceeds like an unbroken stream.

When we focus carefully and persistently on the object of meditation, our meditation becomes effortless. We are now completely absorbed in single-pointed concentration, which is the ninth and final stage, *placement in equanimity*.

Just as somebody well versed in the scriptures can effortlessly chant them, even without fully engaging the mind, we can focus on the object of meditation effortlessly and without any hindrance, holding that concentration for as long as we want.

When we reach the ninth level, we have strong single-pointed concentration, but we have yet to achieve actual shamatha. We still need to meditate again and again, until the intense familiarity that arises for the object of meditation gradually induces first pliancy of body and then pliancy of mind.[102] After that, the bliss of physical and mental pliancy arises. Only when our concentration is supported by this bliss of pliancy have we then achieved shamatha, calm abiding.

The Six Powers and the Four Attentions

To achieve shamatha we need the help of the *six powers* and the *four attentions*, which are four degrees of stability of mind. These six powers are explained in Arya Asanga's *Five Treatises on the Grounds*:

1. the power of study, used on the first stage
2. the power of memory, used on the second stage
3. the power of mindfulness, used on the third and fourth stages
4. the power of awareness, used on the fifth and sixth stages
5. the power of effort, used on the seventh and eight stages
6. the power of familiarity, used on the ninth stage

These powers reflect the main tools we need at each stage. For instance, at the very beginning we need to study about what to do so we can avoid mistakes, which is the *power of study*, whereas beyond that we train to continuously place our mind back on the object when it moves off it: the *power of memory*. After that, the powers of *mindfulness* and *awareness* become even more important, and then, to reach a really high level of concentration, we need *effort*. Finally, when we can concentrate without effort, we need the *power of familiarity* to strengthen even that strong concentration.

The *four attentions* are the four degrees of stability of our mind as we progress toward shamatha:

1. tight focus is used during the first two stages
2. interrupted focus is used during the next five stages
3. uninterrupted focus is used during the eighth stage
4. spontaneous focus is used during the ninth stage

After we achieve the first attention, *tight focus*, whatever analytical meditation we do, the mind is brought single-pointedly onto that object. With the second, *interrupted focus*, although the mind may remain concentrated for some time, every now and then distractions arise, and this type of focus brings the mind back to its object. With *uninterrupted focus* the mind can hold the object of meditation for sustained periods without any distraction.

Finally, with *spontaneous focus*, which occurs during the ninth stage of shamatha, the mind can hold the object of meditation effortlessly. This summary is roughly what is explained in Lama Tsongkhapa and Pabongka's lamrim texts and in other teachings.

SHAMATHA AND INSIGHT

Shantideva starts the ninth chapter of *A Guide to the Bodhisattva's Way of Life*, the chapter on wisdom, by saying,

> The Great Muni [Shakyamuni Buddha] has taught that
> one gathers all this equipment of virtues for the sake of wisdom.
> Therefore, if one seeks nirvana and happiness,
> one should also develop wisdom.[103]

Liberation and enlightenment are impossible without the direct realization of emptiness, which in turn is impossible without shamatha. In the lamrim texts, shamatha is explained after bodhichitta and before emptiness, and the combination of shamatha and emptiness is often called "serenity and special insight." Special insight is *vipashyana* in Sanskrit and *lhaktong* in Tibetan, literally meaning "superior seeing," the type of wisdom that sees reality directly, nonconceptually. *Vipashyana* is the investigation into how things actually exist—in other words, emptiness—which, when conjoined with shamatha, leads directly to liberation.

Of this, Shantideva says,

> One who is properly engaged in the cultivation of insight,
> accompanied by calm, will destroy the afflictions.
> Knowing this, one should first seek to have calm;
> and calm arises from equanimity before the delights of the
> world.[104]

We can think of how Shakyamuni Buddha was once in samsara like us, with an uncontrolled mind, unable to attain perfect concentration because of all the interferences from scattering and sinking thoughts. But afterward, by applying the methods for achieving shamatha given by his teacher, he was able to eliminate these obstacles and achieve both shamatha and penetrative insight, then generate the whole path and become enlightened.

This is also true of the great masters that followed the Buddha, such as the Tibetan yogis like Milarepa, Marpa, and Lama Tsongkhapa. They practiced the Dharma and attained the lamrim realizations, especially the realizations of shamatha and penetrative insight. We can also think of the present living meditators, ascetic sangha and lay people who are practicing the Dharma purely, gaining experience in shamatha and penetrative insight and attaining realizations.

I think the qualities of the current sangha are particularly inspiring, showing us that we too can achieve this. The fundamental nature of our mind is unstained, not mixed with the obscurations. And it is the same with those meditators who have accomplished shamatha and penetrative insight. Like ours are now, their minds were temporally obscured, but with continual perseverance and much patience, they were able to bear the hardships of practicing the Dharma. If we do the same, why can't we also achieve this?

In the *Foundation of All Good Qualities*, Lama Tsongkhapa says,

> By my having pacified distractions to wrong objects
> And correctly analyzed the meaning of reality,
> Please bless me to quickly generate within my mindstream
> The unified path of calm abiding and special insight.[105]

Pacifying distractions to wrong objects means not allowing our mind to wander to any object other than the object of our meditation.

Achieving the ninth level of shamatha, we gradually experience first physical pliancy and then mental pliancy, followed by the extremely refined mental and physical pliancy. We have then achieved shamatha and are able to continually meditate on absolute truth. Then, whenever we analyze emptiness, our mind naturally abides in meditative equipoise on emptiness. The teachings describe it as like a fish that can swim in water without disturbing the surface at all, meaning the analytical meditation does not disturb the single-pointed concentration, and the single-pointed concentration does not disturb the analytical meditation. This is the unification of calm abiding and special insight.

Only when we have attained emptiness directly can we completely cease all disturbing-thought obscurations, including their seed. When that happens, we have achieved liberation, the sorrowless state of nirvana. Once we have entered the Mahayana path by attaining bodhichitta, with the direct perception of emptiness, we cease even the subtle defilements, and we can achieve full enlightenment and liberate numberless sentient beings. That is the ultimate goal of our life.

Calm Abiding, Emptiness, and Bodhichitta

Only when our practice of calm abiding and special insight is combined with bodhichitta does it become the cause for enlightenment. Great teachers like Guru Shakyamuni Buddha have shown us that all suffering comes from having a selfish attitude, whereas to become truly happy depends on turning the mind toward cherishing others.

In *A Guide to the Bodhisattva's Way of Life* Shantideva says,

> All those who live in torment in this life,
> suffer only because of their desire for happiness.
> All those who live in happiness, are in such a condition
> because of their wish to make others happy.

> But why say more?
> Simply compare these two:
> the fool who seeks only his own welfare,
> and the sage who seeks only to benefit others.[106]

The fool in this context means somebody who childishly remains under the control of the self-cherishing attitude, like a small child who only wants to play for their own happiness. We have been following self-cherishing from beginningless rebirths and because of that we have always suffered. Self-cherishing has been like our parents, like our guru, but instead of guiding us wisely, it leads us into more and more problems. That is what has been happening and will continue to happen if we don't transform our mind. The suffering of samsara will be endless. Therefore, while we have this life where we have all the opportunities to learn and practice, we *must* generate the ultimate good heart, bodhichitta.

That is what Shantideva means when he asks us to compare ourselves to the sages, the buddhas. Look at the difference. From being like we are now, plagued with so many problems, Guru Shakyamuni Buddha became fully enlightened.

Shantideva also mentions,

> Whoever fails to replace his own pleasure
> with the suffering of others will not reach, of course,
> the station of the awakened,
> but neither shall he know happiness even in this cycle of
> transmigration.[107]

Unless we give other sentient beings our happiness and take their suffering upon ourselves, we will be unable to completely transform our mind and so will not be able to eliminate all the obscurations and complete all the realizations. In other words, we won't be able to achieve the highest goal. Furthermore, while trapped in samsara there is no real happiness. Leave aside happiness in future lives, by following the self-cherishing even the work for this life will fail.

Without bodhichitta, we can attain the renunciation of samsara and so achieve the five paths of the individual liberation vehicle to nirvana. We can be free from the oceans of samsaric suffering, we can achieve that ultimate happiness—the blissful state for ourselves—but we cannot achieve enlightenment for sentient beings. Only with bodhichitta can we achieve enlightenment.

TANTRA

Accumulating both types of merit, the merit of wisdom and the merit of virtue, in order to achieve enlightenment through a Paramitayana practice is generally said to take three countless great eons. But during those three countless great eons, transmigratory beings are suffering terribly in samsara. We cannot wait that long. Unable to bear the thought that they must endure so much suffering for so long, by practicing tantra, we can become enlightened in an incredibly short time.

Tantra is generally called Vajrayana, the vajra vehicle, *vajra* meaning "adamantine," sometimes translated as "diamond." It is the vajra vehicle because it employs the inseparability of method and wisdom, making it indestructible. Whereas a diamond can cut all other materials like glass and so forth, it cannot be destroyed by anything else. The mind that is unified in method and wisdom has the power to destroy the root of samsara, ignorance. In the *Foundation of All Good Qualities* Lama Tsongkhapa says,

> When I have become a [suitable] vessel by training in the
>   common path,
> Please bless me to immediately enter
> The holy gateway of the fortunate beings—
> The supreme of all vehicles, the Vajrayana.[108]

There are four levels of Vajrayana: *kriya* or action tantra, *charya* or performance tantra, yoga tantra, and highest yoga tantra. The motivation for practicing any of the four classes of tantra is to achieve enlightenment in the shortest time possible to free all transmigratory beings from suffering and to bring them to enlightenment, but with the lower tantras we first achieve long life, living for hundreds and thousands of years, before achieving enlightenment. In highest yoga tantra, however, there is no need to do that; we can achieve full enlightenment in a brief lifetime of these degenerated times.

The reason tantra is so powerful and so fast is because in one method we combine the method and the wisdom sides of the practice. In nontantric meditation, we have to practice method and wisdom separately, therefore our progress is much slower. In tantra, the same mind that practices the method side of the practice—visualizing ourselves as the deity, which is the cause of the *rupakaya*—also practices the wisdom side—dissolving into emptiness to do that, which is the cause of the dharmakaya. Therefore we are continuously creating the cause of the two bodies of a buddha.

Tantra is called the resultant vehicle because we visualize ourselves as a buddha now, bringing the result into the present moment. Because this method has the power to utterly destroy our delusions, tantra is considered the quick path to enlightenment.

That does not mean that all we have to do is practice tantra and disregard any sutra practices. Sutra is the foundation for tantra. Just as it is impossible to build a multistory house without laying the foundations, it is impossible to practice tantra without the foundations, and the very best foundations are bodhichitta and emptiness, based on all the practices of the lower and middle capable beings.

With the visualization of the deity that is integral with any tantric practice, we protect ourselves from ordinary concepts and ordinary appearances—thinking, "I am ordinary, this place is ordinary"—by keeping the mind in pure thought and pure appearance. In tantra, we protect the mind by practicing the four complete purities:

- visualizing our own body as the deity's holy body
- visualizing the place as the completely purified place, the mandala
- visualizing our actions as completely purified actions, the actions of the buddhas
- visualizing what we experience as pure enjoyment, in the nature of transcendental wisdom of nondual bliss and emptiness

This pure enjoyment is the same enjoyment we will experience when we become enlightened. If we change the appearance of the object into a pure one, pure thoughts arise. This becomes an incredibly fast means to purify obstacles and collect extensive merit.

There are two stages in highest yoga tantra: the generation stage and the completion stage. In the generation stage, which is a preparation for the completion stage, we visualize ourselves as the deity with the various channels and chakras, whereas in the completion stage we are actually able to move the mind, riding on the wind energy, into those channels and chakras and allow it to abide and absorb there. During that time the gross mind absorbs, giving the subtle mind and the extremely subtle mind—the clear light—the chance to appear. Having that extremely subtle mind of clear light experiencing great bliss, we then intensively meditate on emptiness, like having put water into the water, having one taste.

Some people try to practice the generation stage of highest tantra just by following what is explained in a sadhana without understanding the profound points of the lamrim commentaries or knowing shamatha and emptiness, which are the vital elements of a tantric practice. Even if we are still a long way from attaining these precious minds, we should at least be doing our best to develop them. It is said that those able to accomplish even the gross level of the completion stage are like stars in the daytime, unbelievably rare.

7. MEDITATING ON THE LAMRIM

THE MAP TO ENLIGHTENMENT

Even having an intellectual understanding of the Buddha's teachings is of great benefit. Therefore, when we are able to attain a realization of the subjects, where they become integrated with our mind at the deepest level, the benefits we gain are inconceivable, not just for ourselves but also for others. With a realization of something like impermanence and death, saying a few words can profoundly transform others' minds, cutting their delusions. Similarly, when we have bodhichitta, whatever we say has the incredible power to cut others' self-cherishing, allowing others to transform their minds. When we listen to teachings from the great teachers who have a realization of bodhichitta, we can really feel this.

Therefore, we must plan to develop our mind through all the subjects of the lamrim, always keeping that great goal in view, the attainment of enlightenment. The map that the lamrim shows us is the best possible way to progress. If we were planning a journey from Paris to Kathmandu, we would need to know how to go—by plane, train, bus, or whatever—and which route to take. Similarly, on our spiritual journey, we need to know the best method to lead us to enlightenment given our level of mind. The Buddha's teachings are vast, and it is very difficult to integrate them into our mind without a clear structure, which is exactly what the lamrim is; it takes us step by step without any confusion. With such a map and with the strong determination to follow it, by studying and meditating each day we get closer and closer to attaining realizations and enlightenment.

Whether we call it Buddhism or meditation or not, to achieve any level of happiness we need the various understandings that the lamrim can provide. Only the Dharma can completely remove the cause of suffering, but we must be sure that the Dharma we study and meditate on is unmistaken and complete, fully able to lead us to liberation and enlightenment. If it has mistakes, if it is incomplete, we won't achieve what we want.

What the Buddha gave us was the very best psychology to help us develop a truly positive mind, the source of inner peace and happiness. Without the lamrim, without developing the three principal aspects of the path—renunciation, bodhichitta, and right view—quite simply, we become even more crazy. Ruled by our delusions, by our self-cherishing attitude, we have no freedom at all, and because of that we are drowned in a quagmire of problems.

Without the lamrim, even meditation cannot free us from problems. We could be an advanced tantric practitioner but still not be free. There is the story of two people who were doing a very long retreat in Pempo in Tibet on the wrathful deity Yamantaka when one of them died. After that, the other meditator continued, doing a *sur* practice every evening, which involves burning *tsampa* (barley flour) and making charity of the smell to the hungry ghosts. One evening he didn't do the practice and a terrifying hungry ghost with many arms that looked just like Yamantaka appeared. When the meditator asked who he was, the hungry ghost replied, "I am your friend, the one who was doing retreat with you before." Even though he had done retreat on the deity for many years, as it turns out, he didn't know how to practice properly. He had practiced with attachment, missing out the lamrim and bodhichitta motivation. There wasn't even a virtuous thought seeking the happiness of future lives, which would at least make the motivation Dharma and save him from being born as a hungry ghost.

When we thoroughly investigate what the lamrim is, we will see that it is the infallible path that we need, the one that can bring us satisfaction, contentment, peace. All those other preliminary practices, such as saying the refuge prayers, offering mandalas, reciting mantras, and so forth are the branches of the tree of buddhahood, while the main trunk is the lamrim.

Of course, preliminary practices are crucial, but if we do them at the expense of meditating on the lamrim, we lose the purpose of meditating. All the other practices are meant to develop the mind in lamrim, in order to generate renunciation, emptiness, and bodhichitta. As Pabongka Dechen Nyingpo puts it, we should not "cherish the branches but ignore the trunk."

Gaining Realizations of the Lamrim Topics

The path to liberation and enlightenment is the actual medicine we take to cure the sickness of karma and delusions. With the meditations on impermanence, compassion, and so forth we are developing the method side of the path; with our meditations on emptiness, we are developing the wisdom side of the path.

One meditation leads to the next. For example, when we meditate on our own suffering, we develop renunciation for samsara, but we can also see that all other sentient beings are suffering in the same way. In that way, compassion naturally grows for all others. That becomes great compassion, the compassion that wishes each and every sentient being to be free from suffering, and that leads to the resolve that we ourselves will free them. From that comes bodhichitta.

Through this whole process our mind is becoming less affected by delusions, freer from the negative emotional thoughts that make us miserable and trap us in samsara, and closer to liberation and enlightenment. Just feeling our mind lightening like that, even if it is a very small experience, shows that we can transform our mind completely, not just partially, until it becomes completely pure. This ability to transform the mind is the precious gift we have with this perfect human rebirth. Understanding that this comes through the power of the Dharma, we see how nothing is important but the Dharma. This gives us a huge incentive to continue on the path.

At present, because we rely on logic and reasoning to enforce our ideas, the experience we gain from meditation requires effort. We cannot attain an effortless experience of a lamrim subject until we have first thoroughly studied and meditated on it. As we progress, that feeling we are aiming for in meditation will arise spontaneously and our mind will actually be transformed into that experience, becoming effortless, spontaneous.

It is sometimes compared to riding a horse. At first, we need to pay a lot of attention just to sit on the horse as it walks. But slowly, as we become an experienced rider, we can handle the horse effortlessly—no matter what it does. Even if we are distracted, there is no danger of falling off or endangering our life, because we respond naturally to the movement of the horse. Similarly, when we have trained our mind well in a lamrim subject, such as perfect human rebirth, if we are reflecting on all the reasons why our human existence is so special, for a long while we will need to return and reinforce those ideas with effortful meditation, but at some stage a feeling of great joy will arise. We naturally have a strong feeling for how precious our life is. Then, in subsequent meditations, this spontaneous feeling will be there, effortlessly.

Believing and practicing what the Buddha taught is not blind faith; it is not superstition. The Buddha himself actualized the complete, unmistaken path and then revealed it to us sentient beings. Since his time, countless great yogis have examined, verified, and experienced what the Buddha taught, gaining realizations of the whole path. Many of Lama Tsongkhapa's disciples achieved enlightenment in one lifetime. Innumerable beings, like stars in the sky at night, have actualized the path exactly as the Buddha explained and have achieved enlightenment.

I think that people who can do a lamrim retreat are extremely fortunate, more fortunate even than people with great psychic or healing powers, because even those whose clairvoyance allows them to see far into the past and the future are still not free from karma. They have no map to lead them from samsara. On the other hand, if we can do even one short lamrim retreat, or even one meditation, we have begun our journey to freedom.

To even have the wish to meditate on the lamrim is extremely rare and wonderful. Of all the people in the world, how many have any interest in meditation at all? Very few. And of them, how many know of the Buddhist path and have an interest in meditating on the lamrim? Whether it is in the West or the East, the number is incredibly small. So, we are extremely fortunate.

Subject by subject, you need to study and meditate on the lamrim, deepening your understanding until it becomes a realization. You can base your meditations on short lamrim texts, like *The Essence of Nectar* by Yeshé Tsöndrü[109] or *A Hymn of Experience* by Lama Tsongkhapa. They are neither too long nor too short and their style is beautiful and very inspiring. Using that as the root outline, you can do analytical and fixed meditations on that subject, using the analytical meditation to transform your mind into that experience and then doing a fixed meditation to hold that experience for as long as possible.

Then, in between sessions, you can look into the subjects in more detail by reading the great lamrim texts such as *Liberation in the Palm of Your Hand* by Pabongka Dechen Nyingpo and the *Great Treatise on the Stages of the Path to Enlightenment* (*Lamrim Chenmo*) by Lama Tsongkhapa. Everything you need to know about the lamrim topics is within these texts and so they can really enhance your meditations.

COMMON LAMRIM MEDITATIONS

Meditating on the Perfect Human Rebirth

The purpose of meditating on the perfect human rebirth is to realize how incredibly rare and unique your life is. Nothing could be more precious than the human life you now have, and there could be no loss greater than failing to use this unique opportunity to realize your potential as a human being. Therefore, once you understand the subject, you need to meditate on it again and again. The more you can understand what a perfect human rebirth is, the more determined you will be to make every moment of your life meaningful.

Meditating on the perfect human rebirth helps you to appreciate how you have been controlled by self-interest and to see the truth in the teachings on the nature of suffering. By going over each of the meditations within the perfect human rebirth, you can make those understandings part of your life. Crucially, you can understand the need for morality and generosity if you are to take the work you are starting now into the next life. You see that taking and keeping the vows offered within Buddhism are like a key to the door to enlightenment. You are also able to develop your compassion until it becomes bodhichitta, enabling you to enter the tantric path and achieve enlightenment quickly.

In lamrim texts you usually see these meditation outlines for the perfect human rebirth:

- recognizing that you have a perfect human rebirth
- understanding the eight freedoms
- understanding the ten richnesses
- recognizing its great value
- recognizing its rarity

As you will see in the meditation in appendix 3, the eight freedoms include four undesirable states you are free from—as a hell being, a hungry ghost, an animal, or a long-life god—and four undesirable situations you are free from—being a barbarian, living at a time where there is no buddha, holding wrong views, or being born with defective mental or physical faculties. Similarly, the ten richnesses are divided into two: the five personal richnesses that include being born as a human being in a Dharma country with perfect mental and physical faculties, and the five richnesses dependent on others, such as being born in the time of a buddha and when the complete teachings still exist, and having the necessary conditions to practice the Dharma, such as the kindness of others.

A common way to meditate on the perfect human rebirth is to go over each of the eight freedoms and ten richnesses individually, reflecting on each one in depth and trying to see just why you are so fortunate to have these eighteen qualities.

If your meditation is in a retreat or as a daily practice where you generally do a lamrim subject, then you can do one freedom or richness each day, or each session, or stay with one freedom or richness for a few days until you have a strong feeling for it. Conversely, you can do a glance meditation on a range of freedoms or all of them to give yourself an overview. The object is to understand each subject at as deep a level as possible so that it really becomes a profound truth.

Meditating on each of the eighteen qualities can be done in conjunction with a deity practice. For instance, if you are doing a Chenrezig practice, after you have been reciting the mantra for a while, bring in this topic and meditate on it as part of developing compassion. His Holiness the Dalai Lama says that when you can no longer concentrate on visualizing yourself as the deity, doing a lamrim meditation stops superstitions arising.

The purpose of meditating on each of the eight freedoms and ten richnesses separately is to convince yourself that there is no possibility of practicing the Dharma while in any realm other than the human one and that even as a human there is no possibility of practicing Dharma unless you are free from living in a suppressive country, having wrong views, and so forth. Only when all eighteen conditions are there will you be free to practice the Dharma unhindered.

You can make each meditation as elaborate or as simple as you like. It really depends on what is most effective for your mind, and of course how much time you have.

The meditation on each freedom and richness follows the same format. For instance, with the first meditation, on the freedom of not being born as a hell being, you can go through the detailed descriptions of each hell that you can find in the lamrim texts. This can happen in one meditation session or many, but the point is to really feel how unbearable that suffering is and how fortunate you are that you are not in that situation. Then you reflect on how having this freedom allows you to practice the Dharma and achieve the three great purposes of obtaining a

happy future rebirth, attaining liberation, and attaining full enlightenment. Finally, you determine to never waste one moment of this perfect
human rebirth but to use it to attain full enlightenment in order to free
all kind mother sentient beings from the unbearable suffering they are
now trapped in.

So, each meditation has these four elements:

- reflecting on the suffering and lack of freedom of that being or
  situation
- reflecting on how you are free of that suffering or situation and
  rejoicing that this is so
- reflecting on how this freedom allows you to attain the three
  great purposes
- determining not to waste a moment of this perfect human rebirth

After you have done the analytical meditations on each freedom and
richness, you then reflect on how, despite the extreme difficulty of gathering all eighteen qualities, you have done so, and therefore appreciate
how precious this rebirth is. As I explained above, when you get a strong
feeling during your analysis, it is very good to stop and do a fixed meditation on that feeling, making it stronger, more profound, and more
stable. Here, you can repeat the idea over and over, "This is so precious,
this is so precious, this is so precious...."

Not only should you reflect on each freedom in this way, you should
also reflect that this freedom will not last. This life is very short and it
can end at any moment, even today. It could even end during this very
meditation session.

If you train your mind in this way, even in the breaktimes between
meditations the thought that your perfect human life is extremely precious will arise effortlessly, just as the thought of hunger or attachment
arises effortlessly. With greater understanding of how precious your perfect human rebirth is, you will automatically stop meaningless actions.

Meditating on Impermanence and Death

We all need to constantly remember impermanence and death. When we do, we will automatically see what is important in life, and the distractions that hinder our Dharma practice will evaporate, giving us unlimited energy to practice the Dharma. Understanding how imminent death is, we see how stupid it is to hold minds of anger, attachment, or ignorance, and by letting go of these deluded minds, we bring peace and happiness in our everyday life. If our goal is to attain a better human rebirth, we can easily do that. If our goal is liberation or full enlightenment, we can do that.

The meditation on impermanence and death is the most powerful method to control the worldly concern that clings to the happiness of this life. To my mind, it is *the* fundamental meditation. As the Buddha said in the *Mahaparinirvana Sutra*,

> Among all the reapings, the autumn harvest is supreme.
> Among all the tracks, the track of the elephant is supreme.
> Among all ideas, the idea of impermanence and death is
>   supreme,
> because with it you eliminate all attachment, ignorance, and
>   pride of the three realms.[110]

Without fully appreciating the fragility of our perfect human rebirth, we will not have the energy to make full use of it. We might logically understand it, but we will still have more feeling for losing money than for losing this life. Our skulls are so thick we need to repeatedly meditate on this to break through the dense fog of our delusions.

Understanding impermanence and death is easy; there is nothing complicated. Every object or situation shows us impermanence all the time. Impermanence and death are all around us; in the city we live, in the sounds we hear, in the newspapers we read or the television and movies we see. Even shopping is a constant reminder of impermanence and death if we want to look for it.

While there are various meditations on gross and subtle impermanence, the impermanent nature of life—how we all must die—is the most important one. The common way to meditate on death, generally called the nine-point death meditation, is using three roots: death is certain; the time of death is uncertain; and nothing can help at death but the Dharma. This meditation, which is taught extensively in Tibetan Buddhism, is presented with three reasons and one conclusion for each root:

Root: Death is certain.
1. No being has ever escaped death.
2. My lifespan is constantly decreasing.
3. There is very little time to practice Dharma.
Conclusion: I must practice the Dharma.

Root: The time of death is uncertain.
1. The lifespan of human beings is not fixed.
2. More conditions endanger life than support it.
3. My body is extremely fragile.
Conclusion: I must practice the Dharma *now*.

Root: Nothing can help at the time of death except the Dharma.
1. Wealth and possessions cannot help.
2. Friends and relatives cannot help.
3. My body cannot help.
Conclusion: I must practice the Dharma *purely*.[111]

This is how to use these points: The only thing you can be sure of at all is that you will die. If you think about all the "certainties" you have in life—your next birthday, tonight's dinner, your favorite television program on Friday—they are all really just assumptions, because no matter how probable they might seem, you might not be here to experience them. That is because the most uncertain thing of all is your time of death. Death can happen at any moment, from your next breath to many years from now. You just don't know. Therefore, this concept of permanence you carry around with you, like a heavy weight, is the great deceiver. You cannot trust anything that is marked by this concept of permanence. We all have this notion that we won't die. It might not be spoken, it might be quite unconscious, but we live with this notion every day. You say to your friends, "See you next week," and the assumption is you won't die before then. You work one more hour in order to get your pay and the assumption is you will still be alive at pay day. Every day you live with this notion you won't die. Right up until the day you die, this notion is there, deceiving you, blinding you to the reality. This assumption is dangerous not just because it is mistaken. Thinking you won't die, you put off what is really important, practicing the Dharma. You need to investigate this deeply in your meditations.

When you profoundly consider not only how death is definite but also how the time of death is uncertain—how it could even be today, this hour, this minute—suddenly there is no reason at all to cling to things. You clearly see how the mind of attachment that wants things for *me* now is a totally childish mind. Before, you couldn't even breathe you were so overwhelmed with attachment, like being sunk in mud, then, at the very moment you remember impermanence and death, you are free from the disturbed, uptight mind of attachment.

As with all the lamrim realizations, once you have generated the realization of impermanence and death, you will no longer have to meditate by going through the outlines, such as the nine-point death meditation. From the depth of your heart, knowing that life is very short and you can die at any moment, as you start the session, you feel uncertain that you will even finish it. If you have to get up from your cushion and go for a pipi, you have no idea whether you will ever be able to return to the cushion. You go to bed with the feeling deep in your heart that you may very well not get up in the morning.

When you constantly have this intuitive, effortless understanding that you *will* die and that you could die *at any moment*, you have attained the realization of impermanence and death. With such a mind, there will be no wish to do anything other than prepare yourself for your next life and lives, which means only purely and consistently practicing the Dharma.

The hindrances to practicing the Dharma generally come from the mind, not from external factors. Once you have realized how impermanent your life is, even if you live in the busiest city in the world, like New York or Hong Kong, not only will there be no hindrances to your Dharma practice, there will be *real* happiness, because you have cut attachment, the root of your problems.

Meditating on the Points of the Paths of the Lower and Middle Capable Beings

The meditations that lead to higher rebirths and freedom from samsara are those that come into the paths of the lower and middle capable beings. They include the suffering of the lower realms; refuge in the Buddha, Dharma, and Sangha; karma; and the renunciation of samsara.

One of the initial meditations you must do is on your own suffering. The Buddha's first teaching was on the four noble truths, in which he not only taught the nature of suffering but how to be free from it. As we have seen, in Buddhism suffering, *dukkha*, refers to all levels of mental and physical suffering.

Without a thorough feeling for how and why you suffer, there is no way to do any of the more advanced meditations, such as on bodhichitta or emptiness, and certainly any tantric practice would be impossible. Unless you can recognize your own suffering, you will have no fear of it, making it very difficult to overcome the difficulties that will certainly arise with your Dharma practice.

In the lamrim texts, after impermanence and death, there are the teachings on the *suffering of the lower realms*: the suffering of the various hell realms, the different types of hungry ghosts, and the animal realm. You should meditate on each of these to generate a profound fear of them and a heartfelt wish to avoid them at all costs.

Having meditated on impermanence and death and on the suffering that awaits after death, you should come to a point where you are desperately looking for a way out. Suppose you went to the doctor for a routine checkup, thinking you were perfectly healthy, only to be told you had terminal cancer and only months to live. Wouldn't you do everything you could to find a cure? In the same way, when you understand just how precarious your situation is within this cycle of eternal suffering called samsara, you determine to do whatever you can to be free from it.

It's not as if you were not suffering before, and you only are now because you have to think about it. You have always suffered, but now—like the patient being shown the x-ray—you have come face to face with the extent of your suffering. And so, you have to turn to the physician who has the treatment to cure that illness: the Buddha, the enlightened being who can show the perfect method to completely destroy your ignorance and so eliminate all suffering.

That leads to *taking refuge* in the Buddha, Dharma, and Sangha. Within the lamrim texts there are extensive teachings on the qualities of the Three Rare Sublime Ones and why you should totally rely on them. These points are perfect for your meditations.

Taking refuge further leads to meditating on *karma* and its four aspects—how it is definite, how it expands, and so forth. Then, meditating on how the whole of samsara is suffering by its very nature leads to developing *renunciation of samsara*, a total aversion for it, having not the slightest interest in samsaric pleasures. You do this by meditating on the particular sufferings of human and god realms, looking at the various sufferings there: three types, six types, and eight types.[112] Then, you investigate the evolution of cyclic existence, the twelve links of dependent origination, and the fundamental cause of samsara: karma and delusions. You meditate on all that until you have a realization of renunciation of samsara, feeling that being in samsara is like being in the center of a fire or like waking up in a cobra's nest—there is not the slightest wish to remain there for even a second.

At that time, with a stable realization of the renunciation of samsara, you have attained the graduated path of the middle capable being.

Meditating on the Three Higher Trainings

To attain liberation, nirvana, you need not only renunciation of samsara but also completion of the three higher trainings:

• the higher training of ethics
• the higher training of concentration
• the higher training of wisdom

Concentration and wisdom are not explicitly mentioned in the lamrim texts within the graduated path of the middle capable being, coming instead immediately after bodhichitta in the graduated path of the higher capable being, where they are often called serenity and insight. The higher training of wisdom refers to realizing emptiness, and as we have seen, when it is conjoined with shamatha, it leads directly to liberation.

Without the higher training of concentration, shamatha, you cannot realize emptiness. The analogy often used is trying to view a beautiful thangka when it is dark. You not only need a candle to see it but you also need to be shielded from any wind that will blow the candle out or cause it to flicker so badly you can't see the painting clearly. To view it perfectly, the candle needs to be bright and the air needs to be still so the flame will be straight. Like this, without a strong shamatha practice, the mind cannot concentrate for a long enough time without disturbance to penetrate the correct view of reality.

If you want to have any level of concentration at all, you need to control the mind, to stop mental distractions, but as we have seen, scattering and sinking thoughts are a constant hindrance until a high level of concentration is reached. The mind is just like that candle flame in the center of the wind, full of distractions, full of superstitions. A lack of ethics causes the disturbed minds of excitement and laxity. So, if you want good concentration, you must develop the higher training of ethics, where you protect your body and speech from negative actions.

A crazy elephant refuses to follow the path its trainer leads it on but runs everywhere—in the fields, in the houses—killing people and destroying whatever is in its path. It harms itself and harms other living beings. In order to make the elephant useful, the trainer must subdue it well. Whenever the elephant is disobedient, it must be disciplined. A mind not trained in ethics is exactly like a crazy elephant. It must be subdued, or you won't reach the destination you are aiming for. Therefore, along with the higher trainings of concentration and wisdom, the higher training of ethics is vital.

In the graduated path of the middle capable being, the higher training of ethics mainly refers to keeping the different types of vows you can take as a Buddhist. This is the main tool you use to not only assure a future rebirth in the upper realms but also to attain shamatha. How quickly that happens depends on how strictly you maintain your moral conduct.

The third higher training is the wisdom realizing emptiness, which is not easy. You need to extensively read texts on emptiness and to study and reflect on them so that you have a good general understanding of what it is. I recommend doing a simple meditation on emptiness every day—even if it is something like reciting the *Heart of Wisdom Sutra*—in order to plant the seed. Even if you don't understand the explanations now, they leave an imprint on your mind so that, sooner or later, you will fully understand the meaning, which will lead to a realization of emptiness.

This might not even happen in this lifetime, but by doing all this work—listening, reading, studying, reflecting, meditating—you create such a deep imprint that it becomes astonishingly easy to realize emptiness in your next life. Just hearing the word "emptiness" will enable you to realize it.

Meditating on the Three Principal Aspects of the Path

In addition to the three higher trainings, which are seen as practices that lead to liberation, in the Mahayana, the fundamental practices that lead to enlightenment are the three principal aspects of the path:

- renunciation
- emptiness
- bodhichitta

Without renunciation you cannot control desire; without the wisdom realizing emptiness you cannot eliminate ignorance; and without bodhichitta you cannot overcome the self-cherishing attitude, the font of all problems.

Renunciation, freeing yourself from the painful dissatisfied mind of desire, means the renunciation of the whole of samsara. Renunciation might sound like you are giving up something precious, but it is exactly the opposite of this. Rather than renouncing your happiness, you are renouncing the cause of all your life's problems: the mind of desire. When you do that, you find real peace, real happiness. Although at present it is natural to mistake samsaric pleasures as happiness, you need to understand how they are really another form of suffering, the suffering of change, so called because whatever is experienced in samsara will change; that is its nature. Renouncing the pursuit of samsaric pleasures, in contrast, brings an inner peace that is pure happiness, a happiness that is not labeled on a feeling that is suffering by its very nature. This is what you must understand and meditate on.

Of the other two principal practices within the Mahayana, bodhichitta and emptiness, bodhichitta is considered the more important, because even if you have realized emptiness, without bodhichitta you still cannot enter the Mahayana and attain enlightenment.

Arhats are completely free from delusions, completely free from samsara. They have incredible knowledge and psychic powers, including a direct realization of emptiness, but they are still unable to enter the Mahayana and attain enlightenment. New bodhisattvas, however, who have just attained bodhichitta but have still not realized emptiness and therefore have less knowledge than arhats, are closer to enlightenment because of the power of their bodhichitta.

Whatever action done with bodhichitta becomes a Mahayana action, an action that leads to full enlightenment. Even if it is a meditation on one of the initial lamrim subjects, such as meditating on impermanence and death, because the mind is imbued with bodhichitta, it is a Mahayana action and a cause of enlightenment.

Pabongka Dechen Nyingpo explains that you cannot generate bodhichitta from a few words. If you wish to enter the Mahayana, you need to study and meditate on the whole lamrim and to train your mind gradually in bodhichitta through the seven points of cause and effect or equalizing and exchanging self with others.[113] He says when you meditate on bodhichitta, even just by leaving a few imprints on your mind from your meditation, those imprints are far more special than any other realization you can have.

LAMRIM PRAYERS AND MEDITATION

In Buddhism, any prayer we do is meditation. When people don't realize that, they can mistakenly think of the many prayers there are in Tibetan Buddhism as just ritual. My feeling is this comes from having grown up in a Christian environment and perhaps having some aversion for the prayers sung in church, which then affects how people see Buddhist prayers.

Unless we understand the profound meaning of the prayers, we might well see them as pointless and quickly get bored. When we appreciate their meaning, however, the prayers become very rich. They become a meditation, like medicine for our disturbed mind. We enjoy them, like relaxing on a beach. After working so hard, we go to the beach and lie in the sun or ride the waves—that's a great holiday! *Here*, when we say prayers and meditate, we are laying the foundations for the greatest holiday, the holiday of liberation.

Prayers are not some empty words that we recite. Every word is for meditation, every word is to subdue our mind, freeing it from attachment, ignorance, anger, and so forth, all the delusions that arise from our selfish attitude.

Most meditation practices begin with the refuge and bodhichitta prayer. It is essential to know how to meditate on this in order to transform our mind into the mind of refuge and bodhichitta so that these two precious attitudes harmonize with our heart. Then, the prayers become incredibly meaningful. Otherwise, they are just words, just noise. We are so preoccupied with distractions, especially nonvirtuous ones, we can spend hours saying prayers while only creating nonvirtue. In that way, we can completely waste our life. Unless we are aware of the prayers we are reciting, we cannot leave a positive imprint on our mind. Therefore, it is very important to keep our mind focused when saying prayers. Then we are meditating.

8. RETREATS

Doing a Retreat Brings Us Closer to Enlightenment

No matter what other priorities fill our life, even if we are working full time at a very exacting job, it is very useful to find time to do a retreat every year, for a week, a fortnight, a month, or even two months—in fact for as long as we like! Of course, our daily practice is vital, but within the framework of a retreat we have more freedom, more time, more energy, to take what we have learned to a much deeper level.

We need to meditate to benefit ourselves and free ourselves from suffering. We have no other choice. We must actualize the path, and to do that, we must meditate on the path. Within a retreat we place ourselves in a situation where there are the best possible circumstances away from distractions, creating the conditions to quickly progress in our meditations.

If we are a Mahayana practitioner, we also need to retreat to benefit others. By developing our own mind in retreat, we are much more able to work for others afterward, benefiting them in whatever way is most appropriate. For instance, with the clarity we have gained from the retreat, when we try to explain the Dharma, people sense that it is coming from our heart and is not mere book learning. Because of that, it has a great effect on them, making it easier for them to turn their minds to the Dharma.

Retreating Away from the Eight Worldly Dharmas
Usually when Tibetan people talk about a retreat, it means they go to a certain place to do a certain practice for a certain time, for a month or two or longer. However, the essence of a retreat does not depend on

where we are. Whatever type of retreat it is—a mindfulness retreat, a lamrim retreat, a tantric retreat—for it to be a retreat, we must live in the discipline of observing our karma, avoiding the negative actions of body, speech, and mind as much as possible. This is the general meaning of the word "retreat."

No matter where we are—in a city, in a train station where there is so much noise, in an American supermarket—if we are living in the discipline of avoiding negative actions, we are in retreat. Conversely, we might be far from the city, alone on a meditation cushion in a cave on a Himalayan mountain, but if we are not living in the discipline of avoiding negative actions, we are not really in retreat. In short, the word "retreat" means retreating away from the thought of the eight worldly dharmas.

Usually, the time that any of us have for retreat is very limited. Therefore, it is unbelievably important to put all our effort into making sure whatever we do within the retreat becomes pure Dharma. Heruka gave this advice to the great yogi Luipa, one of the lineage lamas of the Heruka Chakrasamvara teachings:

> Give up stretching the legs
> and give up entering samsara.
> Generate bodhichitta to achieve Vajrasattva, the Great Victorious
> One, for all sentient beings.[114]

This is not saying that we can't sleep during retreat, that we can't lie down and stretch out our legs at night. That is *not* Heruka's advice. "Giving up stretching the legs" means giving up allowing the mind to be controlled by the thought that seeks only the comfort of this life.

For example, although stretching our legs when we are with other people can be rude, when we are meditating and we feel a little tired, the thought of seeking comfort arises, and following that thought, we can very easily start to miss sessions or even our commitments, or even spend our whole time sleeping, which is *completely* stretching the legs. This is a terrible waste of time, because in those hours, when we could have made our life highly meaningful, we have missed that great opportunity. The fundamental mistake is allowing our mind to be under the control of our laziness, our attachment to comfort.

Wanting comfort, happiness, possessions, reputation, praise, and not wanting their opposites—in other words, the eight worldly dharmas— is what ties us to this life. Whenever we try to have a virtuous thought, one of these eight concerns is there to pull us back into selfish consideration. No action motivated by attachment is Dharma. We might have been meditating in a solitary place for years but still be plagued with problems, attached to comfort and upset by discomfort, concerned that people might dislike us, and so forth. When there are hindrances and our mind becomes more agitated rather than more peaceful, that is due to the thought of the eight worldly dharmas. Until attachment to this life's pleasures has been overcome, our meditation practice will be flawed and ineffective. We are mostly a "mouth" meditator.

Students have sometimes complained to me that they have been meditating for decades, but with few results. They say this, but I'm not actually sure that they have been *meditating* for that long, even though that is what they might believe. Furthermore, some seem to see their lack of progress as somehow the fault of the Dharma, that there is something wrong with the teachings. They don't recognize that the flaw lies with them, that a part of their practice is missing, causing the hindrances that block their progress. They never think that it is their own attitude that must be changed.

Everything we do in retreat should be an antidote to the thought of the eight worldly dharmas, through meditations such as those on the graduated path of the lower capable being, meditating on the perfect human rebirth, on impermanence, and so forth. From the perspective of how precious and fragile this life is, to waste even a second seems quite childish and silly.

A more advanced retreat is our mind retreating away from attachment to future lives' samsaric happiness by living in renunciation of the whole of samsara. Then, on *that* basis, we retreat away from the self-cherishing by living in bodhichitta, working only for others.

More advanced still is retreating away from ignorance, the root of samsara, which is the ignorance apprehending the I to exist from its own side. We use meditations such as seeing that whatever appears to the senses—form, sound, smell, taste, or tangible objects—appears to the hallucinated mind as though it truly exists even though it is totally empty of existing from its own side.

In this way, we retreat in renunciation and away from attachment, we retreat in bodhichitta and away from self-cherishing, and we retreat in emptiness and away from self-grasping and ignorance.

What I want to emphasize, however, is that if we do a retreat with a good heart, then there will be good results. Even though our motivation might still be muddied with attachment to this life, at least we are honestly trying. And because we are *trying* to practice morality, our good heart gives us peace and protection, and we are able to practice the Dharma without major obstacles.

Accepting the Inevitability of Problems

When we come out of the retreat, maybe we will find that the whole world has completely changed. Or maybe not! If we can take the opportunity to retreat as much as possible, no matter how many problems arise during the retreat, by seeing how important it is to develop our mind in this way, we will persevere, and our mind will definitely be transformed. We must remember we are not retreating for the happiness of this life alone, to free ourselves from this life's problems. When this life's problems are over, we will have to face the problems of the next life and all our future lives. No matter how many problems we have to face now, we must never give up our Dharma practice.

When we do a retreat, or even practice meditation on a daily basis, of course we will encounter difficulties, both physical and mental. For instance, when we sit down to meditate, there will always be something not right—we will feel uncomfortable or hungry, or too hot or too cold, or we will be too tired because we haven't been able to sleep. Or perhaps everything will feel just right—and then we start to get itchy because of lice! We can always find some problem to keep us from meditating.

We should not be concerned with problems we notice, thinking they are important. Those problems might seem like a hindrance to our Dharma practice, but we need to understand that without completing our Dharma practice there is no part of life—not even for one moment—when we are completely free of all physical and mental problems. That will only happen when we have totally overcome our delusions. Therefore, it is worthwhile to encourage ourselves to continue without caring so much about those small problems. When we don't give them any importance, they don't bother us, and our meditation practice will progress much more easily.

This is the experience of all of us when we begin meditating. We should just accept problems as natural, instead of putting ourselves down or being obsessed with fixing them. We should think, "I'm living in samsara, which is suffering by its very nature, so of course there are problems, just as it would be hot if I were sitting in the middle of a bonfire." If we didn't know the nature of fire was heat, we might well blame the fire for our discomfort, but when we see that that is its nature and the only thing we can do is get out of it, then we can do something about it. In the same way, when we see that the nature of samsara is suffering, we can determine to do whatever is necessary to escape from it, even if that means bearing some discomfort in our meditations.

When we recollect this, we can reassert our motivation whenever we slip into wanting only comfort. Then there will be much less distraction in our meditation and our Dharma practice, and our retreat will go much more smoothly. This is how all those great meditators started their Dharma practice, trying to have a pure life by constantly recalling their motivation and thinking about the importance of meditating, mainly through understanding the suffering nature of samsara.

Of course, that does not mean we should go looking for problems in our retreat. As we have seen when we looked at the prerequisites for developing shamatha, we can progress more easily when we prepare for a retreat carefully, finding the most conducive place, making ourselves physically and mentally prepared beforehand, and so forth. For long retreats, there are also sets of preliminary practices we are strongly encouraged to do, which we will look at below.

NYUNGNÉS

An unbelievably powerful practice of purification we can do is the two-day *nyungné* practice,[115] a practice that was handed down from Chenrezig to the fully ordained Indian nun Bhikshuni Gelongma Palmo.[116] A nyungné is a tantric practice combining fasting, prostrations, and the eight Mahayana precepts with a Chenrezig meditation, using a combination of very powerful purification techniques, such as visualizing ourselves as the deity and sending out beams of light to purify the countless other sentient beings.

Nyungné means "abiding in the retreat."[117] In other words, we are retreating away from negative karmas of body, speech, and mind. When we think of a nyungné, we should think not only of the physical practices such as the fasting and prostrating; nyungné has a much vaster meaning than just not eating.

Physically, we are in retreat from the nonvirtuous actions mentioned in the one-day eight Mahayana precepts that we take pre-dawn: vowing to abstain from killing, stealing, lying, sexual contact, taking intoxicants, sitting on high seats or beds, eating at an inappropriate time, and singing, dancing, and wearing perfumes and jewelry. In addition to these vows, we abstain from food and drink. On the first day of a nyungné we fast in the afternoon and on the second day we totally fast, neither eating nor drinking anything at all. These are the physical activities we abstain from.

We are also in retreat from the negative verbal activities. On the first day we keep our speech pure, free from idle conversation that might increase our delusions, and on the second day we remain completely silent, except for the prayers within the practice.

Cherishing others is the most important samaya, or commitment, of any Chenrezig practice and is the main practice during a nyungné. If somebody criticizes us, we don't criticize them in return. If somebody is angry with us, we don't get angry in return. If somebody harms us, we don't harm them in return. If somebody beats us, we don't beat them in return. There are these four pieces of advice given, but the essential point is to not retaliate to any harm given. By receiving the blessings of Chenrezig, our heart becomes softer; we naturally feel incredibly strong compassion for other sentient beings.

Purification is the most important thing we can do, especially for us beginners, and a nyungné is an unbelievably powerful practice of purification. It's generally mentioned in the teachings that doing one nyungné purifies forty thousand eons of negative karma. While doing a nyungné, we may experience hunger, thirst, tiredness, pain, and other difficulties, which are signs of great purification. We should feel whatever difficulties we experience are incredibly worthwhile because they are not only to help us to obtain ultimate happiness for ourselves; we also experience the hardships of a nyungné to relieve the suffering of all other sentient beings.

Because a nyungné practice is very easy to do and yet is unbelievably powerful, I recommend everybody to attempt to do it, at least once a year. Besides being the best means of purifying and developing realizations, it is especially powerful in helping us develop compassion for sentient beings. It is also very effective in healing sicknesses, even those that are difficult to cure. With the great purification and accumulation of merit that the nyungné brings, we can easily go to a pure land and to achieve enlightenment, without needing to undergo many hardships for eons.

Although I recommend doing at least one nyungné a year, if you can do more, that's extremely good. Of course, more is always better. Venerable Tenzin Namdrol, a Brazilian nun, has already finished many hundreds of nyungnés, and there are other FPMT students, such as Venerable Ailsa Cameron, from Chenrezig Institute, Australia, and Venerable Charles, from Institut Vajra Yogini, France, who lead nyungnés and who have each completed hundreds.

THE PRELIMINARY PRACTICES

Preliminary practices (*purvaka*, *ngöndro*) are practices you do prior to a long retreat, preparing your mind to ensure the retreat will be successful. The four main practices:

- recitation of the refuge formula
- mandala offerings
- prostrations
- Vajrasattva mantra recitation

The Geluk tradition adds five more:

- guru yoga
- water bowl offerings
- making *tsatsas*
- the Damtsik Dorjé purifying meditation
- the Dorjé Khandro burning offering practice

These practices are done before a retreat to purify obstacles to the success of the retreat, to purify the negativities and broken vows, and to collect extensive merit, the conditions necessary for achieving realizations. The guru will recommend the practices most beneficial for a particular disciple at that time, such as so many thousands of the Dorjé Khandro burning puja, prostrations to the Thirty-Five Buddhas, and so forth. Generally, the disciple will be instructed to do a hundred thousand of each or some of the preliminaries, but that number varies. When I advise people, the number of preliminary practices some people should do is a lot, much more than a hundred thousand, and for others not so many. It doesn't mean everybody gets a big number to do.

The Vajrasattva practice and prostrating and reciting the names of the Thirty-Five Buddhas are done to pacify obstacles, and offering the mandala is done to collect merit. Besides these, I consider guru yoga an essential practice, in order to receive the blessings of the guru to quickly gain realizations.

Where large numbers of preliminary practices are needed, most should be completed in retreat, although it is also possible to do some while at home or working. Whoever gives you the preliminary commitment will explain this. For instance, the hundred thousand Vajrasattva mantras usually take three months in a retreat condition but occasionally a guru will allow a disciple to do some in retreat and some over an extended period out of retreat, with very specific conditions.

When you do a retreat to complete a particular preliminary practice commitment, I recommend that in the first session you concentrate on a guru yoga practice with an emphasis on a guru devotion meditation. Then do a half hour, more or less, of lamrim meditation. For the rest of the session—an hour, an hour and a half, or two hours—do the preliminary practice. The length of the session is up to you.

In this way your preliminary practice retreat also becomes a lamrim retreat, and the lamrim meditations render your preliminary practice very powerful for purification and for the accumulation of merit. Pabongka Dechen Nyingpo explains that the goal should not be just to complete the preliminary practices but to also enrich your lamrim meditations in order to have realizations of the three principal aspects of the path.

You must be careful to protect yourself from even small negative actions that will spoil your preliminary practices, making them ineffectual. Even if you do a hundred thousand of this one and a hundred thousand of that one—even if you do all nine preliminaries—if you continuously create negative karma at the same time, your need to do preliminary practices will never end.

Doing preliminary practices is not just a beginner's practice. If you read the life stories of the great meditators, they do huge numbers of prostrations and other preliminary practices. Even Lama Tsongkhapa did so many hundreds of thousands of prostrations in the cave in Wölka Chölung.[118] Milarepa's preliminary practices were much more than doing many mandalas and Vajrasattva mantras. He achieved enlightenment within a brief life in these degenerate times by doing a special preliminary practice, cherishing his guru, Marpa, more than his own life. He never had a negative thought of anger or heresy no matter how he was treated, despite being constantly scolded and insulted by Marpa. He followed his guru's advice, no matter how difficult the task was. Marpa made him build a nine-story tower without anybody's help and then told him to tear it down after it was built and put every stone back in the same place it came from. He had to do this three times. If you read Milarepa's incredible story, you will know how perfectly he followed his guru's advice. The hard work, beating, and abuse he received were his preliminaries.

Besides these traditional nine preliminary practices, Kirti Tsenshab Rinpoché, a great teacher and one of my gurus, explains that one of the best ways of purifying and collecting merit is by studying great philosophical texts, such as the *Prajnaparamita* (*Perfection of Wisdom*) texts or Maitreya's *Ornament of Clear Realizations* (*Abhisamayalamkara*). The next most effective preliminary is reciting the *Perfection of Wisdom in Eight Thousand Lines* one hundred times. According to Rinpoche, after that come the nine preliminaries: refuge, water bowls, mandala offerings, and so forth. That means that if you persevere in studying these texts despite the hardship, that itself includes these preliminary practices.

Refuge Mantras

The first preliminary is generally listed as saying the refuge mantra or prayer many times. Traditionally, it is said in Sanskrit or Tibetan, but you can also say it in English. The prayer is this:

NAMO GURUBHYA (*lama la kyab su chio*)
I take refuge in the Guru.
NAMO BUDDHAYA (*sanggyä la kyab su chio*)
I take refuge in the Buddha.
NAMO DHARMAYA (*chhö la kyab su chio*)
I take refuge in the Dharma.

NAMO SANGHAYA (*gedün la kyab su chio*)
I take refuge in the Sangha.

In Lama Atisha's tradition, when you offer a short mandala, which is one of the ways of doing the hundred thousand mandalas for the preliminaries, you precede the mandala offering with the refuge prayer to remind yourself of your motivation each time you offer the mandala. If you combine the two in your preliminaries in this way, you complete a hundred thousand refuge mantras along with a hundred thousand mandala offerings.

Mandala Offerings

While reciting the mandala prayer the determined number of times, such as a hundred thousand, you offer to the merit field the whole world and all the other planets, as well as all the precious sense objects that are in this and other worlds. You should especially offer all the objects you cling to: your body, possessions, and friends. Fill space with the highest quality offerings you can think of. By reading and studying the commentaries, you can learn the details of the meditations that go with the mandala offering prayer.

The mandala offering is a method to accumulate extensive merit in a short time. The essential technique is to offer as many best-quality mandalas as possible, with the visualization according to the prayer. As you think of offering many golden mountains or universes as clearly as you can, at that very moment, you accumulate the extensive merit of having actually offered that many golden mountains or universes.

As I just mentioned, an excellent way of doing the two preliminaries together is to recite the refuge prayer with the mandala offering. We have already seen the technique and visualization involved with a long mandala, but within the preliminary practices an abbreviated version of this can be done while reciting the short mandala. I highly recommend you use a mandala set, first cleaning the base of the set, then, on the base, putting heaps for Mount Meru, the four continents, the sun, and the moon, making seven heaps in all.

When you finish a session of offering the mandala, you make a strong request to the merit field for all the interferences and obstacles to generating the whole path to be pacified. White nectar beams are emitted from the merit field, purifying all your obscurations and those of all other sentient beings. Then, to generate realizations, you visualize yellow beams of light coming from the merit field and granting you and all sentient beings all the realizations.

Prostrations and Vajrasattva

According to Lama Tsongkhapa's tradition, the preliminary practices usually include a hundred thousand prostrations, although the number is not the main consideration. In *Liberation in the Palm of Your Hand*, Pabongka Dechen Nyingpo advises that you must try to do them correctly even if you don't manage to complete that many prostrations. You should not rush through them just to get the number done. He says,

> Jé Rinpoché [Tsongkhapa] advised us not to focus on the number of prostrations—doing a hundred thousand as a preliminary practice, and so on; go instead for quality, even if that means not doing as big a number.
>
> Some might claim "I am going to do my preliminary retreat," and then take shortcuts when they do the hundred thousand prostrations. This is wrong. You must build up your accumulations and purify your obscurations right up until you reach enlightenment. Beginners like ourselves must work hard at accumulation and purification all our lives. Accumulation and self-purification are much more important than meditation: you will not achieve anything at all if you claim, "I have finished my preliminary retreat" and take things easy thereafter.[119]

When you finish doing however many prostrations you have to do, that does not mean you should become like a retired person, with the totally lazy mind. You will reach nowhere living your life like that, thinking the job is done and there is no more need for effort. Even after having done the prostrations and the other preliminaries, you still need to continue purifying and accumulating merit.

On the other hand, if you do your prostrations skillfully, you purify so many negativities and accumulate so much merit that realizations will come whether you have done the specified number or not. And, when you understand how wonderful it is that you have done so many prostrations, great joy will naturally arise, and *that* increases your merit immensely.

If you are doing prostrations in a full-time retreat, it is best to do them as part of a practice of guru yoga, (see below) pausing within the practice to do the prostrations to the Thirty-Five Buddhas, using the standard practice, *Confession of a Bodhisattva's Downfall to the Thirty-Five Buddhas.*[120]

Another preliminary practice is Vajrasattva, which means doing a hundred thousand Vajrasattva mantras or more in a retreat situation while prostrating. This is considered one of the most powerful means of purifying negative karma. It is not common in the Geluk tradition to give a commitment of doing a Vajrasattva retreat when giving a Vajrasattva empowerment, but Lama Yeshe, with his skillful means and compassion for us, his students, kindly started this tradition within our organization. Since then, many thousands of people have benefited.

Generally, the preliminary retreat instructions in the texts advise that you should begin and finish a retreat in one place ("on the same seat" the texts say) whether you are doing a hundred thousand, two hundred thousand, or even four hundred thousand of that preliminary. In this way there are far fewer obstacles. However, in a Vajrasattva practice you visualize Vajrasattva on your crown, which also means you can do the practice in different places. There is no question of this being either a strict or a loose retreat; that is just the way it is with Vajrasattva. Therefore, even though it is preferable to do all hundred thousand mantras in the same place, you can complete them elsewhere.

There are different versions of the Vajrasattva practice, including a very short sadhana. You can use whatever version you like.[121] Then, you can feel comfortable completing the required number of mantras. Of course, it is preferable to have both a high number and a high quality of mantras, but if you can't have both, then it's better to have a high quality, because the aim is to purify negative karma.

Guru Yoga

Some people's minds are very easily transformed by just having done some of the preliminary practices, and they start to have great devotion or very powerful compassion or renunciation. Depending on how thick the obscurations are, some people need to do a lot more preliminary practices in order to really develop. For some it takes a long time.

Therefore, you need to persevere with a strong practice of purification and collecting merits, and you need to put effort into developing guru devotion. Even if in the beginning the mind is very stubborn, refusing to feel any devotion for the guru, devotion will come as you continue with the preliminary practices. Then, when you meditate or read a Dharma text, as you purify, as the obstacles diminish, suddenly your heart opens and the experience manifests.

Doing a guru yoga practice within the preliminary practices, such as doing the practice of *Lama Tsongkhapa Guru Yoga* or *Guru Puja*, you generally combine it with prostrations and a lamrim meditation. To do this you begin the day with your guru yoga practice up to the point of the seven-limb prayer of confession. After the confession verse, you do your prostrations to the Thirty-Five Buddhas, complete your guru yoga, and then dedicate.

If you are doing the *Lama Tsongkhapa Guru Yoga* practice, after the prostrations you can complete the seven-limb prayer and recite the *Foundation of All Good Qualities*, doing a short lamrim meditation on whatever topic you have reached. This way, with each session, you do your guru yoga practice, prostrations, and a short lamrim meditation.

If you are doing the practice of *Guru Puja*, the prostrations come after verse 38. In a full retreat, doing between four to six sessions a day, it will probably take you between two to three months to complete a hundred thousand prostrations.

Calling the Guru from Afar,[122] written by Pabongka Dechen Nyingpo, is a very powerful prayer, combining guru yoga practice and lamrim. Because this prayer came from Pabongka Rinpoché's own experience, it is a wonderful way to do a glance meditation on the three principal aspects of the path and the two stages of highest tantra.

When you recite the prayer, visualize your guru on your crown or in front of you as the embodiment of all the gurus, the Buddha, Dharma, and Sangha. The very essence of the meditation is to concentrate on the guru as the absolute guru, the dharmakaya, the holy mind of all the buddhas, the transcendental wisdom of nondual bliss and voidness.

Whatever guru yoga practice you use, after your final session of the day, do extensive dedication prayers together with multiplying mantras.

Water Bowl Offerings

When you do a hundred thousand water bowl offerings, you can use as many bowls for each session as is practical, say fifty or a hundred, setting them up neatly on an offering table. Of course, it is best you do this in your home or retreat place, but you could even do them at the beach. You can fill up the whole beach with bowls, then maybe the next day you will have to go to a psychiatrist!

As you do when you set up your altar on a daily basis, when you clean the bowls after a session, don't just wipe the towel quickly around like some kind of token cleaning. You have to clean the bowls well, so that they are dry inside. And they should be left upside down for the next session.

First of all, you start on the basis of the *Lama Tsongkhapa Guru Yoga* practice, the *Guru Puja*, or a similar practice. Then, when you reach the offering section within the seven-limb practice, you do the water bowl offerings. The texts say the offering should be "beautifully performed," meaning that the line of bowls should not be crooked, and the offering should be done with a focused mind, not one stained with worldly concern.

When you have finished offering all the bowls, you should think that the whole of space is filled with offerings of nectar. The more extensively you can think this, the more merit you accumulate. Think that even a tiny drop of that nectar generates infinite bliss. The bliss that is generated cannot fit in the sky.

You then empty and clean the bowls, to be set up again in the next session. When you have emptied the water from the bowls, you should not throw it on dirty ground or where it will be walked on. This applies generally to anything offered on an altar, such as flowers. You should throw the water in a flower garden or somewhere clean. Remember that this is an offering to the Three Rare Sublime Ones and that it has been taken by them.

Making Tsatsas

Tsatsas are small images of a buddha or a holy object made in clay or plaster from a mold. They can also be made from other materials. You can make a print image on paper or make an impression of the Buddha on water, but that is two-dimensional and there are many less atoms, so a three-dimensional clay or plaster tsatsa is much better. In the *Sutra Requested by King Sengyal*, the Buddha says that those who make holy objects such as stupas will achieve the level of a king of the god realm and the sublime concentration of the form and formless realms for as many eons as there are atoms in that holy object. Even though the tsatsa you are making might be tiny, it still consists of countless atoms, so for each atom of that tsatsa you will achieve that incredible result for that many eons.

As with any offering, the more tsatsas you make the more merit you create. And because tsatsas are small and very cheap to make, you can easily give them to people. Then anybody who sees and makes offerings to the tsatsas you have made also creates so much merit. Those with devotion experience strong purification and collect great merit, but even when animals and people with no understanding or faith in the Buddha, Dharma, and Sangha see, touch, or go round holy objects, they get all the benefits mentioned in the sutras.

This is how, by making holy objects and giving them to others, you bring other sentient beings to enlightenment, even though they may have no wish to learn the Dharma. Somebody who prostrates to one holy object—one tsatsa—creates one cause for enlightenment; somebody who prostrates to two creates two causes. If you have made a hundred thousand tsatsas, you are giving people the chance to create a hundred thousand causes for enlightenment. That is why people doing preparatory practices are encouraged not to make only a few dozen or a few hundred tsatsas but tens of thousands or even hundreds of thousands.

Somebody who receives one of your tsatsas gets incredible merit. If that is true, imagine how much merit you are creating by making it— working so hard, getting plaster dust up your nose and everywhere else, turning your whole room white. And you are making thousands! All the merit that others collect is your gift to them. It is something to rejoice in and feel very happy about (and therefore create even *more* merit).

Your friends can place your tsatsas around their home, such as along the walls, although they should not place them in the toilet or bathroom. Then, whenever they look at them, there is a very nice feeling of respect, because they are the Buddha's form and so even just looking purifies the mind.

You can also build a stupa in your garden and place the tsatsas inside (although never put broken tsatsas into a stupa as that affects the minds of those who circumambulate). This is especially good for your pets and for the birds and insects in your garden. You can pick up your dog or cat and walk it around the stupa, thus making circumambulations.

If you are making a hundred thousand tsatsas for your preparatory practices, you should remember the benefits before you start work and also recall them from time to time while you are working. That way, despite the difficult and messy work you are doing, your mind will be so happy.

Damtsik Dorjé Purification and the Dorjé Khandro Burning Offering

Damtsik Dorjé (Samayavajra) is a powerful purification practice,[123] especially for purifying broken samaya vows, those vows taken during an initiation, and negative karmas created in relation to your guru.

Damtsik Dorjé, who belongs to the mandala of Guhyasamaja tantra, is the essence of the holy mind of all the buddhas.

As well as doing this practice as one of the nine preliminaries, I often recommend doing it daily in conjunction with the Vajrasattva meditation in order to do the confession practice perfectly with the remedy of the four opponent powers: the powers of the object, of regret, of resolve, and of the remedy. When the lamrim lineage lamas, such as Yongzin Yeshé Gyaltsen, did the *Guru Puja*, they alternated the Damtsik Dorjé practice on one day and Vajrasattva on the next.

The last of the nine preliminary practices is the burning offering (*jinsek*) to Dorjé Khandro, which, according to Yongzin Yeshé Gyaltsen, is a very powerful way to purify general obscurations and negative karmas. Dorjé Khandro is Vajra Daka in Sanskrit. *Dorjé* or *vajra* refers to the transcendental wisdom of nondual bliss and voidness, which is the dharmakaya, the absolute guru, and *khandro* or *daka*, which literally means "going in space," refers to not just ordinary space but the space of emptiness. This practice was Lama Tsongkhapa's heart practice.

The essence of the practice is offering sesame seeds into a fire while saying a mantra and visualizing you are offering all your negativities (the seeds) into the mouth of Dorjé Khandro (the fire). Because he eats your negative karma, he is also called "the Eater."

As with other sadhanas, the practice has three parts: the preliminaries, the actual practice, and the completion. For the actual practice, after forming a pile of black sesame seeds into the shape of a scorpion on a flat tray or plate, you sit in front of a fireplace[124] that has a pot to throw the seeds into. The pot should be round and not broken. You can use a specially made iron statue of Dorjé Khandro, with his mouth gaping wide, ready to receive the seeds.

Having done all the preliminaries and visualized Dorjé Khandro, you dispel the interferers, generate the fire first into emptiness and then into the deity, and then you make offerings to Dorjé Khandro, placing a few sesame seeds between your fingers and throwing them into the fire, as you say the mantra OM VAJRA DAKA KHA KHA KHAHI KHAHI

SARVA PAPAM DAHANA BAKMI KURU SVAHA. You do this until all the seeds are gone. You then think that all your negativities have be burned up completely, eaten by Dorjé Khandro. There are short and elaborate versions of this practice you can do.[125]

STRUCTURING A RETREAT[126]

For your lamrim retreat to be successful, one that stabilizes your experiences, you must first train the mind by studying the lamrim from beginning to end, and then do the meditations on all the different subjects. You have to become familiar with them all.

Being familiar with the whole path from beginning to end, you can then slowly work through each subject, doing one subject for one day, or for a few days, then moving to the next. You can start each day by going on from wherever you left off at the end of the previous day. This will certainly give you confidence that you can attain realizations if you try.

For a lamrim retreat, I recommend a daily schedule like this:

- Take the eight Mahayana precepts every morning.
- Do an extensive motivation at the beginning of each session and reflect again on the motivation before beginning the mantra recitation.
- For the first session of the day, do the *Lama Chöpa Jorchö* with a meditation on guru devotion.
- At the beginning of the other sessions, do a glance meditation on the lamrim, with deep reflection on one particular topic. Work your way through the entire lamrim—session after session—then start again from the beginning.
- Begin each session with prostrations to the Thirty-Five Buddhas and the Eight Medicine Buddhas together with the General Confession prayer.[127]
- At the end of the day, do extensive dedication, such as verses from the *Extensive Dedication Prayers* and *Additional Dedication Prayers*, and *King of Prayers*, followed by *Prayers for Multiplying Merit*.[128]

When you are doing a deity retreat, I recommend also including one session of lamrim meditation each day. Besides that, you should do a little guru devotion meditation every day, until you have a stable realization.

A possible timetable for a deity retreat:

4:30–5:00 am	Eight Mahayana Precepts
5:00–7:00 am	*Lama Chöpa Jorchö* beginning with prostrations to the Thirty-Five Buddhas
8:00–9:30 am	Retreat deity sadhana and mantra recitation starting with prostrations to the Thirty-Five Buddhas
10:00–11:00 am	Retreat deity session as above
11:00–3:00 pm	Lunch and break
3:00–4:30 pm	Retreat deity session
5:30–7:00 pm	Retreat deity session
8:00–9:00 pm	Short retreat deity session with extensive dedication prayers or protector prayers

BETWEEN SESSIONS

It is extremely important not to waste your time in between the meditation sessions but do everything you can to make them as highly meaningful as your meditations. In the breaktime, you should try to remember whatever meditation you have done during the session, relating it to whatever activities you are doing. In that way you can best protect your karma by not allowing the three poisonous minds of anger, attachment, and ignorance to arise.

For instance, if the meditation you did was on guru devotion, in the break it is good to read the biographies of the great yogis such as Naropa, Milarepa, Lama Atisha, or Lama Tsongkhapa, how they followed the guru and generated realizations in their minds. Then, after the break, when you continue the meditation, because your mind was not distracted, your experience will be deeper, your understanding clearer, and your devotion to your guru stronger. In this way, the breaktime helps the session and the session helps the breaktime.

Similarly, if you are training your mind in bodhichitta during the session, in the break you should read about the benefits of bodhichitta and about how to meditate on it. This is not just preparation for the meditation; many Kadampa geshés actually generated realizations in the breaktime.

Many people feel meditation is hard work and it feels good at breaktime to let their mind go slack. It's like they have just been released from prison. But in fact it's completely the opposite. By letting the unsubdued mind take over during the break, you are surrendering your freedom to your delusions, completely letting them take control.

You shouldn't spend the breaktime talking or reading about things that have nothing to do the subject you meditated on. You should avoid books or videos filled with all kinds of misconceptions, depicting scenes of violence or couples in strong relationships. A conversation with somebody could easily trigger attachment, jealousy, or anger, rather than renunciation and compassion. Before you know it, you have wasted hours in gossip, chatting about friends, about the things you desire, about sex, and all the subjects that make your mind even crazier. In short, you should stay well away from anything that increases any delusion.

When you read a non-Dharma book or watch a television program, it might not only disturb your mind but also what you read or see could take over your thoughts when you return to the meditation session. Then, even though you are sitting on the meditation cushion, you are a million miles away, utterly unable to concentrate. Your mind is like one of those tornados you see in the south of the United States, out of control, furiously swirling around, throwing all sorts of things into the sky. You recite the prayer, saying you are going to meditate to attain enlightenment for the sake of all sentient beings, but it might as well be a sound coming out of a tape recorder.

The texts say that a complete retreat involves three break-time activities:

- a correct diet eaten at the appropriate time
- the right amount of sleep at the correct time
- watching the three doors at all times

I think your most important breaktime activity is to always be mindful of the three doors of your body, speech, and mind: watching what you do, what you say, and what you think. With great diligence, you need to spy on your mind and see whenever a nonvirtuous thought is about to arise and then do whatever is necessary to avert it. By recognizing any nonvirtuous thought, you are not only able to stop it but also to transform it into virtue. Unless you do this, you can spend every second not on the meditation cushion accumulating negative karma. Whole hours can go by trapped in anger or attachment.

When you look at your retreat day, more time is spent outside the formal meditation session than within it, and that means there is more time to potentially create nonvirtue. Without constant vigilance, it is very difficult to stop the unsubdued mind from contaminating any positive merit you create in the session. That is why you should try to "close the door of the senses" between sessions, meaning guarding your mind whenever you experience the objects of the six senses.[129] You should be acutely aware of everything you see, hear, taste, and so forth, and how your mind reacts to it, to ensure that no negative mind can arise.

Between sessions you should be conscious of how everything comes from your mind—what you hear comes from your mind, what you smell comes from your mind, what you taste comes from your mind, what you think comes from your mind. Practicing mindfulness like this becomes a powerful antidote to anger and other delusions, allowing you to always feel at peace, free from emotional fluctuations such as excitement or depression.

Furthermore, you should watch your mind to see when any sense of self-cherishing arises and actively avert it. Then, everything you do in the breaktime becomes an antidote to selfish concern, everything becomes a practice of bodhichitta, working for the benefit of others. Eating, walking, sitting, sleeping—every activity becomes the best Dharma.

PART III
POSTMEDITATION

9. AWAY FROM THE MEDITATION CUSHION

··

TAKING THE ESSENCE DAY AND NIGHT

Because we spend a lot more time out of meditation than in meditation, it is vital to make every action of body, speech, and mind outside of the session—when we are going about our daily life—as meaningful as possible. We should not get up from the meditation cushion and immediately lose the positive energy of the meditation, spending the rest of the day as if our meditation and our daily activities were completely separate. Instead, we should maintain our awareness in everything we do, taking whatever feeling or experience we generated in our meditation session into our postmeditation day. For instance, if our meditation on the perfect human rebirth concluded with a strong feeling of our great good fortune, that should flavor everything we do during the day.

In *A Hymn of Experience* Lama Tsongkhapa says,

> This body of leisure, more precious than a wish-fulfilling jewel,
> Is found but once. Though difficult to obtain again,
> It finishes as quickly as lightning in the sky.
> Having reflected in this way, realizing that all worldly activities
> Are like winnowed chaff,
> You must take its essence day and night.
> You, the perfect guru, practiced in this way.
> I, who am seeking liberation, will also practice in this way.[130]

Worldly activities are like the husk that gets blown away by the wind when the grain is threshed; they have no essence at all. To get the essence, the kernel, you have to thresh it. In Nepal, people put the grain in bamboo trays and throw it in the air, so the wind separates the valuable kernel from the worthless husk. Like that, we need to take the essence of this life day and night by avoiding the essenceless activities of worldly life.

According to His Holiness the Dalai Lama, a good way to take the essence is to do a meditation session in the morning and then, for the rest of the day, at various times recall the meditation and the feeling it evoked and try to bring our mind back to that experience.

Whatever we have been meditating on will color our attitude. For instance, if we had meditated on guru devotion and generated some devotion though analytical and fixed meditation, for the rest of the day we should try to remember the conclusion, holding the mind in the devotion that was generated in the morning. And this applies to the sense of impermanence gained through the meditation on impermanence and death or the feeling of compassion gained through that meditation. Say, having developed some sense of compassion through meditating on the suffering of sentient beings, what better thing to do when we are out there among others than to observe how, although many appear happy, all are suffering in one way or another? No matter what their situation, they are trapped in delusions and unhappiness. Seeing this, compassion naturally arises.

At other times, we can train the mind to look at sentient beings with loving-kindness by thinking of how each has been the source of all our past, present, and future happiness, starting from our family to each person or animal we see in the street. Then, even if we meet a person who is antagonistic, who criticizes or harms us, we will not become angry but only regard that person with loving-kindness and compassion.

Having created a bodhichitta motivation and dedicated for all sentient beings during the meditation session, for the rest of the day we should try to continue that mindfulness, feeling we have received all our past and present happiness and will receive all our future happiness from all beings, including the bees on the flowers in our garden, the worms in the ground, the pets we see around us, and the people we encounter.

With this mindfulness, we see every being as most precious, most kind. Then, the thought to respect and serve them comes naturally.

By taking these meditations away from the meditation cushion and incorporating them into everything we do in our daily life, we learn to take the essence of our precious human life. Seeing others with compassion, loving-kindness, patience, renunciation, wisdom, and so forth, we not only benefit others greatly but ourselves as well.

With Others, Watch the Speech; Alone, Watch the Mind

We can only really be concentrated and undistracted during our meditation session if we can lead our daily life virtuously. Concentration becomes much easier if throughout the day we can always protect our actions of body, speech, and mind from negativity. This is just as important in daily life as it is in retreat. This is why the texts say we must practice mindfulness at all times, no matter what we are doing.

Meditation time and postmeditation time complement each other. The meditation session helps us become more conscious during our nonmeditation time, and living our life with conscientiousness helps our meditation session. As Atisha advises in his *Bodhisattva's Jewel Garland* (*Bodhisattvamanyavali*),

> When among many, watch your words.
> When alone, watch your mind.[131]

The point is this: If we are among others, although of course the motivation we have is fundamental in whether our verbal or physical action becomes harmful or helpful, we need to be especially watchful of what we say, because we are more likely to hurt others through our speech than through our physical actions. Even if negative thoughts arise while we are with somebody, we should restrain from any unwanted verbal action in order to not harm them or make them angry in any way. By recognizing that our motivation is impure and that it could lead to words that will harm them, we discipline ourselves to not say those words.

Then, when we are alone, we should watch our mind. By ourselves, there is no reason to speak because nobody is around. So, while with others, the danger is harmful speech, when we are alone, the danger is nonvirtuous thoughts. Unless we constantly watch the mind, there is great danger that any negative thoughts we might have increase, and we become habituated to them. When that happens, it becomes harder and harder to control the mind.

What many meditators do in retreat is place around the four walls of their meditation room Dharma quotes emphasizing the need for an undistracted mind. In that way, wherever they look they see the Dharma and their mind is much less likely to slide into negative thoughts or become distracted. This greatly helps them when they are going through difficulties, and it makes continuing the practice easier in breaktimes. No matter what happens they always remain aware of the Dharma; everything becomes a kind of meditation for them.

Even if we are not doing a retreat, it is good to create the conditions where we are always conscious of the Dharma, so that whatever we see can become a teaching. In that way, we can keep our mind peaceful, without ups and downs.

Be a Conjurer of Illusions

It is difficult to take any understanding of emptiness we have gained during our meditation into our daily life, where generally we continue to instinctively see everything as truly existent. To counter that habit, instead of letting our mind believe the appearances to be true, we can practice the mindfulness of seeing things as hallucinations.

In his *Seven-Point Mind Training*, Geshé Chekawa Yeshé Dorjé[132] says,

> Train to view all phenomena as dreamlike.
> Examine the nature of the unborn awareness.
> The remedy, too, is freed in its own place.

Place your mind on the basis-of-all, the actual path.
In the interval be a conjurer of illusions.[133]

Meditating on these incredibly powerful words brings a sense of emptiness. Maybe we are still far from the stage where we can realize emptiness, but here is a training that can give a wonderful taste of it. "Train
to view all phenomena as dreamlike" refers to the emptiness of phenomena; "examine the nature of the unborn awareness" refers to the
emptiness of the mind; and "the remedy, too, is freed in its own place"
refers to the emptiness of the person. So, in our meditation session,
we meditate on these three emptinesses, and outside of the session,
we become "the conjurer of illusions." In other words, we practice the
mindfulness of seeing everything as like an illusion, like a dream.

In meditation we have seen that everything—the I, the action, the
object—appears as real, as not merely labelled by the mind, whereas
nothing is real at all in that way. Although things exist, they do not exist
inherently, and the way they appear to exist is a hallucination. So, when
we leave our meditation, we should continue the mindfulness of seeing
whatever appears as hallucinations. We look at that which is a hallucination as a hallucination; we look at that which is empty as empty.

To take this very profound thought into our busy life, with one part
of our mind we focus on whatever we are doing—working, talking,
driving our car, whatever—while another part of our mind watches
how what appears to be true is in fact a lie, how the solid world around
us is a hallucination. For instance, rather than seeing the food we are
eating as truly existing, we see how the food appears and how it exists
are completely the opposite; that truly existing food is a complete hallucination. We are the "conjurer of illusions" by seeing the illusionary
nature of the solid-seeming objects around us. When we can carry this
mindfulness through the day with whatever we experience, even if we
just have doubts about how things exist, it has the power to destroy
samsara by eliminating its root: ignorance. In *Four Hundred Stanzas*,
Aryadeva says, regarding emptiness,

Even those with few merits
have no doubts about this Dharma.
Even those who still have their doubts
will tear existence to tatters.[134]

Recognizing that what appears as inherently existing has no such inherent existence is not that difficult, even outside of a meditation session. The main problem, however, is that it is difficult to maintain that mindfulness. When we don't consciously think in this way, because of habituation we allow our mind to fall into its old thinking, holding on to those things as true.

That is the root problem. This misunderstanding of seeing people and things as truly existent becomes the basis for all those other emotional negative thoughts to arise—we get attached to "true" desirable things, we become jealous of "true" fortunate people, we get angry with "true" harmful people—which then motivates karmic verbal or physical actions. And then we perpetuate the oceans of samsaric suffering.

To counter that, we must somehow reverse our thinking and start to see that things do not exist in the way they appear. We can do this by trying to remain in the awareness of the dream-like nature of our life. Things do exist, but only as a mere imputation, so although the accurate phrase would be "like a dream" and not "a dream," I think to effectively carry this thought through the day, we can simply practice mindfulness by thinking, "I'm dreaming," "I'm dreaming that I'm meditating," "I'm dreaming that I'm walking," "I'm dreaming that I'm eating." Although philosophically incorrect, this builds our habituation to this new way of viewing the world, until we slowly start to see how the way things appear to us is not at all true. They exist but it is *as if* they don't exist.

Training ourselves to see "real" objects as dream objects is like the "no" in the *Heart of Wisdom Sutra*, where it says, "no eye, no ear, no nose, no tongue, no body, no mind." The *no* is like an atomic bomb to destroy the hallucination. However, we don't throw this bomb on the merely labeled eye that exists, or the merely labeled ear, nose, tongue, mind, or body that exist. We throw this bomb, this *no*, on the target, the object of ignorance, the concept of true existence. We throw it on the eye that appears to us to be not merely labeled by mind. That inherently existent eye is *totally* nonexistent, *totally* empty. And it is the same with all other phenomena: no form, no sound, no smell, no taste, and so forth.

We dream a "real" I but it is only a dream. We dream a "real" friend but it is only a dream. We dream a "real" enemy but it is only a dream. There is no real I or real friend or real enemy at all. Thinking, "I am dreaming," we put the dream on the "real" friend, the truly existent friend that appears to us. Just as in a dream, if we recognize we are dreaming, we feel no desire for a beautiful dream object or anger for an angry dream person, knowing it is just a dream, in the same way, even though we are still living within the hallucination, there is no basis for attachment or anger to arise.

After we wake up in the morning, when we wash, meditate, have breakfast, and then rush to work, we should try to be aware that there is no truly existing washing, eating, meditating, or rushing to work. Although they all appear to exist from their own side, they don't exist like that at all.

Perhaps, rather than thinking of our life as a dream, we can relate it to a movie. It's like we are watching a movie of our life, viewing how the scenes play out, one after the other, each appearing real, and how we believe in them and hold on to them. But this is all just a movie, all completely nonexistent. While we are driving, having a meeting, teaching in a school, or cooking at home, with whatever we are doing, we are watching the movie of our life.

Everything we see on the streets appears as real—the cars, buses, and motorcycles with the men in black leather making a huge noise—but we are always mindful how they do not exist in that way. We can practice seeing an important meeting at work as like a movie, something completely unreal. Practicing mindfulness in this way is so enjoyable. We might be working incredibly hard, but at the same time, because we are no longer bound up in the trap of believing in concrete existence, we are having the best vacation, the vacation from ignorance.

Outside of meditating on emptiness, being a "conjurer of illusions," as the great mind training text *Seven-Point Mind Training* advises, is the best antidote to samsara. We are the magician, the conjurer of illusions. The magician is often used as an analogy for ignorance. The magician uses a mantra to "illusion" the audience's mind, so instead of the piece of wood or some other object, they see beautiful things. The object isn't real at all, but the audience is tricked into thinking it is real. Here, because we ourselves are the magician, we are not fooled like the audience but know that what appears as real is just an illusion. Even though we might not be able to maintain that awareness continuously, we should try to think in that way during the day as much as possible.

A STAR, A DEFECTIVE VIEW, THE BUTTER LAMP FLAME

The Buddha skillfully used different analogies to illustrate how we should view conditioned phenomena. A verse from the *Diamond Cutter Sutra* says,

> A star, a defective view, a butter lamp flame,
> An illusion, a dew drop, a water bubble,
> A dream, lightning, a cloud:
> See all causative phenomena like this.[135]

The first image is *a star* in daytime. Because the sun is too bright, even though the star is there, we cannot see it. In the same way, even though everything is empty of existing inherently, it is much too subtle to see.

Seeing all conditioned phenomena—things that arise due to causes and conditions—as uncaused is compared to *defective view*, such as when we see a mirage appearing in the desert. If we were traveling in the desert, we might see water and rush to it, driven by our great thirst, but it turns out to be a mirage. This is how appearances trick us. Fooled by the appearance of an object, we are dismayed when it lets us down.

A bodhisattva would not be fooled if they saw the mirage. When arhats or arya bodhisattvas are not in meditative equipoise directly perceiving emptiness only—when they are in postmeditation breaktime—they also have the hallucination of inherently existent appearance but, unlike us, they do not have the belief that the hallucination is real. It is like looking back after having crossed a hot desert and seeing a mirage—the appearance of water—but knowing it to be false because we have just been there. Like the bodhisattva, we need to discern reality from fantasy in order to avoid mistakes and suffering.

Then, we should look at conditioned phenomena as like *a butter lamp flame*. All things are under the control of causes and conditions and therefore always changing, always decaying, not only day by day, hour by hour, minute by minute, second by second, but even within a second. Things are changing momentarily and can cease momentarily, just as a candle burns lower and lower and can be extinguished at any moment.

Similarly, just as *a dew drop*, hanging onto a leaf, can fall off and perish, just as *a water bubble* can pop at any moment, the I, the aggregates of body and mind, possessions, and people—friends, enemies and strangers—can perish any time. Khensur Denma Locho Rinpoché[136] used the example of a beautiful bubble, with all its rainbow colors, to show how even the beautiful is ephemeral. By exaggerating the beauty of something, by seeing it as inherently beautiful and clinging to it, we make suffering inevitable. Beautiful or ugly, any object is under the control of causes and conditions and can perish at any moment. This is the truth of impermanence.

We should see conditioned phenomena as like a *dream*, as we have discussed, and like a flash of *lightning* on a dark night, which illuminates the scene for an instant and then all is dark again. In that brief flash we see a tree and a person and we immediately label them, perhaps seeing the tree as a refuge from the rain and the person as a possible enemy. Although it is absurd, based on the fleeting appearance in a lightning flash, that is the way our mind works. In our life it is just like this. From birth until death we see objects and label them, assigning them to roles of "friend," "enemy" or "stranger," with no more evidence than a fleeting appearance. If we knew how little time we had left, we would know how foolish this discrimination is.

Finally, we should look at causative phenomena as like *a cloud*. Not only are clouds constantly changing as we observe them, but also, due to the heat of the sun, they are there in the sky one moment and the next they have vanished. Causative phenomena are just like that.

The reality of any phenomenon—a beautiful flower or body or whatever—is that it is changing, decaying momentarily; it cannot last. Because this is the reality, there is nothing to cling to, nothing to get angry about. This concept of permanence, that things last a long time, is another form of ignorance. Things appear to be permanent, and we believe this, but there is nothing at all like that, including our own life. We should bring this truth into our everyday life as much as we can.

10. THE DHARMA IN EVERY ACTION

The Dharma in Our Daily Life

How to Eat and Drink[137]

With this perfect human rebirth we have, we can turn everything we do into Dharma—even actions like eating and sleeping—making our life highly meaningful. It doesn't have to be an overt Dharma activity such as meditation; any action done purely, with a perfect motivation, benefits ourselves and all others. Because we all eat and drink many times each day, if we can make eating and drinking virtuous, then every day we will create so much merit. Having the correct motivation is vital.

There are Hinayana and Mahayana ways of offering food. The Hinayana way is expressed in a prayer by Nagarjuna, where he says that the purpose of eating food is not to have a beautiful or fit body—aims that come only from attachment—but simply to sustain ourselves in order to practice the Dharma. A common prayer when offering food is this.

> This food with a hundred flavors,
> which is mouth-watering and well-made,
> to the Conqueror and his Children we offer with faith.
> By this, may all migrators become wealthy
> and enjoy the food of concentration.
>
> Seeing this food as medicine,
> we eat it without attachment or hatred,
> not to have an enviable body, not out of pride,
> not to look strong, only to sustain the body.

Food should be eaten without the three poisonous minds of ignorance, attachment, and anger. With the motivation of seeking our own freedom from samsara, we offer the food to the Three Rare Sublime Ones and then eat it. This is the Hinayana way of eating food.

The Mahayana Sutra way of eating food is to dedicate every spoonful of food and mouthful of drink to all sentient beings, including those living in our body. In this way we make a connection with all sentient beings such that when, in future lives, they eventually become human, we can reveal the Dharma to them and lead them to enlightenment. Because this is done with a bodhichitta motivation, it becomes a cause for achieving enlightenment.

As I always emphasize, we must always check our motivation and ensure it is as pure as possible. Any action done with a motivation of attachment is nonvirtuous and results only in suffering. As we eat breakfast, we should ask ourselves what our motivation is. If it is done with attachment, then every spoon of food we eat is nonvirtuous, every mouthful of tea or coffee we drink is nonvirtuous, resulting in only suffering. With a nonvirtuous motivation, the more tea or coffee we drink, the bigger the mug we use, the greater the negativity. And similarly, the more food we eat, the bigger the plate, the more negative karma we create.

Conversely, when we eat or drink with a positive motivation, the more we eat and drink the more positive karma we create. This is especially so if we do it with a bodhichitta motivation or with guru devotion where we see the guru as inseparable from the buddhas. In that case, we should use *huge* mugs to drink our coffee from, like the mugs designed for truck drivers you find in gas stations in the US. Meditating on bodhichitta or guru devotion as we drink our huge mug of coffee, we are continuously creating inconceivable merit, making our life so beneficial, so productive.

The choice is completely in our own hands—every day, every minute, every second—to stay in samsara or to end it, to create the causes for the lower realms or for enlightenment. With every sip we drink and every mouthful we eat, we make this choice. When we eat or drink something solely for our own happiness, we totally disregard others. Misguided by a selfish attitude, we fail to see how every mouthful of food or drop of drink only happens through the great kindness of countless sentient beings, who have suffered greatly to produce it. If we could really feel this, there is no way we could continue to eat or drink just for our own pleasure. We must feel at least a little guilty! And if we consider this more deeply, the thought must come to try to repay their great kindness.

With that thought we can think, "In order to receive enlightenment for the sake of all mother sentient beings, I offer this food to Guru Shakyamuni Buddha as well as offer it as charity to all sentient beings." Then, thinking that the food belongs to the Buddha and to all sentient beings—that it is theirs, not ours—we recite the mantra OM AH HUM three times to bless it.[138] As we eat or drink, we can stay conscious of this, and when we have finished, we can really rejoice. How fantastic! We have made our life highly meaningful if we can do that much.

As I have said, the more food we have on the plate, the more good karma we collect—as long as we don't get a pain in the stomach! The amount we should eat is indicated in the Vinaya. Of course, it is less important if we are not doing a meditation session right after lunch, but the texts say that we should never eat more food than would disturb our meditation. It suggests that if four portions would normally fill our stomach, we should only eat three and leave one. To eat until we are completely full not only makes meditation difficult, but in general it makes us uncomfortable. Our body feels heavy and tired, and it is easy to fall asleep. Then, I suppose, we can do a sleeping session.

The Vajrayana way of eating is to see ourselves, our guru, and the deity as one, and make every bite of food and every mouthful of drink a tsok offering, an offering to them. If we do that, it becomes an extraordinarily powerful means of purifying all negative karma, defilements, and degenerated samaya vows and collecting vast amounts of merit.

As the great Tibetan yogi Milarepa says, "Every step I take becomes circumambulating all the holy beings; everything I eat becomes a tsok offering." Everything he did became a powerful means of purifying his mind and creating merit, and therefore, a quick path to enlightenment.

Similarly, whatever we do—eating, walking, washing, and so forth—can become a very powerful method for quickly achieving enlightenment, making our life most meaningful, most satisfying.

How to Sleep and Wake Up

In the same way as there is the practice of how to eat and drink, we can also make going to sleep a Dharma practice. As we are about to go to bed, we think, "In order to enlighten all sentient beings, I must achieve enlightenment, therefore I am going to practice the sleeping yoga practice." Then, we visualize Guru Shakyamuni Buddha at our pillow, facing us, sitting on a throne on a lotus, sun, and moon seat. Before getting into bed, while holding that visualization, we can do three prostrations and then lie down.

The best position for sleeping is the lion's posture the Buddha took when he was passing into parinirvana, lying on his right side, stretched out with his two legs straight and feet together, his left arm along his side and his right hand under his head, one finger closing the right nostril. Remembering that this is how the Buddha passed away, if we can lie in that position too, we will sleep deeply, free from any fearful dreams caused by spirits that might try to harm us in the night.

Having assumed this position or another comfortable one, we visualize that our head is in the Buddha's lap as we are falling asleep. The Buddha is totally protecting us. White light comes from his heart, purifying us and filling us with great bliss. While continuously concentrating on this, we allow ourselves to fall asleep. Then, however many hours we sleep, it all becomes a virtuous action, mainly by the motivation we had at the beginning.

Then, when we get up in the morning, remembering the visualization of Guru Shakyamuni Buddha we did as we were falling asleep, we think, "How fortunate I am that I didn't die last night! How fortunate that I am still alive today and have another chance to create positive karma." With that, we determine that every action of body, speech, and mind during the day will be done with only a pure bodhichitta motivation.

Shopping with Renunciation, Bodhichitta, and Wisdom

With the right motivation, the bodhichitta motivation, we can shop, we can eat, we can work, we can go to the movies, we can go to parties—we can do anything—with no danger of the activity becoming nonvirtuous. In fact, whatever we do in our daily life can help us develop the three principal aspects of the path: renunciation, bodhichitta, and the right view of emptiness.

In *Liberation in the Palm of Your Hand*, Pabongka Dechen Nyingpo explains that shopping is the perfect example of covetousness.[139] Without examining it, shopping seems quite harmless, but when we really investigate, we can see its dangers. In every shop we visit, we see thousands of items and we want them all, our covetousness getting stronger all the time. When we first arrived it wasn't that big, so where did it all come from? We feed our covetousness by buying lots of things and we feel so happy, but when we get back home and look in our shopping bag all we see is a huge pile of negative karma. Actually, it was always there, just waiting to ripen.

We can start to turn our attitude around by using whatever we do as a means to develop *renunciation* rather than to strengthen our attachment. When we buy something, instead of focusing on its attractive qualities, which increase our attachment, we look instead at what it has cost us and what it has cost others in terms of the labor and suffering. Many beings have sacrificed so much, sometimes even their lives, just so we can have that object. We can also consider the hard work involved in earning the money needed to buy all the stuff we think we need.

Looking around, we see the shopping mall is full of others doing the same thing we are. They believe themselves to be happy as they spend all their money, but this is just the suffering of change. Rather than seeing shopping malls as pure lands full of everything we want, we can see them as hungry ghost countries filled with beings buying and buying and buying without being able to find the slightest satisfaction.

As we shop, we can remember how everything we buy is impermanent and in the nature of suffering. It might give us some pleasure, but that pleasure won't last. Here is the lamrim, not just in some abstract sense but right here and now in our daily life. We need to shop, but we can shop with the renunciation of samsara, not in order to perpetuate it.

By generating a *bodhichitta* motivation, we can buy food to prolong our life so we are better able to help others; we can buy clothes to protect ourselves so we are capable of being of service. With a good heart, even though we might not actually reflect on all sentient beings as we shop, our shopping will be of immense benefit. We might be buying food or clothing for ourselves, but if our life is dedicated to helping others, then our purchases are for them, and so shopping with bodhichitta creates only positive karma. It also means our shopping bill becomes very small. Instead of those hundreds of things we thought were vital, with a bodhichitta motivation we realize we actually need only a few things.

We can also shop with *right view*, which is a perfect way of integrating emptiness into our busy life. Then, even if we are buying only our basic necessities, it will ensure that attachment does not arise. As we have discussed above, we can see the happiness our consumer items offer us as just like a dream. It is like somebody offering us a billion counterfeit dollars. There is so much clinging when we think the money is real, but that clinging disappears as soon as we realize we have been tricked and the money is worthless. Shopping in this way ensures our mind will not be disturbed. We see the same objects, we might even buy them, but they are a teaching on the shortcomings of samsara, not an invitation to create negative karma.

Doing any daily action with the mind of renunciation, bodhichitta, and wisdom means the action is no longer mundane and the cause for future samsara but a Dharma action and the cause for liberation and enlightenment. Really there is no other choice. Without renunciation, bodhichitta, and the right view of emptiness, we are left with their opposites: greed, selfishness, and ignorance.

Bodhichitta Mindfulness in Everyday Activities

We can accompany every single action we do with a mindfulness practice that turns our mind toward bodhichitta. That means everything we do—whatever it is—is motivated with the wish to benefit all sentient beings.

If we are truly intent on attaining enlightenment in order to benefit each and every one of the numberless sentient beings, we need to collect merit and purify defilements in as many ways as we possibly can. The Buddha has explained myriad ways to do this. For those of us who have not yet attained the realization of bodhichitta, he has given us instructions on how to conduct ourselves in our daily activities.

With this bodhichitta mindfulness practice, there is a prayer we can say as we go about any activity to ensure we always remain mindful. Whether we directly relate the prayer to all sentient beings or to our own realizations in order to better help others, the main motivation is bodhichitta.

For instance, the minute we wake up in the morning, we can think, "May all sentient beings achieve the holy body of the Buddha." And when we rise—sitting up from bed, standing up, and so forth—we think, "May all sentient beings rise up from the great oceans of samsaric suffering." As we leave our home, we can think we are liberating all sentient beings from the prison of samsara bound by karma and delusions. Opening a door, we can think we are opening the door of wisdom for all sentient beings, allowing them to go beyond samsara. And as we close a door, we can think we are closing the door of samsara for all beings. If we are going somewhere particular, we imagine it to be a pure land, a place we can best develop to benefit all sentient beings.

We do this practice with every possible activity, no matter how mundane. We can even practice this bodhichitta mindfulness when we go to the toilet! When we wash our clothes, we can imagine we are washing away the stains that cloud our own mind and the minds of all sentient beings with the water of bodhichitta. The dirt we scrub from the pots and dishes is the defilements, our own or those of all sentient beings. When cleaning the house, the vacuum cleaner or broom is the realizations we are trying to achieve, and the dirt is the wrong concepts we need to remove. The knife we chop vegetables with can be imagined as bodhichitta cutting the self-cherishing thought, or it can be emptiness cutting ignorance. Again, we can relate this to ourselves or to all other sentient beings.

At a Dharma center or a holy place, such as when we are on pilgrimage, or even where we usually meditate at home, on entering we should imagine we are leading all sentient beings to the city of liberation. The moment we see any holy object like a stupa or thangka, we can pray that all sentient beings achieve enlightenment quickly. And when we meet our guru, we can pray that every sentient being may also quickly meet a perfectly qualified guru who can lead them to enlightenment. In that way every tiny thing we do becomes a cause of enlightenment.[140]

11. THOUGHT TRANSFORMATION

Enjoying Problems

We will have to face problems until we have overcome the whole of samsara. Illnesses, other beings, and adverse situations and circumstances will continue to harm us. As long as our mind is conditioned to identify such experiences as problems, more and more things will seem to be problems to us. Unless we learn how to control the mind, the most insignificant matter can overwhelm us, upsetting us very quickly.

Until now, our habitual response to a problem has been unhappiness and even anger. Over countless lifetimes our mind has become conditioned to respond in that way. But just as we have trained our mind well in anger, feeling aversion for any problem, we can retrain it to see whatever problems that arise as beneficial. This is the practice called "Mahayana thought transformation" or "mind training" (lojong).[141] Rather than seeing a problem as something harmful and repulsive, we can see it as a chance to develop our mind on the path. That way we can remain calm and happy whenever a problem confronts us.

No matter how many problems we have, there is no point at all in being disturbed or irritated by them. As Shantideva explains in *A Guide to the Bodhisattva's Way of Life*,

> If there is a solution,
> what good is discontent?
> If there is no solution,
> what good is it anyway?

No matter what happens, there is no point in being angry or depressed. Furthermore, there is always a reason to feel that this problem could ultimately be something very beneficial. It depends on our point of view. For instance, nobody would choose to be cut by a knife; it is painful and terrifying. But if we have been bitten by a poisonous snake and somebody can immediately cut the poison out, then we welcome the cut. It is still as painful, but we do not see it as a problem at all.

By applying Mahayana thought transformation techniques, we train to identify all problems as beneficial, learning not only to face each one without aversion but to actually welcome it. Trained in thought transformation, we immediately and effortlessly recognize any miserable condition or obstacle we meet as good. The thought of liking problems arises naturally, like the thought of liking ice cream or the thought of liking music. When we hear a favorite song, we feel happy; we have no need to consider the reasons. Similarly, when we meet an undesirable situation, we feel happy, spontaneously recognizing it as good. Problems seem enjoyable, as light and soft as cotton.

Accepting problems rather than rejecting them can make a big difference to our experience, not only helping us to stop worry and fear but also to actually turn our action into Dharma. The nature of samsara is suffering, so we will naturally experience problems. (Of course we have a problem! It's samsara!) Seeing the inevitability of this helps us develop the first of the three principal aspects of the path, renunciation.

If we can deal with our problem with a lightness, without being filled with despair, we have the space to consider others, seeing how they are likewise suffering, and so our problem fosters compassion, lovingkindness, and a bodhichitta attitude.

We can also use the problem as a means to develop wisdom by seeing how it is not some inherent situation but is caused by the arising of various conditions. Conditions coming together have caused the problem and they will cause it to end, something which is difficult to see when we are overcome with despair. In that way, problems become the best possible teaching on the three principal aspects of the path.

When we believe that happiness comes from external objects and we chase sense pleasures, the world is a disappointing place. We are bound to be let down. At present, we are like the tourists who stop in Kathmandu on their way to trek in the Himalayas. They are often horrified. The hotels are dirty, shabby, and without facilities. The food is terrible and gives them diarrhea. The people are uneducated, unable to speak a word of English, and utterly untrustworthy. The streets of Kathmandu are filthy, with cows and beggars everywhere; stepping in cow dung is a constant problem. Many people come for a month's holiday and leave after a week because it is so horrible, desperate to return to their comfortable existence.

On the other hand, the local village people see Kathmandu as the most wonderful place, with great, wide roads full of life and the most delicious food. And many Western and Asian students who come to meditate find the atmosphere very special. The Himalayas are a wonderful, spiritual experience for them. For each, the Kathmandu experienced is a product of their own minds.

This is true of everything. There is no inherent experience; it is how we interpret it. Therefore, just as we can interpret an event as bad and a source of suffering, we can also interpret it as good, beneficial, even pleasurable. When we see how we create our reality like this, we understand how we have the power to experience every situation as positive because every situation gives us the chance to progress toward enlightenment. This is the essence of thought transformation.

Turning the Mind from Self-Cherishing

One way to transform our mind is to realize that countless sentient beings face the same problems we do, and countless more face far greater problems. We could be buried in a mountain of terrible problems, but there is nothing to be depressed about; we are just one person and others are countless. We could be divinely happy, but there is nothing to get excited about; we are just one person and others are countless. Like us, everybody wants to have happiness and to avoid suffering. We and all others are equal in this, but by sheer number, because others are infinite, they are infinitely more important than this single one.

Therefore we should think, "Since I have to go through this problem, why don't I make it beneficial for all sentient beings? How wonderful

210 POWER OF MEDITATION

it would be if I could take all their suffering and its causes upon myself and experience my problem on their behalf so that they could be free from all suffering." This thought of great compassion, wishing to free all sentient beings from suffering and its causes by ourselves alone, is the first part of the important taking and giving meditation, or *tonglen*, in which we take upon ourselves all of the sufferings and obscurations, as well as the causes, of other beings' problems. We will look at this below.

In this way, no matter what problem we face—a life-threatening illness, a lawsuit, or whatever—experiencing the problem itself becomes a very powerful method of purification and of accumulating infinite merit, because we are experiencing it on behalf of all sentient beings. Because the number of sentient beings is infinite, the merit we accumulate is infinite.

By understanding that all problems stem from our self-cherishing, we can use them to destroy our self-cherishing. Being criticized, failing in business, our partner leaving us, losing a million dollars—whatever problem we experience, we immediately remember that it is a present from our self-cherishing attitude. In the past, because of self-cherishing, we harmed others, and now we are experiencing the result of those negative actions. Just by recognizing that these problems are the results of our selfish attitude, we can do something about them. That alone immediately makes us feel less upset, less depressed.

The core of thought transformation is to take the problem that has been given to us by our self-cherishing and give it right back to the self-cherishing, using it as a weapon to destroy this attitude that has been harming us from beginningless rebirths until now, and which will continuously harm us as long as we follow it. By destroying the self-cherishing in this way, we are destroying the cause of our problems.

The Wheel of Sharp Weapons Effectively Striking the Heart of the Foe by Dharmarakshita, a ninth-century Indian scholar, combines teachings on thought transformation with the lamrim, especially karma, to clearly show the source of all our problems. He explains that because all problems come from our self-cherishing, that is where we should put the blame. For instance, he says,

When my mind falls prey to suffering,
it is the weapon of evil karma turning upon me
for definitely causing turbulence in the hearts of others;
from now on I will take all suffering upon myself.

When I am tormented by extreme hunger and thirst,
it is the weapon of evil karma turning upon me
for engaging in deception, theft, and miserly acts;
from now on I will take all hunger and thirst upon myself.[142]

When we blame external sources, there will always be problems; when we blame our self-cherishing, our problems will evaporate. Furthermore, we should train ourselves to use every problem to destroy our self-cherishing.

In *Seven-Point Mind Training*, the great Kadampa geshé Chekawa says,

When the world and its inhabitants boil with negativity,
transform adverse conditions into the path of enlightenment.
Banish all blames to the single source.
Toward all beings contemplate their great kindness.[143]

"Banish all blames to a single source" means putting all the blame on just one thing, our own self-cherishing. Since everything undesirable comes from it, no matter what problem we experience, the most important practice is to blame just that one thing, our self-cherishing. By doing that, the situation that seemed a huge problem before immediately stops being so. Even without talking about this as a route to enlightenment, it is vital for peace of mind in daily life.

The next line is "Toward all beings contemplate their great kindness." This means we must meditate on the kindness of every sentient being, even our enemy. By meditating on the kindness of others, loving-kindness and compassion naturally arise.

These two lines, which embody the fundamental thought transformation, are summed up by Nagarjuna's wonderful prayer:

Whatever suffering transmigratory beings experience,
May it all ripen on me.
Whatever happiness and virtue I accumulate,
May it all ripen on others.[144]

Eight Verses of Thought Transformation

Geshé Chekawa was inspired to write his *Seven-Point Mind Training* by
another Kadampa geshé, Langri Thangpa, who wrote the quintessential
thought transformation text, *Eight Verses of Thought Transformation*.
Chekawa said his admiration for the Kadampas first arose by hearing
the eight verses, and that whenever he encountered a problem, he found
them very beneficial.[145]

The two main practices we need in order to live a meaningful life are
bodhichitta and emptiness. The *Eight Verses* shows us how to use these
to transform any problem into the path to enlightenment.

The first verse:

Determined to obtain the greatest possible benefit
From all sentient beings,
Who are more precious than a wish-fulfilling jewel,
I hold them most dear at all times.[146]

This verse is very important to understand because it is the basis of
all other Mahayana practices. The wish-granting jewel is something
unbelievably rare, much rarer than a diamond, a sapphire, or any other
jewel. Someone who has collected a great deal of merit can obtain a
wish-granting jewel and, through its power, effortlessly gain whatever
worldly needs they pray for, for themselves and others—wealth, cars,
TVs, luxurious apartments, or anything else. It just happens like that.
But it cannot grant a higher rebirth as a human or a god. It cannot
purify negative karma, the cause of being reborn in the lower realms.
Only by practicing and developing pure morality, generosity, and other

peerless qualities can we attain a perfect human rebirth and go on to attain enlightenment.

Therefore, because these qualities come only from working for others, sentient beings are much more precious than a wish-granting jewel. Serving sentient beings with our body, speech, and mind, trying to free them from their problems and to lead them to happiness and full enlightenment, is the ultimate practice.

The second verse:

> Wherever I am and whoever I am with,
> I always consider myself the lowest of all
> And, from the depths of my heart,
> Hold others dear and supreme.

The essence of the bodhichitta attitude, to solely care for others more than ourselves, is total thought transformation. We turn our mind around a hundred and eighty degrees, from seeing all others as there only for our own benefit to becoming a willing servant to them.

There are many ways we create negative karma by discriminating against others, such as seeing the color of their skin, their caste, their level of education, or their position as inferior or contemptible. So many problems happen because people in one category hate those of another, judging and discriminating because others are different.

In the government, in businesses, in universities, and even in schools, people argue over positions. For instance, someone in a low position who wants a promotion may be jealous of those in a higher position, with a higher status and salary. They watch and listen, trying to take advantage of any mistakes that are made so they can take advantage of them and climb the ladder. They can exaggerate or lie in order to have the other person kicked out.

Perhaps they gain that promotion, but then there is the problem of pride, feeling superior to those below them. They have the money and status they craved, but they are still riven with dissatisfaction. And with pride and arrogance, they can easily create heavy negative karma.

Feeling superior to somebody else is a big problem in the world. The rich often feel superior to the poor, the educated to the uneducated, the high caste to the low caste, white people to black people (and sometimes black people to white people). People can even feel proud because they have a more beautiful singing voice than others.

How can we overcome such prejudice? Langri Thangpa says we should always consider ourselves to be the lowest of all, seeing others—teachers, friends, enemies, strangers, any other sentient beings—as superior to us. Thinking we are lower in knowledge or any other quality than others means we don't discriminate against them. Rather than feeling proud or arrogant, we feel humble.

"From the depths of my heart" means this is not just being diplomatic; it's not just show—saying the words while thinking the opposite—but actually feeling we are lower than others and greatly respecting them because of that. Seeing how kind and precious they are, we genuinely hold them dear and are happy to be their willing servant.

The third verse:

> In all actions, I examine my mental continuum
> And the minute a delusion arises,
> Since it endangers myself and others,
> I forcefully confront and avert it.

Because we have not eliminated the seeds of delusion, we feel attachment whenever we encounter a desirable object and aversion whenever we encounter an undesirable one. Although we might be able to intellectually understand the disadvantages of attachment and aversion, unless we are constantly vigilant, these deluded emotions can arise without warning, causing us to act negatively.

Mindfulness and awareness are the most important tools we can have to guard our mind and make sure we never create nonvirtue. We need to always watch what arises in the mind, and when it is a nonvirtuous thought, we need to immediately be aware of it to give ourselves the chance to avert it. We must be vigilant all the time—Langri Thangpa says "the minute a delusion arises"—no matter what activity we are doing. The basic activities we all do every day—eating, walking, sitting, sleeping, and so forth—might seem so automatic that there is no conscious thought involved, but they can be the trigger for nonvirtuous thoughts.

We need mindfulness and awareness, like a guard standing at the door of a house, constantly alert, watching for any thief that might try to sneak past to steal our valuables. Our delusions, such as attachment and anger, have been with us since beginningless time and have only ever brought us suffering. Understanding this, we do everything possible to destroy or at least avert them.

Anger is the most damaging affliction and the one we must do everything to eliminate. Shantideva explains one of the most effective ways to do this in *A Guide to the Bodhisattva's Way of Life*:

> If I forget the stick, which is the nearest cause of pain,
> and feel anger toward the one who wields the stick,
> then it would be better to hate hatred,
> since it is hatred that moves the one who brandishes the stick.[147]

If somebody beats us with a stick, we get angry with the person, we don't get angry with the stick. But there is no reason to get angry with the person. Just as the stick is blameless because it is controlled by the person, the person is blameless because they are controlled by their delusions, by their anger. And so, if we must get angry, we should get angry at anger. Seeing the person had no choice, the only thing we can do is practice patience and compassion.

In the fourth verse of *Eight Verses* Langri Thangpa tells us to not only see such as person as blameless but as a treasure:

> Whenever I see sentient beings who are wicked in nature
> And overwhelmed by negative actions and heavy suffering,
> I hold such rare ones dear,
> As if I had found a precious treasure.

"Beings who are wicked in nature" refers to people who are overwhelmed by negative karma and suffering, those with strong attachment, ignorance, and so forth, which causes them to be unbelievably selfish, angry, or impatient. Even if they had committed one of the five heavy negative karmas without break, we should feel very fortunate to have met them, seeing them as extremely dear.

We should not be repulsed by anyone but, instead, cherish all beings, even somebody with a terrible disease, such as leprosy, as in the story of the old woman wanting to be taken across a river. She was rejected by the great yogi, Ngakpo Chöpawa but, when his disciple, Getsul Tsimbulwa, moved by compassion and not at all repulsed by her horrible leprosy, carried her across the river, she transformed into the enlightened deity, Dorjé Phakmo,[148] and, without him needing to die, took him in that body to Vajrayogini's[149] pure land. Although she was Dorjé Phakmo, because of his obscurations he had been unable to see this until his unbelievable compassion purified those obscurations.

There is also the story of Angulimala, who lived in India during the Buddha's time. Angulimala's guru told him to kill a thousand people and to give him a mala made of one finger from each person. As he was about to kill the thousandth person—his own mother—the Buddha appeared and told him to come to him. Even though the Buddha was walking very slowly, Angulimala was unable to catch up with him because of the Buddha's psychic power. In that way, the Buddha was able to completely subdue him. Hated and feared by everybody because he was so evil, after being ordained by the Buddha, Angulimala became very humble and patient and was universally respected.

There are people who have committed such heavy negative actions that they repulse everybody. Nobody wants to be anywhere near them. Because it is our training to cherish all beings regardless of who they are or what they have done, we train to see such beings as a treasure. We can only attain enlightenment and then benefit countless others when we have deep love and compassion for all beings, and that includes these objects of others' repulsion and hatred. Even though there are numberless sentient beings, it is with these particular sentient beings that we can progress most quickly.

We can also see that, because of their great suffering, such beings need our help, so while they are shunned by all others, we should do whatever we can. But we must be realistic. If we can befriend them and win them over to being gentler and less aggressive, we should, but possibly they cannot be swayed by words alone. We can try to be kind to them, maybe giving them small gifts or food, and in that way try to move them away from doing negative actions.

If none of that is possible, we can at least sincerely do tonglen for them, taking on their terrible suffering and mentally giving them every good thing, imagining that their mind is turned toward enlightenment. If we can do this, we are actually doing the sincerest practice for that person, a practice utterly unpolluted by self-interest.

If we train to see those afflicted with great suffering or overwhelmed by strong negativities as extremely precious, as more precious than gold or diamonds, we progress to enlightenment incredibly quickly.

The fifth verse:

> When, out of envy, others mistreat me
> With abuse, insults, or the like,
> I accept defeat
> And offer the victory to them.

This practice, which we all need to do, can also be seen in Christianity. It was the advice of Saint Francis, who always asked his disciples to criticize him because he disliked praise. (However, they could never find anything to criticize him for.) Saint Francis was a great bodhisattva and had a lot in common with the great Tibetan meditators, the Kadampa geshés. I think it is important to know that this advice is not just a Buddhist thing; otherwise, people might think we are a bit crazy.

It might be natural to become upset when somebody criticizes or abuses us, but we should understand how, by destroying our pride, that person is actually doing us a great favor. Pride, arrogance, anger, and so forth are great faults, blocking our spiritual progress.

Worldly people don't offer the victory to others; they do the opposite, trying to defeat others in order to gain the victory. We live in a very competitive society, especially in the West. Generally, people like to win. Businesspeople, athletes, students, gamblers—people get so excited about defeating someone else.

However, this practice is completely different. In it, we see that winning—causing others defeat—is a victory for our self-cherishing. When our self-cherishing wins, in the next life or in thousands of lifetimes in the future, we will have to experience the result similar to the cause and to take a loss while somebody else wins. On the other hand, when we take the defeat on ourselves and offer the victory to others—the exact opposite of normal thinking—we are the one who wins, because we defeat the competitive mind, our self-cherishing, which only ever attempts to harm us and destroy our happiness. By cherishing sentient beings and offering them the victory, we not only help them but we create the cause to experience success for thousands and millions of lifetimes.

The only adversaries we should be competing against are our delusions, especially the king of delusions, our self-cherishing. That is the best competition. The more we are able to free ourselves from our self-cherishing, the more we are able to open our heart to all the kind, precious sentient beings who are the source of all our own past, present, and future happiness. We not only hold others as superior, as in the second verse, but we also offer them the victory. Taking the defeat is no defeat at all; offering the victory to others is the real victory.

The sixth verse:

> When someone whom I have benefited
> And in whom I have great hopes
> Gives me terrible harm,
> I regard them as my virtuous friend.

When Atisha was in Tibet, he had a servant called Atara who was very bad tempered and who always caused other people to get angry. Asked why he kept him, Atisha explained that he did so in order to practice patience, for without patience you could not become a great yogi. It is very useful to think like this.

Just as we can never develop generosity and compassion without a needy person, we can never develop patience without an angry person. Rather than seeing somebody who harms us as the cause of our suffering, we can see them as the means for our transformation. Enlightenment is impossible without the perfection of patience, and patience is impossible without somebody testing our patience by trying to harm us in some way. Thinking like that, returning anger with anger seems utterly senseless.[150]

Langri Thangpa shows us that our greatest friend is somebody who has more than just overtly harmed us, they are somebody we have placed great hope and trust in who has betrayed us. Normally, that would be the person we feel angriest with, but that is not right, because they can teach us the most, so in that respect they are our greatest teacher. Geshé Chen Ngawa says we should recognize our patience and our harmer as disciple and guru; the relationship is that strong.[151] In that way, we can see this person who has returned our help and trust with harm as the embodiment of our guru, manifested as this harmful person in order for us to develop our patience.

That is not to say that they had the motivation to lead us to enlightenment or that they were as wise and compassionate as the bodhisattvas. From their side, they could be completely evil and self-cherishing, doing everything for their own benefit and quite happy to harm us or anybody else. But from our side, because they are the greatest possible help on our quest to enlightenment, we should respect them as our most sublime teacher.

The seventh verse:

> In short, both directly and indirectly,
> I offer every happiness and benefit to all my mothers.

I secretly take upon myself
All their harms and sufferings.

We can benefit others in two ways: directly, where we offer some substantial help to them, and indirectly, where we visualize taking their suffering from them and giving all our happiness and merits to them, in a practice such as tonglen.

The eighth verse:

Also, I do not defile all these practices with the stains
Of the superstitions of the eight worldly concerns,
And by knowing all phenomena to be illusory,
Without trusting in them, I am freed from bondage.

As we have seen, the eight worldly concerns are craving material possessions, happiness and comfort, a good reputation, praise, and feeling aversion for their opposites.

These eight minds cause our mood to fluctuate greatly. We are up when things are going well and down when they are not, up when we are given gifts and down when we are forgotten, up when we are flattered or have a good reputation and down when we are criticized or have to endure a bad reputation. Because we are always chasing desirable things and trying to avoid undesirable ones, our life is like being on a roller coaster, always up and down. Isn't that true for most of us?

Most people in the world fail to gain any satisfaction because they try to achieve happiness from external things. Naturally, we suffer when we have to experience the four undesirable things, but obtaining the four desirable ones only increases our attachment and is therefore also suffering. On the other hand, ensuring our practice is free from these worldly concerns, as Langri Thangpa exhorts, brings great inner happiness and satisfaction. When we can free ourselves from these eight worldly dharmas, we are yogis, pure practitioners, and we have great inner satisfaction and happiness.

Furthermore, he tells us to understand all things "to be illusory." All things—the I, action, object, all phenomena—do exist. They exist in mere name, merely designated on a valid base. However, the way they exist is so subtle that it is *as if* they don't exist. They are *like* illusions, and as we have seen, we should train ourselves to see them as illusions.

The two main tools we need to live the most meaningful life are bodhichitta and a realization of emptiness. As we progress, we will certainly encounter problems, and here Langri Thangpa in the *Eight Verses* has given us a profound means to deal with them, transforming them into the path to enlightenment, overcoming our self-cherishing and learning to cherish others.

TONGLEN

Tonglen is a special meditation we can do as part of the bodhichitta technique of equalizing and exchanging the self with others. In tonglen we renounce our self-cherishing attitude and cherish others instead by visualizing taking all the sufferings from all other sentient beings in the form of black smoke and giving them all our possessions, positive qualities, and merit in the form of white light. This very special meditation is a vital part of developing our bodhichitta, where we develop great compassion with the taking part and great loving-kindness with the giving part.

We can do this in a general way or in a more specific way, taking from others the same sort of problem that we have. Say we have cancer. We can imagine taking all the cancer from all the other people suffering from it. Visualizing others' suffering pouring into us—the first part of the meditation—does not actually bring us more suffering. Instead, we visualize it pouring into our self-cherishing, which we imagine as a dense, black ball in our heart, completely destroying it. No matter what problem we have, no matter how serious, since we have to experience the problem anyway, we might as well make it beneficial.

Many people have been cured by doing a tonglen practice. A Chinese student in Singapore with AIDS was given this special meditation by his guru, Rato Rinpoché. After doing the meditation for only four days, when he went for a checkup, the doctors in the hospital found no trace.

This meditation is not only for diseases. It can be used with any problem, such as relationship problems, anxiety, depression, even suicidal wishes. In fact, it is the best meditation for depression because the mind is lifted up by generating a loving heart. The meaning of life is to serve others, whether we serve one or many, so this practice brings great happiness. Most importantly, tonglen helps us to develop our loving-kindness, compassion, and bodhichitta, which are the main causes of full enlightenment.

Tonglen is not just something to do within a sitting meditation session. It can be done while we are walking, lying down on the beach, traveling, or at home. We can even do it as we are dying—in fact it's the best meditation, the best preparation, to deal with death. There are special meditation techniques to transfer the consciousness into a pure land at death, but tonglen meditation is the most reliable. Even though we are dying, rather than being terrified, we are incredibly happy. Our death becomes the most beneficial death possible because we are experiencing it with strong compassion on behalf of all sentient beings.

The Practice

To do the actual practice of taking and giving, start with the *taking*. First generate compassion by thinking how living beings constantly experience suffering, even though they have no wish to do so, because they are ignorant of its causes or unable to abandon them even if they do know them. Think, "How wonderful it would be if all living beings could be free from all suffering and the causes of suffering." Then generate great compassion by thinking, "I myself will free them from all their suffering and its causes."

You then relate the meditation to your breathing. As you breathe in, imagine that you take in all the suffering and causes of suffering of other living beings through your nostrils in the form of black smoke. If you have an illness or some other problem, focus first on all the other beings with that same problem, then think of all the other problems experienced by living beings, as well as their causes.

As you slowly breathe in the black smoke, you immediately free all the numberless living beings from all their suffering. The black smoke comes in through your nostrils and absorbs into the self-cherishing mind, visualized as a dense black ball at your heart chakra, completely destroying it.

Next, do the *giving* part. Generate loving-kindness by thinking that even though living beings want happiness, they lack it because they are ignorant of its causes or unable to create them. Even if they achieve some temporary happiness, they still lack the ultimate happiness of full enlightenment. Think, "How wonderful it would be if all living beings had happiness and the causes of happiness." Then generate great loving-kindness by thinking, "I myself will bring them happiness and its causes."

Visualize your body as a wish-granting jewel that can grant all the wishes of living beings. Then, as you breathe out, give everything you have to every living being in the form of pure white light. Give all your good karma of the three times, the past, present, and future, and all the happiness that results from it up to enlightenment; give your possessions, your family, your friends, and your body, all visualized as wish-granting jewels. Also make offerings to all the enlightened beings.

All the living beings receive everything they want, including all the realizations of the path to enlightenment. Those who want a friend find a good friend; those who want a job find a satisfying job; those who want a doctor find a qualified doctor; those who want medicine find excellent medicine; those who want a guru find a perfect guru. For those with incurable diseases, you become the medicine that cures them.

By visualizing this extensive practice of generosity, you incidentally create the cause of your own wealth and success in this life and in future lives, meaning you can then benefit others even more. In addition to these temporary benefits, you will receive the ultimate benefit of enlightenment.

After everyone has become enlightened in this way, rejoice by thinking, "How wonderful it is that I have enlightened every single living being."

There are much more extended versions of this meditation, where you separately visualize the beings of each realm, taking their particular suffering and giving them what they most need.[152]

MEDITATION IS TRANSFORMING THE MIND

Learning to meditate opens a door for us, releasing us from the prison of wrong concepts that currently trap us. It opens the door to liberation, which means not just freeing ourselves from the temporary sufferings that plague our life now, but from the whole of samsara, causing us to be totally liberated. It especially opens the door to bodhichitta, the ultimate good heart. And that door leads us straight to full enlightenment, where we are able to perfectly lead each and every sentient being to liberation and enlightenment. When we start to meditate to generate compassion for every living being, the door that is opened brings benefits that are as limitless as the sky.

Whatever meditation we do should bring peace and calmness to our life, allowing us the space to transform our mind from nonvirtue to virtue. Because meditation is the antidote to disturbing, negative emotions, it is the medicine we need. It transforms the mind from the painful states of attachment and anger and brings the contentment of renunciation. It clears the murky misconceptions that are at the root of all our problems, dispelling our ignorance and allowing wisdom to grow. Most of all, it allows us to develop our good heart, overcome our selfish tendencies, and transform self-cherishing into cherishing others, the heart of bodhichitta.

Anything we do that transforms the mind from a deluded, ignorant one to a clear, wise one, from one trapped in self-cherishing to one cherishing others, is meditation. Meditation is transforming the mind. This is what we must practice. This is what gives meaning to our life.

APPENDICES

APPENDIX 1
MEDITATION ON THE CONTINUITY
OF THE CONSCIOUSNESS[153]

THE PURPOSE OF THIS meditation is to see that each moment of consciousness must be the result of the previous moment, and because of that it is impossible to posit a first moment, one without a prior cause. This means that consciousness is beginningless; it did not magically begin with the first moment of this life.

To realize this, you need to start by understanding that although there are many conditions that influence the type of mind you experience, the principal cause of *any* moment of mind *must* be the immediately preceding moment of mind. It is necessary to investigate this and to come to understand this crucial point.

This moment of consciousness you are experiencing at this very moment must have had a cause. There are probably many things going on in this brief split-second of mind. Perhaps there is a visual consciousness operating or an aural one, perhaps there is an emotion about what you see, and maybe some conceptualization as you think about the object. Almost all of these things are mental factors, embroidering the basic consciousness. They are all conditions; none are the principal cause of the main mind. The main cause of that moment of consciousness must be a similar moment of consciousness. This is one of the fundamental aspects of karma, that the result must be concordant with the cause. Thus, the mind flows in a continuous stream of momentary cause-and-effects.

When you accept this, you can start to take that train of cause-and-effects back and back. The moment of consciousness that you are experiencing at this moment must have had a cause, and that cause must have been the immediately preceding moment of consciousness. Check and ascertain that this is true. Be sure about this in your mind.

That immediately preceding moment of consciousness—the cause of this moment of consciousness—also had a cause, which must have been the previous moment of consciousness. In that way, take it back to the one before that and the one before that. The consciousness of this evening is linked to this morning's consciousness by a continuing stream of cause-and-effects.

The consciousness you experienced the moment you woke up this morning must have had a cause. What was that? It must have been the consciousness you had during the last moment of your sleeping state, which was caused by the previous moment of sleep, and so on, back to the first moment of last night's sleep and the last moment of being awake yesterday.

Yesterday's consciousness was caused by the consciousness of the day before, which was caused by last week's, which was caused by last year's. Last year's consciousness was caused by the consciousness you had as a teenager, which was caused by the consciousness you had as a child. That was caused by the consciousness you had as a baby.

Take that back to the very first consciousness you had as a baby, the first moment you left your mother's womb. What was the cause of that? It had to have been the last moment of the consciousness you had as a fetus, which was caused by the consciousness of the moment before that.

Take that further back. What was the cause of the very first moment of consciousness of this life? Now, *this* is the interesting question. Either there wasn't one, and so there is no such thing as karma, or there was one. That means it had to have been a previous moment of consciousness in the same continuity.

That means the consciousness must have already existed and that it existed *before* this life began. Otherwise, without the previous continuity of that very first moment of consciousness, it is impossible for consciousness to come into existence. Therefore, the cause of the mind of the very first moment of this life, the moment your consciousness joined the sperm and egg of your parents, must have been the very last moment of the mind of the intermediate state being. The consciousness of the intermediate state being came from the consciousness of the previous life, and the life before that and the one before that. There is no end to the line of previous lives that the mind has experienced in this way.

You can take the chain of cause-and-effects the other way too. Joining with the fertilized egg, the first moment of consciousness of this life is the cause of the second, which is the cause of the third, and so on. The last moment of consciousness as a fetus is the cause for the first moment of consciousness as a baby, right up to this morning's consciousness and to the consciousness of this very moment.

This moment's consciousness must have a result, and that is the consciousness that comes immediately after, the next moment's consciousness. That moment's consciousness will give rise to the next, and that one to the next, and so on.

In this way, you can see a continuing stream of consciousness, from beginningless lives to the first moment of this life all the way to now and into the future, with each moment of consciousness being the result of the previous moment of consciousness and the cause of the next moment of consciousness.

This moment of consciousness will lead to the consciousness you experience in the very last moment of this life, the moment before you die. What happens then? Does the mind just go out like an extinguished candle? The consciousness, the mind, cannot just cease to exist. There cannot be a cause without a result. And so there must be another moment of consciousness, the consciousness of the first moment of the intermediate state that leads to the next life.

APPENDIX 2
THE NINE-ROUND BREATHING MEDITATION[154]

....

THE MAIN PURPOSE of any breathing meditation is to keep the mind focused and positive and not let it slip into having nonvirtuous thoughts that would make concentration difficult. If you can do this by simply focusing on the breath, that is excellent, but there is also the nine-round breathing meditation practice, which is slightly more forceful and, as such, is a very skillful means to ensure your meditation remains virtuous.

For the first three rounds, close your left nostril with the index finger of your right hand and breathe in through the right nostril. Then close your right nostril and breathe out through the left. Do this for three breaths.[155]

For the next three rounds, close your right nostril and breathe in through the left and close the left nostril and breathe out through the right. Do this for three breaths.

Then, for the last three rounds, breathe in through both nostrils and out through both nostrils. Do this for three breaths.

This is one set of the nine-round breathing meditation. To make this kind of meditation more beneficial, it is also good to do it with a visualization, rather than just concentrating on the breath as many people do.

First watch your mind to see whether there is any attachment, anger, or ignorance, whether your mind is virtuous, nonvirtuous, or neutral.

Then, cultivate the motivation, "In order to attain enlightenment for the sake of all sentient beings, I am going to do the purifying breathing meditation."

Now do the first three rounds. Close the left nostril with the index finger of your right hand and breathe in through the right nostril slowly, visualizing white light coming from all the buddhas and bodhisattvas living in all directions. The essence of the white light is all the buddhas' perfect power, perfect knowledge, and perfect compassion, as well as the power, knowledge, and compassion of the bodhisattvas. As you breathe in, think, "I am receiving the light that is the essence of these qualities." Every single atom of your body, from the head down to the toes, becomes full of this white light. As it spreads over all the body you feel completely blissful. Think, "Now I have received the perfect power, knowledge, and compassion of all buddhas and bodhisattvas." Try to feel great happiness for having received it.

Next, close the right nostril with the index finger of your right hand and breathe out through the left. As you do, visualize that all your negative karma and delusions, in the form of black smoke, pour out of you with your outbreath. Think the black smoke has completely gone, beyond the Atlantic Ocean, and has completely disappeared. Just like when a valley darkened with thick fog clears, leaving a sunny day, all the black smoke disappears, making you feel very happy, very light. If you feel happy, that is a good sign that the visualization is working. Do this for three breaths.

With the next three rounds, reverse the process. Close the right nostril this time and breathe in through the left, doing the same visualization of taking in the white light. Then, close the left nostril and breathe out through the right, visualizing all the black smoke pouring out of you. Do this for three breaths.

Finally, for three rounds, breathe through both nostrils, visualizing white light filling your whole body with the in-breath and black smoke pouring out with the outbreath. Do this for three breaths.

An alternative is to only visualize white light entering you during the first three rounds and black smoke leaving you during the second three rounds, the third three rounds being the same.

If your mind is so disturbed that even this meditation has little effect, you can try doing it more forcefully, by closing one nostril while blowing strongly out of the other, even if it makes a bit of noise. Putting a little bit of energy into it like this makes it easier to concentrate. If you are alone, of course, there is no problem, but you might have to be careful if you are meditating with other people. And don't do it so strongly that your whole face becomes red and all your veins stand out! After doing this for one set of nine rounds, you can go back to breathing softly and quietly. In that way, even five minutes of breathing meditation can be extremely effective.

APPENDIX 3
A MEDITATION ON THE
PERFECT HUMAN REBIRTH[156]

A COMMON WAY TO meditate on the perfect human rebirth is to go over each of the eight freedoms and ten richnesses individually, reflecting on each one in depth and trying to see just why you are so fortunate to have these eighteen qualities.

If your meditation is in a retreat or as a daily practice and you are purely doing lamrim subjects, then you can do one freedom or richness each day or each session, or stay with one freedom or richness for a few days until you have a strong feeling for it. Conversely, you can do a glance meditation on a range of freedoms or all of them to give yourself an overview. The object is to understand each subject in as much depth as possible so that it really means something very profound to you.

Meditating on each of the eighteen qualities can be done in conjunction with a deity practice. For instance, if you are doing a Chenrezig practice, when it is time to recite the mantra, after a while you can bring in this topic and meditate on it as part of developing compassion. His Holiness the Dalai Lama says that when you can no longer concentrate on visualizing yourself as the deity, doing a lamrim meditation stops superstition arising.

By going over each of the freedoms and richnesses, you become aware of how other beings lack these vital qualities and so you naturally develop great compassion for them. You are also aware of how having that quality yourself allows you to practice the holy Dharma so you can truly help those beings. After remembering each of them, conclude: "This human body is extremely precious. Without wasting time, I must attain bodhichitta."

The method to make that experience of your perfect human rebirth deeper is to move from the analytical meditation on that quality into a fixed meditation. There will hopefully come a time as you are analyzing the topic when you get a strong feeling about it. Rather than continue with the next part of the analysis, do a fixed meditation on that point by thinking over and over, "This is so precious, this is so precious, this is so precious...." You can either recite, "This is so precious" over and over again or recite a mantra, such as Chenrezig's, while you do fixed meditation on how precious your perfect human rebirth is. If you do analytical meditation followed by a little fixed meditation, your understanding of the preciousness of your perfect human rebirth will become stronger and more stable.

You should not hurry. This is not fast food to be gobbled down but a wonderful meal to be slowly enjoyed. Meditation needs time to see each point clearly, to see what is missing and what needs to be developed more. You should savor each point and try to fully understand it.

The purpose of meditating on each freedom and richness separately is to convince yourself that there is no possibility of practicing Dharma while in any realm other than human and that even as a human there is no possibility of practicing Dharma unless you are free from living in an irreligious country, having wrong views, as so forth. And so you conclude that the only chance of practicing Dharma is to have exactly the set of conditions that you do have at this very moment.

You can make each meditation as elaborate or as simple as you like. It really depends on what is most effective for your mind, and of course how much time you have.

The meditation on each freedom and richness follows the same format:

- Reflect on the suffering and lack of freedom of that being or situation.
- Reflect on how you are free of that suffering or situation and rejoice this is so.

- Reflect on how this freedom allows you to attain the three great purposes.
- Determine not to waste a moment of this perfect human rebirth.

For the richnesses, rather than the fortune of being free from an unfavorable situation, you feel fortunate at having a wonderful quality. Relate to each freedom and richness in this way and then consider how meaningful it is, and how it will be difficult to find again. Also reflect on the fact that this situation you have now will not last. Life is not only very brief but it can also be stopped at any moment, even today. It could even be stopped during this very meditation session. When you consider each freedom and each richness in this way, you realize how unbelievably precious all these eighteen qualities are.

If you train your mind in this way, even in the breaktimes, the thought that this life is extremely precious will arise effortlessly, just as the thought of hunger or attachment arises effortlessly, and you will automatically stop meaningless actions.

Meditating on the Eight Freedoms

The Freedom of Not Being Born as a Hell Being

For the first meditation, think about the suffering of the hell realms that you have read about. Go through the various hells in some detail.

Think that a spark from a match or a stick of incense that touches your skin for a second is unbearable to you. At that moment you have no thought of Dharma at all, no compassion for others, no understanding, just a blind desire to be free from pain. Think that if you were born in any of the hot hells, the suffering would be billions of times worse, not only in the intensity of the pain, but in that it is all over your body and that it lasts for eons. If you were such a being suffering in that way of course you could not practice Dharma.

Think of what it would be like to be trapped in an iron house that is consumed with fire that is hotter than the fire at the end of this world system. Imagine yourself trapped in an iron cauldron of boiling water. Think of the horror. There is no way you could have any rational thought; your mind would be overwhelmed by the suffering.

In the same way go through the cold hells and the surrounding and occasional hells.

Then realize how, even though the vast majority of sentient beings are in this situation, you are not. Furthermore, you have a perfect human rebirth, that rarest of all rebirths. Think, "How incredibly fortunate I am." Reflect on the cause of being born in the hell realms—hatred and ignorance—and determine you will never, even for a second, create those causes.

Think that having this freedom of not being a hell being gives you the freedom to practice the Dharma and achieve the three ways a perfect human rebirth is meaningful (a fortunate rebirth, liberation and enlightenment, and being meaningful in every moment of this life). Think especially how you can attain enlightenment for the sake of all sentient beings. But this highly meaningful life can stop at any moment. Death is definite and its time is completely unknown.

Conclude the meditation by determining to never waste even one second of this perfect human rebirth but use every second to actualize the great potential of this life by developing bodhichitta and attaining enlightenment.

The Freedom of Not Being Born as a Hungry Ghost

As with each subsequent meditation, start the meditation by thinking, "Even if I wasn't born as a hell being, I have still been born as a hungry ghost numberless times." Reflect on the freedom of not being born as a hungry ghost by thinking about what you have learned about the conditions of the hungry ghosts. Think about the types of hungry ghosts and how their principal sufferings are terrible hunger and thirst, where they must go for hundreds of years without getting even a scrap of food—not even a tiny piece of dried spit—or a drop of putrid water.

Reflect on how you expect to always have enough food and drink, and even more than that, you always expect it to be delicious and nutritious. You couldn't go even two days without food. Remember a time when you were really hungry (if there has ever been such a time) and how obsessed with food you got at that time. If you were starving, would you be able to think of anything but food? Would you be able to think about the Dharma? I'm sure the answer to that is no; Dharma would be the last thing on your mind. Think about this and see how such a basic need drives all other thoughts away.

Think of how the suffering of a hungry ghost is billions of times worse than the worst hunger you could ever imagine, and how the chance of their finding food is virtually zero. Visualize the hungry ghosts wandering around, mad with desperation. Of course they can't practice morality or generosity. They would kill over a scrap of food. How terrible that is.

Then think how, although there are far more hungry ghosts than either animals or humans, you are not a hungry ghost. You have enough to eat and drink and you have the luxury of not having to spend all your time thinking about and trying to obtain sustenance. Even among humans this is a luxury. Furthermore, you have a perfect human rebirth, that rarest of all rebirths. Think, "How incredibly fortunate I am." Reflect on the causes of being born as a hungry ghost, such as attachment and ignorance, and determine you will never, even for a second, create those causes.

Think that not being a hungry ghost gives you the freedom to practice the Dharma and achieve the three ways a perfect human rebirth is meaningful.

But this highly meaningful life can stop at any moment. Determine to never waste a second of this perfect human rebirth but use every second to actualize the great potential of this life by developing bodhichitta and attaining enlightenment.

The Freedom of Not Being Born as an Animal

With this meditation on the freedom of not being born as an animal, as with the others, start by thinking, "Even if I wasn't born as a hell being or a hungry ghost, I have still been born as a being of the animal realm numberless times." Reflect on the situation of the beings of the animal realm that you can see in this world: the animals, birds, fish, and insects. Although a few, like pets, are pampered, the vast majority have to face terrible suffering every day. There is never a moment of peace or happiness for them. Take time to go through the different types of animal beings, reflecting on what they face every day and how their lives are dominated by suffering and fear.

Think of what it would be like if you were born as an animal, even as your own pet. Dominated by stupidity, you would have no ability to understand anything except the most rudimentary commands from your owner. Even if your owner explained the Dharma to you for a hundred years, there would still be no hope; you would have no chance to accumulate even a tiny shred of good karma. And here we are talking about the most favored of all animals. Take any wild animal or farm animal. Reconstruct its life and see how trapped it is in suffering.

You are born as a human and not an animal, and furthermore you have a perfect human rebirth with the eight freedoms and ten richnesses.

Think, "How incredibly fortunate I am." Reflect on the causes of being born in the animal realm, such as ignorance and stupidity, and determine you will never, even for a second, create those causes.

Reflect on how incredibly precious this life is, how highly meaningful it is in every moment, unlike the poor animal's, and determine never to waste one second of it.

Determine to do everything possible to attain the realization of bodhichitta and to attain enlightenment.

The Freedom of Not Being Born as a Long-Life God

Think, "Even when I wasn't born as a hell being, a hungry ghost, or an animal numberless times, I have still been born as a long-life god numberless times." Then reflect on the various types of gods of the desire realm, the form realm, and the formless realm. Think of the overwhelming indulgence of sense pleasure that is the life of the desire realm gods and the dream-like state that is the life of the form and formless realm gods.

Think of a time when you were under the control of attachment and desire occupied your whole mind—for a possession, for a friend, for success in studies or business. Was there space for anything else at that time, such as compassion? Just as the long-life gods have no chance to practice Dharma, neither do human beings when they are controlled by the thought of the eight worldly dharmas.

Think how, although you haven't overcome attachment yet, you can see its great disadvantages and so you have the choice not to follow it. Think, "How incredibly fortunate I am." Reflect on the causes of being born as a god, such as attachment and ignorance, and determine you will never, even for a second, create those causes.

Consider that not having been born as a god gives you the freedom to practice the Dharma and achieve the three ways a perfect human rebirth is meaningful, making every moment of this perfect human rebirth highly meaningful.

Determine to never waste even one second of this perfect human rebirth, but to use it to actualize bodhichitta and attain enlightenment.

The Freedom of Not Being Born Where No Buddha Has Descended

Think, "Even though I wasn't born in the three lower realms or as a long-life god, even if I was born as a human being, I have still been born numberless times during periods when there is no buddha and no teachings of a buddha." In this period, the teachings of the Buddha exist. Even though Shakyamuni Buddha passed away, the lineage of his teachings still lives on in highly realized teachers, and the transmission of his holy Dharma is still pure and undiluted.

Imagine if this were not so. There are certain periods without the existence of the Dharma, where the teachings of the Buddha have disappeared and the future buddha has not yet appeared. Even though you may be born as a human being, sometimes, due to karma, you are born in those dark periods where there is no Dharma. Imagine a world where the light of the Dharma does not shine, one which is shrouded in the darkness of ignorance. Being born in such a time, you would have almost no chance to understand what virtue is, let alone create it.

Think, "How incredibly fortunate I am to be born in a time when a buddha has descended." Reflect how we are coming to the end of the period of the Buddha's teachings and will soon be entering another dark period. Therefore, see the urgency of doing everything possible now to actualize the Dharma in your heart as quickly as possible.

Think how death can happen at any moment and there is no assurance of what lies beyond death. Will you still have this precious opportunity in the next life? Hell beings don't, hungry ghosts don't, animals don't, gods don't, nor do barbarians or heretics,[157] even living in a world that has the teachings of the Buddha. You do, for now.

Determine to spend every moment developing bodhichitta in order to attain enlightenment for the sake of all sentient beings.

The Freedom of Not Being Born as a Barbarian

Think, "Even though I wasn't born in the three lower realms or as a long-life god, even if I was born as a human being during a period in which a buddha had descended, I have still been born as a barbarian numberless times." Think of the places where people live completely without the Dharma, where religion is suppressed or seen as superstition. Such people are "barbarians," those uncivilized by the touch of the Dharma. There is no understanding of the Dharma and no wish to practice it. Think of how the people who live under these delusions are always looking for happiness in the wrong places, through attachment to worldly pleasure.

Think of how, if you were in that situation, you would be completely unable to create the causes for happiness and be trapped in suffering forever. How terrible that would be. But you are not like that, you have the freedom that allows you to understand and appreciate the Dharma.

Think, "How incredibly fortunate I am." Reflect on the causes of being born as a barbarian, such as attachment and ignorance, and determine never to create those causes. Being free from this state, you are able to practice the Dharma and achieve the three great purposes of a perfect human rebirth.

Conclude the meditation by determining to use every second to develop bodhichitta and attain enlightenment.

The Freedom of Not Being Born as a Fool

Think, "Even though I wasn't born in the three lower realms or as a long-life god, even if I was born as a human being during a period in which a buddha had descended, and even though I was not born as a barbarian, I have still been born numberless times as somebody who, through some mental or physical condition, is unable to understand or communicate at all." Even if such a person were given an explanation of the Dharma, they could not even understand the words, let alone the profound meaning. How terrible to be in such a condition.

Think, "How incredibly fortunate I am to be able to understand and practice the Dharma." Reflect on the cause of being born with defective reasoning—ignorance—and determine you will never, even for a second, create that cause.

Think that having this freedom means you can achieve the three great purposes of a perfect human rebirth, making every second you have highly meaningful.

Determine never to waste one moment of this perfect human rebirth but use it to attain bodhichitta and enlightenment.

The Freedom of Not Being Born as a Heretic

Think, "Even though I wasn't born in the three lower realms or as a long-life god, even though I was not born as a human being during a period in which no buddha had descended, nor as a barbarian, or a fool, I have still been born as a heretic numberless times." Reflect that being a heretic means holding wrong views—the mistaken belief that karma, reincarnation, and concepts like that don't exist. Imagine what it would be like to be trapped in such wrong views. There is no cause and effect;

there is no life after this; the Buddha never existed, and his teachings are therefore false. With no idea about ultimate truth, the nature of reality, what is there to stop such a person sliding into nihilism? Not only would there be no way of practicing the Dharma, there would be little chance of doing anything worthwhile at all.

You are not trapped in wrong views. Think, "How incredibly fortunate I am." Reflect on the main cause of being born as a heretic—ignorance—and determine you will never create that cause. Think how highly meaningful this perfect human rebirth is, with the freedom of not holding wrong views, but that it can finish at any moment. There is no telling whether in your next life you will be a heretic or not.

Determine to do everything possible to have another precious human body. Make a firm conviction to use every moment remaining in this life to develop bodhichitta and attain enlightenment.

At the end of this meditation or this series of meditations, think on all eight of the freedoms that you have and rejoice at how amazing this precious opportunity is. At any moment you could create the causes to be born as a hell being, a hungry ghost, an animal or a long-life god. At any moment you could create the causes to be born as another human but in an irreligious country or with wrong views, or have such severe mental problems that understanding anything is impossible. At any moment you could create the causes to be born in a place where the teachings of the Buddha don't exist.

How amazing that instead of being born in any of these eight states, you have been born with these incredible freedoms. Be aware how easy it is to create the causes for these unfortunate states, however, and determine never to do that, but only to create the causes for another perfect human rebirth.

MEDITATING ON THE TEN RICHNESSES

The meditations on the ten richnesses can be done in the same way as the meditations on the eight freedoms, although here you don't reflect on the freedom from a negative state but on the advantages of having a positive one. There are five personal richnesses and five richnesses relating to others.

For the first richness, think, "For countless lifetimes I have been born as other than a human being, but this time I have the great richness of *being born as a human being*. This gives me the great opportunity to practice the Dharma." And meditate in this way on the points you have studied.

Think, "For countless lifetimes I have been born as a human being but not in a religious country, but this time I have the wonderful richness of *being born as a human being in a religious country*. This gives me the great opportunity to practice the Dharma." And meditate in this way on the points you have studied.

Think, "For countless lifetimes I have been born as a human being in a religious country but without perfect organs that allow me to practice Dharma, whereas now I have the wonderful richness of *being born as a human being in a religious country, with perfect organs*. This gives me the great opportunity to practice the Dharma." And meditate in this way on the points you have studied.

Think, "For countless lifetimes I have been born as a human being in a religious country with perfect organs, but weighed down by the five heavy negative karmas without break, blocking any chance of a good rebirth, whereas now I have the wonderful richness of *being born as a human being free from the five heavy negative karmas without break*. This gives me the great opportunity to practice the Dharma." And meditate in this way on the points you have studied.

Think, "For countless lifetimes I have been born as a human being but have lacked devotion to the teachings, whereas now I have the wonderful richness of *being born as a human being with strong devotion to the teachings.* This gives me the great opportunity to practice the Dharma." And meditate in this way on the points you have studied.

Think, "For countless lifetimes I have been born as a human being but not in a place where a buddha has descended, whereas now I have the wonderful richness of *being born as a human being in a place where a buddha has descended.* This gives me the great opportunity to practice the Dharma." And meditate in this way on the points you have studied.

Think, "For countless lifetimes I have been born as a human being where a buddha as descended but not where the teachings have been revealed, whereas now I have the wonderful richness of *being born as a human being in a place where a buddha has descended and the teachings have been revealed.* This gives me the great opportunity to practice the Dharma." And meditate in this way on the points you have studied.

Think, "For countless lifetimes I have been born as a human being where the teachings have been revealed, but not all the teachings, such as the Sutrayana and the Vajrayana, whereas now I have the wonderful richness of *being born as a human being in a place where a buddha has descended and the complete teachings exist.* This gives me the great opportunity to practice the Dharma." And meditate in this way on the points you have studied.

Think, "For countless lifetimes I have been born as a human being where all the teachings exist, but I have not had devotion to the teachings, whereas now I have the wonderful richness of *being born as a human being in a place where the complete teachings exist, and I have devotion to them.* This gives me the great opportunity to practice the Dharma." And meditate in this way on the points you have studied.

Think, "For countless lifetimes I have been born as a human being where all the teachings exist and I have had devotion to them, but there have not been the necessary conditions to practice the Dharma, such as having a compassionate guru to guide me, whereas now I have the wonderful richness of *being born as a human being where the complete teachings exist, and I not only have devotion to them but all the necessary conditions exist.* This gives me the great opportunity to practice the Dharma." And meditate in this way on the points you have studied.

Really try to feel the preciousness of each freedom and each richness and use that feeling to motivate your Dharma practice. The more precious you feel your rebirth to be, the happier you will feel. Just as a beggar finding a diamond in the garbage would be overjoyed, you should feel that degree of joy. In this ordinary, mundane life full of work and problems, you have suddenly discovered this priceless jewel. When that happens and your Dharma practice becomes a ceaseless joy, that is a sign that you are making the most of your perfect human rebirth.

NOTES

1. In Sanskrit, *duhkha*.
2. Over the years, Lama Zopa has tended to use the Sanskrit term *shamatha* more than either the Tibetan *shiné* or the English, *calm abiding*, so we will generally use *shamatha* in this book.
3. Lawudo is a small area in the Solu Khumbu region of Nepal near Namche Bazaar where the Lawudo Lama—Lama Zopa was his most recent reincarnation—meditated for more than twenty years. An FPMT retreat center is now there.
4. The First Panchen Lama (1570–1662) composed *Guru Puja* and *Path to Bliss Leading to Omniscience*, a famous lamrim text. He was a tutor of the Fifth Dalai Lama.
5. Quoted in Zopa 2012a, 113.
6. Quoted in Paltrul 2010, 125.
7. Ch. 5, v. 17; Gómez forthcoming.
8. Ch. 5, v. 18; Gómez forthcoming.
9. Quoted in Zopa 2012b, 119.
10. Potowa Rinchen Sel (1031–1105) was one of the three great disciples of Dromtönpa. He was an important figure within the Kadam tradition, the order founded by Atisha that was the forerunner of the Geluk tradition.
11. Dromtön Gyalwai Jungné (1005–1064) was a great Kadampa master and one of Atisha's three main disciples. For his biography, see Jinpa 2008, 575–76.
12. *Dhammapada*, v. 183. Taken from FPMT 2021a, 79, where it is excerpted.
13. Of the four main traditions within Tibetan Buddhism—the others being Nyingma, Sakya, and Kagyü—the Geluk school is the most recent, being founded in the early fifteenth century by Lama Tsongkhapa.
14. V. 1. Quoted in Sonam 1997b, 17.
15. Jé Tsongkhapa (1357–1419) was the founder of the Geluk tradition of Tibetan Buddhism and revitalizer of many sutra and tantra lineages as well as the monastic tradition in Tibet.
16. Available as Lamrim Chenmo Translation Committee 2000–2004, 1:109–10 (my italics).
17. Hinayana (Small or Lesser Vehicle) and Mahayana (Great Vehicle) are the two general divisions of Buddhism, according to the Mahayana tradition. They can also be called Pratimokshayana (Individual Liberation Vehicle) and Bodhisattvayana (Bodhisattva Vehicle).
18. The six perfections are the perfections of generosity, morality, patience, perseverance, concentration, and wisdom. The four means of drawing disciples to the Dharma are giving, speaking kind words, teaching to the level of the student, and practicing what we teach.

19. Rinpoche often refers to the historical Buddha as Guru Shakyamuni Buddha, placing "Guru" before his name to remind us of the inseparability of our own guru and the Buddha.

20. Ch. 6, v. 14 (part); Gōmez, forthcoming.

21. The monastery near Boudhanath in Kathmandu Valley founded by Lama Zopa and Lama Yeshe in 1969 that holds month-long meditation courses every year, attracting hundreds of students.

22. The teaching on the four noble truths was the Buddha's first teaching, the first turning of the wheel of Dharma. They are the truth of suffering, the truth of the origin of suffering, the truth of the cessation of suffering, and the truth of the path that leads to the cessation of suffering. Also, within the *Four Noble Truths Sutra* that comprise this teaching, the Buddha laid out the noble eightfold path, the quintessential Hinayana practice, which in the Mahayana is subsumed in the three higher trainings of ethics, concentration, and wisdom. The noble eightfold path is right view and right thought (wisdom); right speech, right action, and right livelihood (ethics); and right effort, right mindfulness, and right concentration (concentration). See Tsering 2005, 121–39.

23. Chen Ngawa Tsultrim Bar (1038–1103) was one of Dromtönpa's main disciples and the founder of the Kadam lineage of instructions.

24. Puchungwa Shöna Gyaltsen (1031–1106) was the founder of the Kadam lineage of pith instructions.

25. A *sadhana* (*drupthab*), literally "method of accomplishment," is a tantric meditation manual: step-by-step instructions related to a particular meditational deity.

26. His Holiness Zong Rinpoché (1905–84) was a great Gelukpa lama with an impeccable knowledge of Tibetan Buddhist rituals, art, and science.

27. A *thangka* is an image of a deity, usually painted and set in a brocade border.

28. In tantric visualization, a seed syllable is a Sanskrit syllable arising out of emptiness and out of which the meditational deity in turn arises.

29. This practice is available on the FPMT website: https://shop.fpmt.org/A-Daily-Meditation-on-Shakyamuni-Buddha-eBook-PDF_p_3548.html. See also Chöden 2020, 58–61, for another description of how to visualize Shakyamuni Buddha.

30. Within the desire realm, there are three fortunate rebirths (human, demigod, and god) and three suffering rebirths (animal, hungry ghost, and hell being). The hungry ghosts' main suffering is unbearable hunger and thirst that lasts thousands of years.

31. The chakras (*tsankhor*) are energy wheels situated along the central channel. The main chakras are the crown, throat, heart, navel, and secret place (the sex organ). In advanced meditations, such as in highest yoga tantra, the mind is concentrated on one of these chakras and, in the completion stage, actually enters and abides there. The channels (*nadi, tsa*) are constituents of the subtle psychic body through which energy winds and drops flow throughout the body. There are 72,000 channels in all, the main ones being the central channel (*avadhuti, tsa uma*) running just in front of the spine, flanked by the right (*rasana, roma*) and left (*lalana, kyangma*) channels.

32. Rinpoche uses the term "conventional nature" to distinguish it from the ultimate

nature of the mind, its emptiness, so here he means the mind as it is observed by a conventional consciousness not analyzing the ultimate.

33. "Superstitions," in the sense Rinpoche uses the term here, is the very broad idea of all deluded minds that block us from seeing reality. Although we can simply call these "delusions," "superstitions" has that added sense of confusion and befuddlement.

34. The four vital points of analysis are (1) recognizing the object to be refuted, (2) determining the definite pervasion of what is possible, (3) determining that the I and the aggregates are not inherently the same, and (4) determining that the I cannot exist separately from the aggregates. See Zopa 2020c, 128–32.

35. Of the four foundations of mindfulness—of the body, of feeling, of mind, and of phenomena—the Buddha cites six ways of reflecting on the body: reflecting on the breathing, on the postures, on the actions, on the constituents (blood, bile etc.), on the elements, and on the repulsiveness of the body. There is a very neat correlation between each mindfulness, the particular misconception, and the noble truth involved: the mindfulness of the body leading to recognizing the mistake of seeing an unclean body as clean (the truth of suffering); of feelings as seeing what is unsatisfactory as pleasure (the cause); of mind as seeing what is impermanent as permanent (cessation); and of phenomena as seeing what is selfless as having a self (the path). See Gyatso and Chodron 2014, 116–26.

36. For an extensive teaching on the eight worldly dharmas, see Rinpoche's *How to Practice Dharma* (Zopa 2012b).

37. These are the six Rinpoche usually explains, but there are other ways of enumerating them. For instance, in *Steps on the Path to Enlightenment, Vol. 1*, Geshé Sopa explains the fifth as the seven-limb prayer and the sixth as offering a mandala and does not mention requesting the lineage lamas (Sopa 2004, 165–211).

38. To find out how to create a meditation space, see appendix 1, "Preparing for Practice," in Zopa 2022, 173–85.

39. Vairochana is one of the five buddha families, representing the five classes of enlightened mind. White in color, he represents mirror-like wisdom and the purification of the form aggregate.

40. Geshé Ben Gungyal was a robber before he renounced the life of crime and ordained, becoming a Kadampa practitioner and a follower of Atisha. For more stories of Ben Gungyal, see Pabongka 2006, 117, 268–69, and 419.

41. A mudra (*chakgya*), literally "seal" or "token," is a symbolic hand gesture, endowed with power similar to a mantra.

42. See LC9–LC14 (that is, verses 9–14 of the actual Lama Chöpa, which are designated "LC" to distinguish them from the Jorchö practice that is included) of FPMT 2011, 14–16. *Lama Chöpa* is the Tibetan for the Sanskrit *Guru Puja*.

43. Vajradhara (*Dorjé Chang*) is the form through which Shakyamuni Buddha revealed the secret tantric teachings.

44. These are the main beings we visualize in an elaborate merit field. The direct gurus are our own gurus, whereas the lineage gurus are the lamas of the particular lineage of that practice. The *yidams* (*ishtadevata*), literally "mind bound" are our main meditational deities, such as Chenrezig or Tara; the *dakas* (*khandro*)—the Jorchö prayer calls them "heroes"—and *dakinis* (*khandroma*) are male and female beings

respectively who help arouse blissful energy in qualified tantric practitioners. Protectors or Dharma protectors (*dharmapala, chökyong*) are those enlightened or non-enlightened beings who protect the Dharma and the Dharma practitioners. In the merit field, they are always enlightened.

45. The fifth and sixth limbs are sometimes reversed in short prayers for euphony, as in "Please remain until the end of cyclic existence / and turn the wheel of Dharma for living beings."

46. The four aspects of karma are (1) karma is definite—a definite cause will bring a definite result; (2) karma is expandable—a small cause can bring a great result; (3) once created the karma is never lost; and (4) conversely, without creating the cause you cannot experience the result.

47. The refuge and bodhichitta prayer, in its simplest form, is this:

> I take refuge until I am enlightened
> In the Buddha, the Dharma, and the Supreme Assembly.
> By my merit of generosity and so forth,
> May I become a buddha in order to benefit all transmigratory beings.

The four immeasurables (loving-kindness, compassion, sympathetic joy, and equanimity) are expressed in a prayer such as this:

> May all sentient beings have happiness and the causes of happiness.
> May all sentient beings be free from suffering and the causes of suffering.
> May all sentient beings never be separated from the happiness that knows no suffering.
> May all sentient beings abide in equanimity, free of attachment and hatred for those held close and distant.

Both are taken from FPMT 2021a, 73.

48. Taken from FPMT 2021a, 76. Italics are mine.

49. The ten directions are the four cardinal directions—north, south, east, and west—the four intermediate directions, and the zenith and nadir.

50. This and the following verses are taken from FPMT 2021a, 237–39.

51. A buddha in the sambhogakaya aspect displays thirty-two major signs and eighty minor exemplifications, which together are known as the marks of a great being (*mahapurushalakshana; kyebu chenpö tsen*). Not all texts agree entirely what they are, but the most commonly cited text listing them in Tibetan Buddhism seems to be Tsongkhapa's *Golden Garland of Eloquence* (*Lekshé sertreng*). See also Alexander Berzin's *Thirty-Two Major Marks of a Buddha's Physical Body. studybuddhism.com/en/advanced-studies/lam-rim/refuge/the-32-major-marks-of-a-buddha-s-physical-body.* Accessed 05/28/2023.

52. Taken from Quarcoo 2021, 256.

53. The term "gompa," which roughly refers to the main meditation hall or temple in a Tibetan monastery, has been appropriated by many Western Tibetan Buddhist

centers as the name for their meditation/teaching room. It is a term Lama Zopa usually uses.

54. See Pabongka 2006, 191.

55. A *mala* (*trengwa*) is a rosary for counting mantras, usually of 108 beads.

56. The eighty-four thousand teachings the Buddha gave during his lifetime are categorized in three "turnings." The first turning of the wheel of Dharma was the four noble truths given at Sarnath and was the Buddha's first discourse; the second turning refers to the prajnaparamita (wisdom) teachings given at Rajgir; and the third turning refers to teachings on the nature of the mind (buddha nature) and addresses seeming contradictions between the first two turnings.

57. The final nirvana a buddha attains. This was the state the historical Buddha attained at Kushinagar 2,500 years ago.

58. "Heresy," *lokta* in Tibetan, in this context means having mistaken views, rejecting the existence of what exists, such as karma and reincarnation, and believing in what does not exist, such as the truly existing self. There is no appropriate, exact word for it in English, and this is the term Lama Zopa invariably uses.

59. The mandala offering is sometimes included in the seven-limb prayer but is separate in Lama Tsongkhapa's tradition. Geshé Sopa says that the last preparatory practice is both the mandala and the request to the merit field (Sopa 2004, 1:209).

60. Taken from FPMT 2021a, 28.

61. For all the offerings, see the mandala offering prayer in FPMT 2021a, 87–89. For an extensive explanation on the practice, see https://fpmt.org/media/streaming/teachings-of-lama-zopa-rinpoche/lama-zopa-rinpoche-teachings-in-taiwan-2016/, accessed 12/2/2023.

62. These can be found in FPMT 2020a, 124.

63. Originally from the *Heruka Lama Chöpa*, taken from FPMT 2020a, 124.

64. It is our convention to use lower case when talking about the guru as a particular being but upper case as an object of refuge. This corresponds to talking about "a buddha" but "the Buddha."

65. The white, red, and dark appearances are the final appearances in the death process, which are mimicked in the tantric practice of taking the ordinary death into the path of the dharmakaya.

66. *Samaya* vows are commitments made by a disciple at an initiation to keep tantric vows for life or to perform certain practices connected with the deity, such as daily sadhana recitation.

67. The Kadam lineages are the Kadam Lamrimpa Lineage, the Kadam Shungpawa (Scripture) Lineage, the Kadam Men Ngagpa (Pith Instructions) Lineage, and the Kadam Sarma (Geluk) Lineage.

68. Taken from FPMT 2020a, 139.

69. Ch. 1, v. 5; Gómez forthcoming.

70. Ch. 4, v. 21; Gómez forthcoming.

71. A *tsatsa* is a small bas relief deity image made by pressing clay or plaster into a mold.

72. The hundred-syllable Vajrasattva mantra is OM VAJRASATTVA SAMAYA MANUPA-LAYA / VAJRASATTVA TVENOPATISHTHA / DRIDHO ME BHAVA / SUTOSHYO ME BHAVA / SUPOSHYO ME BHAVA / ANURAKTO ME BHAVA / SARVA SIDDHIM ME

PRAYACCHA / SARVA KARMA SU CHAME / CHITTAM SHRIYAM KURU HUM / HA HA HA HA HO / BHAGAVAN SARVA TATHAGATA / VAJRA MAME MUNCHA / VAJRA BHAVA MAHA SAMAYA SATTVA AH HUM PHAT. The short Vajrasattva mantra is OM VAJRASATTVA HUM.

73. The five heavy negative karmas without break (*panchanantarya*; *tsamé nga*) are killing our mother or father of this life, killing an arhat, maliciously drawing blood from a buddha, and causing disunity within the sangha. The five nearing heavy negative karmas without break (*anantarya sabhagah*; *nyeba tsamémä nga*) are killing a bodhisattva, killing an arya being not yet an arhat, defiling our mother or a female arhat through sexual misconduct, stealing property from the sangha, and destroying a stupa.

74. There are different ways of listing the four opponent powers and, hence, doing the actual practice. Lama Tsongkhapa in *Lamrim Chenmo*, lists them as regret, remedy—relying on sutras, emptiness, reciting names, etc.—resolve, and refuge. (Geshé Sopa in *Steps on the Path to Enlightenment* follows this outline.) Pabongka Rinpoché in *Liberation in the Palm of Your Hand* lists them as refuge (the basis), regret (repudiation), resolve (restraint), and remedy. Lama Zopa Rinpoche has ordered them differently over the years, but the majority of times has used the Pabongka ordering. He has also used other names such as the *power of putting the blame* or *confession* for regret and the *power of the holy object* for refuge. For a very brief practice using Vajrasattva and the four opponent powers, see Zopa 2020a.

75. Fried or steamed dumplings, usually filled with meat, that are a favorite meal of Tibetans.

76. Quoted in Zopa 2009, 90.

77. Taken from FPMT 2021a, 111.

78. Kunga Gyaltsen (1182–1251), called Sakya Pandita, was a master of the Sakya tradition who spread Tibetan Buddhism in Mongolia and China.

79. Quoted in Zopa 2009, 239.

80. For the *Guru Puja* see Gyältsen and Lhundrub 2016; for *Lama Tsongkhapa Guru Yoga* see FPMT 2021. Both *Guru Puja* and *Six-Session Guru Yoga* are only for those who have taken a highest yoga tantra initiation.

81. *Migtsema* (*Praise and Request to Lama Tsongkhapa*) is a short prayer of four, five, or nine lines praising Lama Tsongkhapa as Avalokiteshvara, Vajrapani, and Manjushri. (Migtsema is an abbreviation of the first line.) It is usually recited at the beginning or end of teachings or prayer sessions within the Geluk tradition. *Tsok* (*ganachakra*), literally "gathering" (of substances or disciples), is often a section of a puja where offerings are made.

82. See FPMT 2021a, 237–46.

83. Another term often used is *samadhi* or *ting ngé dzin*, which in Sanskrit comes from the same root and refers to the single-pointed mind placed on a particular object. Because Rinpoche has very rarely mentioned this term, for simplicity we have not used it.

84. Taken from FPMT 2021a, 129.

85. Chöden Rinpoché says, "If we mentally shrink the holy body of the lama Thupwang [Shakyamuni Buddha] and take that as our objective support, a firm stability factor

of mind will arise, so we reduce the size of the lama Thupwang to a mere finger width. If that mere finger width is too high in front of us, excitement will arise, and if it is too low, laxity will arise, so imagine it in the space in front at the level of one's navel and meditate." Chöden 2020, 59.

86. Atisha 1997, v. 41.

87. V. 14.FPMT 2021a, 121.

88. Here Rinpoche is using one of the commentaries on Most Secret Hayagriva to explain about retreats in general.

89. Geshé Lamrimpa (1922–97?), Ngawang Phuntsok, was a highly learned lama from Drepung Monastery, who remained in Tibet after the invasion, rather than going into exile.

90. They are earth (the solid elements such as flesh, bone, etc.), water (the liquid elements such as blood, bile, etc.), fire (the heat generated within the body), and air (the wind element).

91. Ch. 8, v. 2; Gómez forthcoming.

92. Taken from FPMT 2021a, 115.

93. His Holiness the Dalai Lama's *Stages of Meditation* contains Kamalashila's root text as well as His Holiness' commentary on it (Dalai Lama 2019).

94. See Pabongka 2006, 599–612. See also Chöden 2020, 55–58, and Gyatso and Chodron 2014, 106–8.

95. General actions to be avoided so as not to create negative karma. There are three of body (killing, stealing, and sexual misconduct); four of speech (lying, speaking harshly, slandering, and gossiping); and three of mind (covetousness, ill will, and wrong views).

96. See Pabongka 2006, 602–3.

97. Also known as Khachen Yeshé Gyaltsen, Yongzin Yeshé Gyaltsen (1713–93) was a tutor of the Ninth Dalai Lama. He composed a commentary on Chökyi Gyaltsen's Mahamudra text, entitled *The Lamp of the Clear and Excellent Path of the Oral Tradition Lineage*.

98. An eleventh-century Indian yogi and spiritual master who traveled widely throughout his life and brought Indian Buddhist teachings to China and Tibet. He is revered by all schools of Tibetan Buddhism.

99. A highest yoga tantra practice where the consciousness is forcibly ejected from the body into a pure land just before the moment of death.

100. Over the years, Rinpoche used various terms for these stages, so for consistency I have applied the terms used in Gyatso and Chodron 2019, 198–201. For an exceptionally clear explanation of these nine stages, see His Eminence Chöden Rinpoché's *Mastering Meditation* (Chöden 2020), 81–88.

101. Quoted (as a table) in Gyatso and Chodron 2019, 197. (My brackets.)

102. Tenzin Gache, in his introduction to Chöden Rinpoché's *Mastering Meditation*, says, "Physical pliancy is an actual physical phenomenon, as the subtle energy channels of the body are physical in nature but exist at a more refined level than the gross matter we experience with our sense organs. Next arises the bliss of physical pliancy, the corresponding bodily sensation. ... Soon one also experiences a corresponding

mental pliancy, and at first this bliss is so strong that it temporarily disturbs mental stability." Chöden 2020, 8.

103. Ch. 9, v. 1; Gómez forthcoming.
104. Ch. 8; v. 4; Gómez forthcoming.
105. Taken from FPMT 2021a, 113.
106. Ch. 8, v. 129–30; Gómez forthcoming.
107. Ch. 8, v.131; Gómez forthcoming.
108. Taken from FPMT 2021a, 114.
109. I have not been able to ascertain whether Rinpoche is referring to the LTWA book *The Essence of Nectar*, which is a translation of the text by Yeshé Tsöndrü, or the lam-rim text in verse, found in Geshé Rabten's *Essential Nectar* (Rabten 2014), 173–243. *The Essential Nectar* is itself Geshé Rabten's commentary on Yeshé Tsöndrü's text. I highly recommend both.
110. Quoted in Tsongkhapa 2000, 1:147. The full sutra is available as *Great Nirvana Sutra* from www.nirvanasutra.net. Accessed 05/15/2021.
111. For the meditation, see McDonald 1984, 69–79.
112. The three types of suffering are (1) the suffering of pain (or suffering of suffering), (2) the suffering of change, and (3) pervasive compounding suffering. The six types of suffering are (1) nothing is definite in samsara, (2) nothing is satisfactory in samsara, (3) we have to leave this samsaric body again and again, (4) we have to take rebirth again and again, (5) we forever travel between higher and lower, and (6) we experience pain and death alone. The eight types of suffering are the suffering of (1) birth, (2) aging, (3) sickness, and (4) death, (5) encountering what is unpleasant, (6) separation from what is pleasant, (7) not getting what we want, and (8) having deluded aggregates.
113. The seven points of cause and effect and equalizing and exchanging self with others are two main methods used in Tibetan Buddhism for developing bodhichitta. See Zopa 2019, 117–216, for explanations on these.
114. Quoted in Zopa 2012a, 71–72, where alternate versions of the verse are given.
115. This is extracted from Rinpoche's *Abiding in the Retreat*, which has an extensive commentary on nyungné (Zopa 2017).
116. Gelongma Palmo (Bhikshuni Lakshmi) was an Indian princess, daughter of the king of Oddiyana, who cured herself of leprosy and achieved enlightenment through the nyungné practice. See Zopa 2017, 23–27, for her story.
117. *Nyung* literally means "fast," but Rinpoche prefers to translate it as "retreat" to reduce the emphasis on this physical aspect of the practice.
118. Wölka Chölung is the hermitage founded by Tsongkhapa in 1393 on the slopes of Mount Odé Gungyal, in southern Tibet. According to Dr. Alexander Berzin's biography of Tsongkhapa, because Manjushri advised him to do a very long retreat, Tsongkhapa entered a four-year retreat with eight close disciples there, doing thirty-five sets of a hundred thousand prostrations, one each to the Thirty-Five Buddhas, and eighteen sets of a hundred thousand mandala offerings, with many Yamantaka self-initiations. See *Study Buddhism: The Life of Tsongkhapa*, study-buddhism.com/en/tibetan-buddhism/spiritual-teachers/tsongkhapa/the-life-of-tsongkhapa. Accessed 04/28/2021.

119. Pabongka 2006, 173–75.

120. For the practice of prostration to the Thirty-Five Buddhas, see Zopa 2022, 152–55, or FPMT 2011.

121. For a short Vajrasattva meditation, see Zopa 2022, 130–34, or Zopa 2020a.

122. The full title is *Calling the Guru from Afar: A Tormented Wail, Quickly Drawing Forth the Blessings of the Guru, the Inseparable Three Kayas.* For the full and abbreviated text, see FPMT 2021a, 99–110.

123. See FPMT 1999 for the sadhana. Note that you must have received a highest yoga tantra initiation for this practice.

124. Rinpoche has sometimes specified this should be a white fireplace as used in pacifying fire pujas.

125. See Zopa, Zangpo, and Donyo 2010 for the sadhana and commentary.

126. This section comes from Zopa 2011, 131–38. At the end of the section, Rinpoche says, "More and more all over the world, I would like retreats to be done in this way. The point is not just to get the mantras done. It is to purify and accumulate as much merit as possible. To practice like this is the solution to everything."

127. FPMT 2021a, 38–55. See also FPMT 2011.

128. The standard and extended dedication prayers can be found in FPMT 2021a, 191–214; *King of Prayers* is on 237–46; and *Prayers for Multiplying Merit* is on 233–34.

129. To the traditional five senses of seeing, hearing, smelling, tasting, and touching, Buddhism adds the mental sense consciousness. The category of the six main minds or principal consciousnesses is an important aspect of Buddhist psychology, where the mind is divided into main minds and mental factors.

130. Taken from FPMT 2021a, 126.

131. Lhakdor 2020 (concluding session XXIV).

132. Chekawa Yeshé Dorjé (1101–75) was a great Kadampa master who, inspired by Geshé Langri Thangpa's *Eight Verses on Mind Training*, studied thought transformation and later composed *Seven-Point Mind Training.*

133. Quoted in Jinpa 2006, 83.

134. Ch. 8, v. 5. Quoted in Pabongka 2006, 623.

135. Taken from FPMT 2021a, 79, where it is excerpted.

136. Khensur Denma Locho Rinpoché (1928–2014) was one of Rinpoche's gurus. After fleeing Tibet in 1959, he became an influential teacher, traveling to the West many times. He was abbot of the Dalai Lama's Namgyal Monastery from 1986 to 1991.

137. This is adapted from Zopa 2003, which is available from Lama Yeshe Wisdom Archive as a download.

138. Rinpoche has made many references to ways of offering food. On another occasion, he suggested this. "As you recite OM AH HUM, you can visualize all the buddhas and bodhisattvas blessing the food with the qualities of their holy body, speech, and mind. All these qualities then absorb into the food. Then, visualize every grain or every part of the food as a blue HUM." (From "Blessing Food in a Factory," Lama Yeshe Wisdom Archive, accessed 06/01/2023.)

139. See Pabongka 2006, 449.

140. This mindfulness practice can be found in *Cultivating Mindfulenss of Bodhicita in*

Daily Activities by Lama Zopa: https://shop.fpmt.org/Cultivating-Mindfulness-of-Bodhicitta-in-Daily-Activities-eBook-PDF_p_2695.html

141. For an extensive teaching on thought transformation, see Zopa 2001a.
142. Jinpa 2006, 134, verses 10–11. Also available in Ngawang Dhargyey 2002.
143. Jinpa 2006, 83.
144. Taken from FPMT 2021a, 176.
145. See "A Commentary on Eight Verses on Mind Training" in Jinpa 2006, 277.
146. Zopa, trans. 2019.
147. Ch. 6, v. 41; Gómez forthcoming.
148. Dorjé Phakmo (Vajravarahi) is a female meditational deity, a consort of Heruka.
149. Vajrayogini (Dorjé Naljorma) is a female meditational deity from the mother class of highest yoga tantra, sometimes a consort of Heruka.
150. Rinpoche explores this idea extensively, especially the chapter on the kindness of the enemy, in Zopa 2020b, 93–104.
151. See "Geshé Chen Ngawa's Four Ways of Controlling Anger" in Zopa, 2020b, 63.
152. For an extended meditation, see Zopa 2001b, 123–34.
153. This meditation is an amalgamation of teachings given at the Heart Sutra Retreat, April 1997; the twenty-ninth Kopan course, November 1996; and the twelfth Kopan course, November 1979.
154. This meditation is extracted from one given by Rinpoche at a lamrim course at Chenrezig Institute, Queensland, Australia, June 1976.
155. There are variations on the way you close the nostrils. This seems the method Rinpoche has most used, which concords with the method described in Chöden Rinpoché's commentary on the mahamudra text, *Highway of the Conquerors* by Losang Chökyi Gyaltsen, where it explains the preparatory practices. See Chöden 2020, 189.
156. This meditation has been extracted from the one in Zopa 2013, 176–92.
157. Lama Zopa has consistently used "barbarian," "fool," and "heretic," these being the terms commonly used in texts such as Nagarjuna's *Friendly Letter* (See Pabongka 2006, 271, for the quote). As there are no simple English terms to cover what they mean, we have kept them here. "Barbarian" refers to someone living in a place where there is no way to meet the Dharma; "fool" refers to someone who is so severely mentally incapacitated that they can neither communicate nor understand communication (and hence have no access to the Dharma); and "heretic" is someone with heresy, *lokta* in Tibetan, which means having mistaken views, rejecting the existence of what exists (such as karma and reincarnation), and believing in what does not exist (such as the truly existing self).

GLOSSARY

··

afflictions. See delusion.

aggregates (*skandha*). The psychophysical constituents that make up a sentient being: form, feeling, discrimination, compositional factors, and consciousness. Beings of the desire and form realms have all five, whereas beings in the formless realm no longer have the form aggregate. The aggregates are considered "contaminated" because they have arisen due to karma and delusions.

analytical meditation (*ché gom*). Of the two main types of meditation, this is a meditation where the subject is examined, as opposed to single-pointed concentration or fixed meditation (*jok gom*) where the mind stays fixed on one single object. *See also* fixed meditation.

anger. A disturbing thought that exaggerates the negative qualities of an object and wishes to harm it; one of the six root delusions.

arhat (*drachompa*). Literally, "foe destroyer." A person who has destroyed their inner enemy, the delusions, and attained liberation from cyclic existence.

arya (*phakpa*). Literally, "noble." One who has realized the wisdom of emptiness.

Asanga, Arya (c. 300–70). The Indian master who directly received from Maitreya Buddha the extensive, or method, lineage of Shakyamuni Buddha's teachings. Said to have founded the Chittamatra school of Buddhist philosophy.

Atisha Dipamkara Shrijnana (982–1054). The renowned Indian master who went to Tibet in 1042 to help in the revival of Buddhism and established the Kadam tradition. His text *Lamp for the Path to Enlightenment* (*Bodhipathapradipa*; *Jangchup lamgyi drönma*) was the first lamrim text.

attachment. A disturbing thought that exaggerates the positive qualities of an object and wishes to possess it; one of the six root delusions.

attachment scattering thought (*auddhatya*; *göpa*). Also known as excitement, this is a mental factor that disrupts concentration through the force of attachment and is one of the three kinds of scattering. With gross excitement, the meditator loses the object of meditation altogether. With subtle excitement, the mind holds the object of meditation, but a part of the mind is distracted by another object. *See also* lethargy; scattering thought; sinking thought.

Avalokiteshvara. See Chenrezig.

awareness (*samprajanya*; *sheshin*). Also called introspection, awareness is the mental factor that is aware of what the rest of the mind is doing. It is a vital element, with mindfulness, in keeping the mind on the object of concentration. *See also* mindfulness.

bhagavan (*chomdendé*). Epithet for a buddha; one who has destroyed (*chom*) all the defilements, possesses all qualities (*den*), and has transcended the world (*dä*).

bodhichitta (*jangchup sem*). A principal consciousness that combines the two factors of wishing to free all beings from suffering and wishing to attain enlightenment in order to accomplish that.

bodhisattva (*jangchup sempa*). One who possesses bodhichitta.

bodhisattva vows. The vows taken upon entering the bodhisattva path.

buddha, a (*sangyé*). A fully enlightened being. One who has totally eliminated (*sang*) all obscurations veiling the mind and has fully developed (*gye*) all good qualities to perfection. *See also* enlightenment.

Buddha, the. The historical Buddha. *See* Shakyamuni Buddha.

buddha nature. The clear light nature of mind possessed by all sentient beings; the potential for all sentient beings to become enlightened by removing the two obscurations to liberation and to omniscience.

calm abiding. See shamatha.

capable being (*lower, middle, or higher*). *See* graduated path of the three capable beings.

chakra (*tsankhor*). An energy wheel situated along the central channel. The main chakras are the crown, throat, heart, navel, and secret place (the sex organ). In advanced meditations, such as in highest yoga tantra, the mind is concentrated on one of these chakras and, in the completion stage, it actually enters and abides there. *See also* channel.

channel (nadi; tsa). A constituent of the subtle psychic body through which energy winds and drops flow throughout the body. There are 72,000 channels in all, the main ones being the central channel (*avadhuti*; *tsa uma*) running just in front of the spine, flanked by the right channel (*rasana*; *roma*) and the left channel (*lalana*; Tib: *kyangma*).

checking meditation. See analytical meditation.

Chekawa Yeshé Dorjé, Geshé (1101–75). The Kadampa geshé who was inspired by Geshé Langri Thangpa's *Eight Verses of Thought Trans-formation* and later composed the famous thought-transformation text *Seven-Point Mind Training.*

Chen Ngawa Tsültrim Bar, Geshé (1033–1103). Kadampa master and one of Dromtönpa's three main disciples, the other two being Geshé Potowa and Phuchungwa Shönu Gyaltsen.

Chenrezig (Avalokiteshvara). The compassion buddha. The meditational deity embodying the compassion of all the buddhas. The Dalai Lamas are said to be emanations of this deity.

compassion (karuna; nyingjé). The wish that others be free from suffering.

completion stage (dzok rim). The second of the two stages of highest yoga tantra, during which control is gained over the vajra body through such practices as inner fire. *See also* generation stage.

cyclic existence. See samsara.

daka (khandro). A male dakini.

dakini (khandroma). Literally, a "female sky-goer." A female being who helps arouse blissful energy in a qualified tantric practitioner.

Dalai Lama (b. 1935). Gyalwa Tenzin Gyatso. Revered spiritual leader of the Tibetan people and tireless worker for world peace; winner of the Nobel Peace Prize in 1989; a guru of Lama Zopa Rinpoche.

defilement. See delusion.

deity (ishtadevata; yidam). An emanation of the enlightened mind used as the object of meditation in tantric practices.

delusion (klesha; nyönmong). Also called affliction, destructive emotion, disturbing thought. An obscuration covering the essentially pure nature of the mind, causing suffering and dissatisfaction; the main delusion is ignorance, and all the others come from this. *See also* three poisons.

desire realm. One of the three realms of samsara, comprising the hell beings (*naraka*), hungry ghosts (*preta*), animals (*tiryanch*), humans (*manushya*), demigods (*asuras*), and the six lower classes of gods (*devas* or *suras*); beings in this realm are preoccupied with desire for objects of the six senses. *See also* form realm; formless realm.

Dharma (chö). The second refuge jewel. Literally, "that which holds or protects (from suffering)" and hence brings happiness and leads you toward liberation and enlightenment. In Buddhism, absolute Dharma consists of the realizations attained along the path to liberation and enlightenment, and conventional Dharma is seen as both the teachings of the Buddha and virtuous actions.

dharmachakra. Literally, Dharma wheel, a symbol of the teachings of the Buddha, often with eight spokes representing the noble eightfold path.

dharmakaya (chöku). The ultimate reality of a buddha's enlightened mind, which is unborn, empty of true existence, free from conceptual thought, naturally radiant, beyond duality, and spacious like the sky. One of the three embodiments of a buddha. Dharmakaya can be divided into the wisdom body (*jnanakaya*; *yeshé nyiku*) (the blissful omniscient mind of a buddha) and the nature body (*svabhavikakaya*; *ngowo nyiku*) (the emptiness of the buddha's mind). *See also* rupakaya.

direct meditation. See glance meditation.

disturbing-thought obscurations (kleshavarana; nyöndrip). Also known as *gross obscurations*, these are the grosser of the two types of obscurations, the ones that block liberation. *See also* obscurations to knowledge.

dorjé (vajra). *See* vajra.

Dorjé Khandro burning offering practice (jinsek). Also called fire puja, a practice where black sesame seeds, representing your delusions or hindrances, are thrown into a fire visualized as the mouth of Dorjé Khandro, while saying mantras. This practice is often done at the end of a retreat in order to purify any negativities created during the retreat.

Dorjé Phagmo (Vajravarahi). Female meditational deity; consort of Heruka.

Dromtönpa (Dromtön Gyalwai Jungné) (1005–64). Kadampa master and one of Atisha's three main disciples.

eight antidotes to the five hindrances. These are specific antidotes to the five hindrances to attaining shamatha. They are confidence or faith, determination, perseverance, and pliancy or tranquility (all of which oppose laziness); mindfulness (which opposes forgetting the object); awareness or introspection (which opposes sinking and scattering thought); application of the appropriate antidote (which opposes any of the above); and equanimity (which opposes overapplying an antidote). *See also* five hindrances.

eight freedoms. The eight states from which a perfect human rebirth is free: being born as a hell being, hungry ghost, animal, long-life god, or barbarian, or in a dark age when no buddha has descended, holding wrong views, and being born with defective mental or physical faculties. *See also* ten richnesses.

eight Mahayana precepts. One-day vows to abandon killing, stealing, lying, sexual contact, taking intoxicants, sitting on high seats or beds, eating at an inappropriate time, and singing, dancing, and wearing perfumes and jewelry.

Eight Verses of Thought Transformation. A short essential mind training text composed by Geshé Langri Thangpa.

eight worldly dharmas. The worldly concerns that generally motivate the actions of ordinary beings: being happy when given gifts and unhappy when not given them; wanting to be happy and not wanting to be unhappy; wanting praise and not wanting criticism; wanting a good reputation and not wanting a bad reputation.

emptiness (*shunyata*; *tongpanyi*). The absence, or lack, of true existence. Ultimately, every phenomenon is empty of existing truly or from its own side or independently.

enlightenment (*bodhi*; *jangchup*). Full awakening; buddhahood; omniscience. The ultimate goal of a Mahayana Buddhist, attained when all limitations have been removed from the mind and the positive potential has been completely and perfectly realized. It is a state characterized by infinite compassion, wisdom, and skill.

eon (*kalpa*). A world period, an inconceivably long period of time. The life span of the universe is divided into four great eons, which are themselves divided into twenty lesser eons.

equanimity. The absence of the usual discrimination of sentient beings into friend, enemy, or stranger, deriving from the realization that all sentient beings are equal in wanting happiness and not wanting suffering and that since beginningless time all beings have been all things to each other. An impartial mind that serves as the basis for the development of great love, great compassion, and bodhichitta.

five heavy negative karmas without break (*panchanantarya*; *tsamé nga*). The five actions that are so heavy that they are the cause to be reborn in hell immediately after death. They are killing your father or mother, killing an arhat, maliciously drawing blood from a buddha, and creating a schism in the sangha.

five hindrances to shamatha. Laziness, forgetting the object, sinking and scattering thought (also called excitement and laxity), not applying the appropriate antidote, and overapplying an antidote. They are opposed by the eight antidotes. *See also* eight antidotes.

five nearing heavy negative karmas without break (*anantarya sabhagah*; *nyeba tsamé nga*). Similar to the five heavy negative karmas without break in that they are the cause to be reborn in hell immediately after death, they are killing a bodhisattva, killing an arya not yet an arhat, defiling your mother or a female arhat through sexual misconduct, stealing property from the sangha, and destroying a stupa.

five paths. The paths along which beings progress to liberation and enlightenment: the path of merit, the path of preparation, the path of right seeing, the path of meditation, and the path of no more learning.

fixed meditation (jok gom). Also called stabilizing, or placement meditation. The meditation that holds the mind single-pointedly on one object, as compared to the other main type of meditation, analytical meditation. *See also* analytical meditation.

form realm (rupadhatu; sukkyi kham). The second of samsara's three realms, with seventeen classes of gods. *See also* desire realm; formless realm.

formless realm (arupadhatu; sukmé kyi kham). The highest of samsara's three realms, with four classes of gods involved in formless meditations: limitless sky, limitless consciousness, nothingness, and neither existence nor nonexistence (also called *tip of samsara*). *See also* desire realm; form realm.

four aspects of karma. The four ways karma will ripen, either in this life or a future life. They are the ripening result, the possessed result, experiencing the result similar to the cause, and creating the result similar to the cause.

four attentions. The four degrees of stability developed as the practitioner advances toward shamatha. They are tight focus, which happen on the first two stages of shamatha; interrupted focus, which happens on the next five stages; uninterrupted focus, which happens on the eighth stage; and spontaneous focus, which happens on the ninth stage. *See also* six powers; nine stages of shamatha.

four classes of tantra. The division of tantra into *kriya* (action), *charya* (performance), yoga, and highest yoga tantra (*anuttara yoga tantra*; also sometimes referred to as *maha-anuttara yoga tantra*).

four foundations of mindfulness. A fundamental Theravadin practice; they are the mindfulness of the body, of feeling, of mind, and of phenomena.

four immeasurables (apramana). Also known as the *four immeasurable thoughts* or the *four sublime attitudes (brahmavihara)*, these are four states of mind or aspirations: loving-kindness (*maitri*; *jampa*), compassion (*karuna*; *nyingjé*), sympathetic joy (*mudita*; *gawa*), and equanimity (*upeksha*; *tang nyom*).

four maras. The four external and internal hindrances or obstacles to spiritual progress. They are the mara of the Lord of Death, the mara of the delusions, the mara of the (contaminated) aggregates, and the mara of the deva's son, the personification of desire and temptation.

four means of drawing disciples to the Dharma. The second of two sets of practices of the bodhisattva (the other is the *six perfections*): giving, speaking kind words, teaching to the level of the student, and practicing what you teach.

four opponent powers (*nyenpo topshi*). The four practices used to purify nonvirtuous imprints on the mindstream. They are the *power of object*, taking refuge in the Three Rare Sublime Ones and generating bodhichitta; the *power of regret*, feeling deep regret for the negativity committed; the *power of resolve*, determining not to repeat that negativity; and the *power of remedy*, a practice such as Vajrasattva that effectively acts as an antidote to the negativity.

four-point analysis. Also known as the four vital points of analysis. One of the main techniques for meditating on emptiness. They are determining the object to be negated, determining that an inherently existent self must either be identical with the aggregates or separate from them, determining that an inherently existing self cannot be identical with the aggregates, and determining that an inherently existing self cannot be separate from the aggregates.

Ganden Lha Gyama. The *Hundred Deities of the Land of Joy*, the *Lama Tsongkhapa Guru Yoga* practice, performed daily in Geluk monasteries. See also *guru yoga*.

Geluk. One of the four main traditions of Tibetan Buddhism, the others being Nyingma, Kagyü, and Sakya. It was founded by Lama Tsongkhapa in the early fifteenth century and has been propagated by such great masters as the successive Dalai Lamas and Panchen Lamas.

Gen. Literally, "elder." A title of respect.

generation stage (*kye rim*). The first of the two stages of highest yoga tantra, during which you cultivate the clear appearance and divine pride of your chosen meditational deity. *See also* completion stage.

geshé. Literally, "a spiritual friend." The title conferred on those who have completed extensive studies and examinations at Geluk monastic universities.

glance meditation. A meditation that reviews the overall points of a lamrim subject or the lamrim in general, rather than going into detail.

god (*deva*). A being dwelling in a state with much comfort and pleasure in the god realms of the desire, form, or formless realms.

graduated path. See lamrim.

graduated path of the three capable beings. Also known as the *three scopes* or *three levels of practice,* the three levels of the lower, middle, and higher capable being, based on the motivations of trying to attain a better future rebirth, liberation, and enlightenment, respectively. *See also* higher capable being; middle capable being; lower capable being.

great compassion (*mahakaruna*; *nyingjé chenpo*). The compassion that includes not only the wish for all sentient beings to be free from suffering and its causes but the heartfelt determination to accomplish this on your own. *See also* immeasurable compassion.

Great Treatise on the Stages of the Path to Enlightenment (*Lamrim Chenmo*). Lama Tsongkhapa's most important work, a commentary on Atisha's *Lamp for the Path*, the fundamental lamrim text.

Guide to the Bodhisattva's Way of Life (*Bodhicharyavatara*; *Jangchup sempé chöpala jukpa*). The inspirational text written by the eighth-century Indian master, Shantideva.

guru (*lama*). A spiritual guide or teacher. The one who shows a disciple the path to liberation and enlightenment. Literally, "heavy"—heavy with knowledge of the Dharma. In tantra, your teacher is seen as inseparable from the meditational deity and the Three Rare Sublime Ones.

guru devotion. The sutra or tantra practice of seeing the guru as a buddha, then devoting yourself to him or her with thought and action.

Guru Shakyamuni Buddha. The historical Buddha. Lama Zopa Rinpoche often adds "Guru" to remind us of the inseparability of the guru and the Buddha.

guru yoga. The fundamental tantric practice, whereby your guru is seen as identical with the buddhas, your personal meditational deity, and the essential nature of your own mind.

Gyaltsap Jé (1364–1432). Gyaltsab Dharma Rinchen was one of the two main disciples of Lama Tsongkhapa, with Khedrup Jé. After Lama Tsongkhapa died he became his successor as abbot of Ganden Monastery.

Heart (of Wisdom) Sutra (Prajnaparamitahridayasutra; Sherab kyi pharöl tu chinpai nyingpö do). The shortest and most recited of the Prajnaparamita Sutras, literally, "perfection of wisdom," the teachings of Shakyamuni Buddha in which the wisdom of emptiness and the path of the bodhisattva are set forth.

hell (narak). The samsaric realm with the greatest suffering. There are eight hot hells, eight cold hells, and four neighboring hells. (Some texts also cite occasional hells.) *See also* samsara.

heresy (mithyadrishti; lokta). Also called *mistaken wrong views,* one of the five afflicted views that are part of the root afflictions. A deluded intelligence that rejects the existence of something that exists, such as karma, reincarnation, the Three Rare Sublime Ones, and so forth, and ascribes existence to that which is nonexistent, such as inherent existence. It is also the holding of incorrect views about the guru.

Heruka. Male meditational deity from the mother tantra class (which emphasizes attaining the clear light) of highest yoga tantra.

higher capable being. The highest of the three levels of practice or scopes, it has the goal of full enlightenment. *See also* graduated path of the three capable beings; lower capable being; middle capable being.

highest yoga tantra (anuttara yoga tantra). The fourth and supreme division of tantric practice, sometimes called *maha-anuttara yoga tantra.* It consists of generation and completion stages. Through this practice full enlightenment can be attained within one lifetime. *See also* kriya tantra.

Hinayana. Literally, "Small, or Lesser, Vehicle." One of the two general divisions of Buddhism, the other being the Mahayana. It can also be called *Pratimokshayana* (Individual Liberation Vehicle) as compared to *Bodhisattvayana* (Bodhisattva's Vehicle). Hinayana practitioners' motivation is principally their intense wish for personal liberation from samsara. Two types of practitioner are identified: hearers (*shravaka*) and solitary realizers (*pratyekabuddha*). *See also* Mahayana; individual liberation.

hungry ghost (*preta*). The hungry ghost realm is one of the three lower realms of cyclic existence, where the main suffering is hunger and thirst. *See also* samsara.

ignorance (*avidya*; *marikpa*). Literally, "not seeing" that which exists or the way in which things exist. There are basically two kinds: ignorance of karma and ignorance of ultimate truth. The fundamental delusion from which all others spring. The first of the twelve links of dependent origination.

impermanence (*anitya*; *mitakpa*). The gross and subtle levels of the transience of phenomena, gross being the observable changes in things and events, and subtle being the moment-by-moment disintegration that happens as soon as they come into existence.

impermanence and death. One of the initial practices of the graduated path of the lower capable being, showing the fragility of this precious life and how you must not waste a moment of it.

imprint (*bakchak*). The seed, or potential, left on the mind by positive or negative actions of body, speech, and mind.

individual liberation. The liberation achieved by the hearer (*shravaka*) or the solitary realizer (*pratyekabuddha*) within the Hinayana tradition, as compared with enlightenment achieved by a practitioner of the Mahayana tradition.

inherent (or *intrinsic*) *existence*. What phenomena are empty of; the object of negation or refutation. To ignorance, phenomena appear to exist independently, inherently.

initiation. A transmission received from a tantric master allowing a disciple to engage in the practices of a particular meditational deity.

It is also referred to as an *empowerment* and can be given as a full empowerment (*wang*) or a permission to practice (*jenang*).

intermediate state (*antarabhava*; *bardo*). The state between death and rebirth.

Kadam. The order of Tibetan Buddhism founded in the eleventh century by Atisha, Dromtönpa, and their followers, the Kadampa geshés; the forerunner of the Geluk school, whose members are sometimes called the New Kadampas. *See also* Atisha; Dromtönpa.

Kadampa geshé. A practitioner of Kadam lineage. Kadampa geshés are renowned for their practice of thought transformation.

kaka. Slang for feces.

karma (*lé*). Action; the working of cause and effect in relation to the mind, whereby positive (virtuous) actions produce happiness and negative (nonvirtuous) actions produce suffering.

Kopan Monastery. The monastery near Boudhanath in the Kathmandu Valley, Nepal, founded by Lama Yeshe and Lama Zopa Rinpoche.

kriya tantra (*ja gyü*). Action tantra: The first of the four classes of tantra, it emphasizes external activities, such as prayers, mudras, and so forth. *See also* highest yoga tantra.

lama (*guru*). A spiritual guide or teacher; one who shows a disciple the path to liberation and enlightenment.

Lama Atisha. See Atisha Dipamkara Shrijnana.

Lama Tsongkhapa. See Tsongkhapa, Lama Jé Losang Drakpa.

lamrim. The graduated path. A presentation of Shakyamuni Buddha's teachings in a form suitable for the step-by-step training of a disciple. The lamrim was first formulated by the great Indian teacher Atisha when he came to Tibet in 1042. *See also* Atisha; three principal aspects of the path.

Lamrim Chenmo. See Great Treatise on the Stages of the Path to Enlightenment.

Langri Thangpa (1054–1123). Dorjé Sengé. Author of the famous *Eight Verses of Thought Transformation.*

laxity. See sinking thought.

Lethargy or fogginess (*styana*; *mukpa*). A foggy mind that causes sleepiness, apathy, and the inability to focus on the object of meditation. Lethargy, which is a grosser mind than sinking thought, is an afflictive mental state that occurs in ordinary people as well as meditators. *See also* attachment-scattering thought; sinking thought; scattering thought.

liberation (*nirvana* or *moksha*). The state of complete freedom from samsara; the goal of a practitioner seeking escape from suffering.

lineage lama. A spiritual teacher who is in the line of direct guru-disciple transmission of teachings, from the Buddha to the teachers of the present day.

lojong. See thought transformation.

long-life god. See god.

loving-kindness (*maitri; yiong jampa*). In the context of the seven points of cause and effect, the wish for all beings to have happiness and its causes, with the added dimension of *yiong* ("beautiful" or "affectionate"); often translated as "affectionate loving-kindness." Lama Zopa Rinpoche suggests this is the "loving-kindness of seeing others in beauty."

lower capable being. The first of the three levels of practice or scopes, the lower capable being has the goal of a better future existence. *See also* graduated path of the three capable beings; higher capable being; middle capable being.

lower realms. The three realms of cyclic existence or samsara with the most suffering: the hell being (*naraka*), hungry ghost (*preta*), and animal (*tiryanch*) realms. *See also* samsara.

Mahayana. Literally, "Great Vehicle." It is one of the two general divisions of Buddhism. Mahayana practitioners' motivation for following the Dharma path is principally their intense wish for all sentient beings to be liberated from samsara and to attain the full enlightenment of buddhahood in order to accomplish this. The Mahayana has two divisions, *Paramitayana* (*Sutrayana*) and *Vajrayana* (a.k.a. *Tantrayana* or *Mantrayana*).

Maitreya (*Jampa*). After Shakyamuni Buddha, the next (fifth) of the thousand buddhas of this fortunate eon to descend to turn the wheel of Dharma. Presently residing in the pure land of Tushita (*Ganden*). Recipient of the method lineage of Shakyamuni Buddha's teachings, which, in a mystical transmission, he passed on to Asanga.

mala (*trengwa*). A rosary of beads for counting mantras.

mandala (*kyilkhor*). A circular diagram symbolic of the entire universe. The abode of a meditational deity.

Manjushri (*Jampalyang*). The buddha (or bodhisattva) of wisdom. Recipient of the wisdom lineage of Shakyamuni Buddha's teachings, which he passed on to Nagarjuna.

mantra (*ngak*). Literally, "mind protection." Mantras are Sanskrit syllables usually recited in conjunction with the practice of a particular meditational deity; they embody the qualities of the deity with which they are associated.

maras. *See* four maras.

Marpa Chökyi Lodrö (1012–96). Also known as Marpa Lotsawa; founder of the Kagyü tradition of Tibetan Buddhism. He was a renowned tantric master and translator, a disciple of Naropa, and the guru of Milarepa.

Medicine Buddha (*Buddha Bhaiṣajya-guru*; *Sangyé Menla*). A buddha who vowed as a bodhisattva to be able to completely free all sentient beings from their illnesses.

meditation (*gom*). Familiarization of the mind with a virtuous object. There are two types: single-pointed (*jok gom*), also called *stabilizing*, *placement*, or *fixed*; and analytic or insight meditation (*ché gom*).

merit (*punya*; *sönam*). Positive imprints left on the mind by virtuous, or Dharma, actions. The principal cause of happiness.

merit field (*punyakshetra*; *tsokshing*). The visualized or actual holy beings that you accumulate merit with by going for refuge and making offerings to, and so forth.

merit of virtue (*punyasambhara*; *sönam kyitsok*). The merit accumulated by developing the method side of the path through practicing patience, ethics, compassion, and so forth, in order to achieve the buddha's holy body, the rupakaya.

merit of wisdom (*jnanasambhara*; *yeshé kyitsok*). The merit accumulated by developing the wisdom side of the path through meditating on emptiness in order to achieve the buddha's holy mind, the dharmakaya.

method. All aspects of the path to enlightenment other than those related to emptiness, principally associated with the development of loving-kindness, compassion, and bodhichitta.

middle capable being. The second of the three levels of practice or scopes, the middle capable being has the goal of liberation from suffering. *See also* graduated path of the three capable beings; higher capable being; lower capable being.

migtsema. A short prayer of four, five, or nine lines praising Lama Tsongkhapa as Avalokiteshvara, Vajrapani, and Manjushri. The name is an abbreviation of the first line. It is usually recited at the beginning or end of teachings or prayer sessions within the Geluk tradition.

Milarepa (1040–1123). Tibet's great yogi, who achieved enlightenment in his lifetime under the tutelage of his guru, Marpa, who was a contemporary of Atisha. One of the founders of the Kagyü school.

mind (*chitta; sem*). Synonymous with *consciousness* and *sentience.* Defined as that which is "clear and knowing"; a formless entity that has the ability to perceive objects. Mind is divided into six principal consciousnesses and fifty-one mental factors.

mind training (*lojong*). *See* thought transformation.

mindfulness (*smrti; drenpa*). In Tibetan Buddhism, the mental factor that holds the mind on the object of meditation, a key factor along with awareness in developing shamatha. In a broader context, mindfulness meditation is a practice, either Buddhist or secular, which remains aware of a broad experience, such as the sensation of the body or the breath. *See also* awareness.

Mount Meru. The center of the universe in Buddhist cosmology.

mudra (*chakgya*). Literally, seal or token; a symbolic hand gesture, endowed with power similar to a mantra's.

nadis. The energy channels that flow through a body. *See also* channel; chakra.

nine stages of shamatha. The nine stages that the mind progresses through before attaining shamatha. They are placing the mind (*chittasthapana*), continual placement (*samathapana*), repeated placement (*avasthapana*), close placement (*upasthapana*), taming (*damana*), pacifying (*shamana*), thoroughly pacifying (*vyupashamana*), making single-pointed (*ekotikarana*), placement in equanimity (*samadhana*). *See also* four attentions; six powers.

nine-point death meditation. An important meditation in Tibetan Buddhism to develop an appreciation of impermanence and the fragility of this human existence. The nine points are contemplated as three roots, each of which has a conclusion. They are that *death is certain*, concluding that we must practice the Dharma; that *the time of death is uncertain*, concluding that we must practice the Dharma now; and that *nothing can help at the time of death except the Dharma*, concluding that we must practice the Dharma purely.

nirvana (*nyang dé*). Liberation; the state of complete freedom from samsara; the goal of the practitioner of the individual liberation path. "Lower nirvana" is used to refer to this state of self-liberation, while "higher nirvana" refers to the supreme attainment of the full enlightenment of buddhahood. "Natural nirvana" is the fundamentally pure nature of reality, where all things and events are devoid of any inherent or independent reality.

noble eightfold path (*aryastangamarga*; *paklam yenlak gyé*). The eight components of the path to cessation of suffering taught by the Buddha. They are right view, right thought, right speech, right action, right livelihood, right effort, right mindfulness, and right concentration.

nonvirtue. Negative karma; that which results in suffering.

nyungné. A two-day Thousand-Arm Chenrezig retreat that involves fasting, prostrations, and silence.

object of refutation (*gakcha*). Also known as object of negation; the object that appears to a mistaken nonanalyzing consciousness as truly or inherently existing, and hence the object that must be refuted or negated in the ultimate analysis on emptiness.

obscuration. *See* delusion.

obscurations to knowledge (*jneyavarana*; *shedrip*). One of the two obscurations, these are the more subtle ones that block enlightenment; also known as *subtle obscurations, obscurations to enlightenment*, and *cognitive obscurations. See also* disturbing-thought obscurations.

Pabongka Dechen Nyingpo (1871–1941). An influential lama of the Geluk order, the root guru of His Holiness the Dalai Lama's senior and junior tutors. He gave the teachings compiled in *Liberation in the Palm of Your Hand.*

Pali canon. Also called the *Tripitaka* or *Three Baskets*, the teachings of the Buddha written down soon after his parinirvana, using the Pali language, hence the name. Refers to the texts used within the Hinayana. The later texts, written in Sanskrit, compose the Mahayana canon.

Panchen Lama. The Panchen Lamas are incarnations of Amitabha Buddha. Within the Geluk lineage and originally from Tashi Lhunpo Monastery, Shigatse, they are the highest spiritual leaders of Tibet along with the Dalai Lamas.

Panchen Losang Chökyi Gyaltsen (1570–1662). The first Panchen Lama, who composed *Guru Puja* and *Path to Bliss Leading to Omniscience*, a famous lamrim text; a tutor of the Fifth Dalai Lama.

Paramitayana. Literally, "Perfection Vehicle." The Bodhisattva Vehicle; a section of the Mahayana sutra teachings; one of the two forms of Mahayana, the other being Vajrayana. Also called *Bodhisattvayana* or *Sutrayana.*

parinirvana. The final nirvana the Buddha attained when he passed away in Kushinagar.

perfect human rebirth. The rare human state, qualified by eight freedoms and ten richnesses, which is the ideal condition for practicing the Dharma and attaining enlightenment. The eight freedoms are being free from being born as a hell being, hungry ghost, animal, long-life god, or barbarian; or in a dark age when no buddha has descended; holding wrong views; and being born with mental or physical problems that preclude you from understanding the Dharma. The ten richnesses are being born as a human being, in a Dharma country, and with perfect mental and physical faculties; not having committed any of the five heavy negative karmas without break; having faith in the Buddha's teachings; being alive when a buddha has descended, the teachings have been revealed, the complete teachings still exist, and when there are still followers of the teachings; and having the necessary conditions to practice the Dharma, such as the kindness of others.

Perfection of Wisdom (*Prajnaparamita*). Sutras pertaining to the Buddha's second turning of the wheel of Dharma, in which the wisdom of emptiness and the path of the bodhisattva were set forth.

prajnaparamita. *See* Perfection of Wisdom.

preliminary practices (*purvaka*; *ngöndro*). The practices that prepare the mind for a successful meditation retreat by removing hindrances and accumulating merit. These practices are found in all schools of Tibetan Buddhism and are usually done 100,000 times each; the four main practices are recitation of the refuge formula, mandala offerings, prostrations, and Vajrasattva mantra recitation. The Geluk tradition adds five more: guru yoga, water bowl offerings, Damtsig Dorjé purifying meditation, making *tsatsas*, and the Dorjé Khandro burning offering practice. The term is also used to refer to the practices done on a daily basis before the main meditation session, such as cleaning the room, setting up the altar, doing a breathing meditation, and the preliminary prayers.

prostrations. Paying respect to the guru-deity with body, speech, and mind; one of the tantric preliminaries.

protector (*dharmapala*; *chökyong*). A being, either worldly or enlightened, who protects Buddhism and its practitioners.

puja (*chöpa*). Literally, "offering"; a religious ceremony. The term is usually used to describe an offering ceremony such as the *Offering to the Spiritual Master* (*Guru Puja*).

pure land (*buddhakshetra*; *dakshing*). A pure land of a buddha is a place where there is no suffering. In some but not all pure lands, after taking birth, the practitioner receives teachings directly from the buddha of that pure land, allowing them to actualize the rest of the path and then become enlightened.

purification (*sansargi*; *jangwa*). The elimination of negative imprints from the mind left by past nonvirtuous actions, which would otherwise ripen into suffering. The most effective methods of purification employ the four opponent powers—the powers of the object, regret, resolve, and remedy.

realization (*tokpa*). A valid mind that holds a stable, correct understanding of a Dharma subject, such as emptiness, that effects a deep change within the continuum of the person. The effortless experience resulting from study and meditation supported by guru devotion and ripened by purification and merit-building practices.

refuge (*sharana*; *kyap*). The door to the Dharma path. Having taken refuge from the heart, you become an inner being or Buddhist. There are three levels of refuge—Hinayana, Mahayana, and Vajrayana— and two or three causes necessary for taking refuge: *fearing* the sufferings of samsara in general and lower realms in particular; *faith* that Buddha, Dharma, and Sangha have the qualities and power to lead you to happiness, liberation, and enlightenment; and (for Mahayana refuge) *compassion* for all sentient beings.

renunciation (*nihsarana*; *ngéjung*). The state of mind of not having the slightest attraction to samsaric pleasures for even a second and having the strong wish for liberation. The first of the three principal aspects of the path to enlightenment. *See also* bodhichitta; emptiness.

rinpoché. Literally, "precious one." Epithet for an incarnate lama, that is, one who has intentionally taken rebirth in a human form to benefit sentient beings on the path to enlightenment.

rupakaya (*zukku*). The form body of a fully enlightened being; the result of the complete and perfect accumulation of merit. It has two aspects: *sambhogakaya* (*longku*, enjoyment body), in which the enlightened mind appears to benefit highly realized bodhisattvas; and *nirmanakaya* (*tulku*, emanation body), in which the enlightened mind appears to benefit ordinary beings. *See also* dharmakaya.

sadhana (*drupthap*). Method of accomplishment; the step-by-step instructions for practicing the meditations related to a particular meditational deity.

samadhi (*ting ngé dzin*). A virtuous single-pointed mind focused on a particular object; a mind in meditative absorption.

samaya (*damtsik*). The pledges and commitments made by a disciple at an initiation, such as to keep tantric vows for life or to perform certain practices connected with the deity, like a daily sadhana recitation or a *tsok* practice twice a month.

samsara (*khorwa*). Cyclic existence; the six realms of conditioned existence, three lower—hell being (*naraka*), hungry ghost (*preta*), and animal (*tiryanch*)—and three upper—human (*manushya*), demigod (*asura*), and god (*deva* or *sura*). The beginningless, recurring cycle of death and rebirth under the control of karma and delusions, fraught with suffering. Also refers to the contaminated aggregates of a sentient being.

sangha (*gendun*). Spiritual community; the third of the Three Rare Sublime Ones. In Tibetan, *gendun* literally means "intending (*dun*) to virtue (*gen*)."

scattering thought (*visarana*; *trowa*). When the mind wanders from the object of meditation to an unintended object. Scattering to another object is induced through either (1) the force of attachment; (2) the force of anger; or (3) virtuous thoughts. Scattering through attachment is most common, the other two less so, but all are obstacles to single-pointed concentration. *See also* attachment-scattering thought; lethargy; sinking thought.

self-cherishing. The self-centered attitude of considering your own happiness to be more important than that of others.

sentient being. An unenlightened being; any being whose mind is not completely free from gross and subtle obscurations.

seven points of cause and effect. One of the two techniques within Mahayana Buddhism for developing bodhichitta. There are six causes: recognizing that all beings have been your mother, recalling the kindness of those beings, resolving to repay that kindness, loving-kindness, great compassion, and special attitude. These lead to the one result: bodhichitta. The other technique is *equalizing and exchanging self and others.*

seven-limb practice. The seven limbs are prostrating, making offerings, confession, rejoicing, requesting to turn the Dharma wheel, requesting the teachers to remain in the world, and dedicating.

Shakyamuni Buddha (563–483 BC). Fourth of the one thousand founding buddhas of this present world age. Born a prince of the Shakya clan in North India, he taught the sutra and tantra paths to liberation and enlightenment; founder of what came to be known as Buddhism. (From *buddha*, "fully awake.")

shamatha (shiné). Calm abiding; single-pointed concentration; a state of concentration in which the mind is able to abide steadily, without effort, and for as long as desired on an object of meditation. There are nine stages in its development. *See also* nine stages of shamatha.

Shantideva (685–763). The Indian Buddhist philosopher and bodhisattva who wrote the quintessential Mahayana text, *A Guide to the Bodhisattva's Way of Life (Bodhicaryavatara).*

shiné. See shamatha.

single-pointed concentration. See shamatha.

sinking thought (laya; jingwa). Also called laxity or sluggishness, sinking thought is a mental factor that causes the object of meditation to lack clarity and intensity. Gross sinking thought is a dull and heavy mind that holds the object of meditation unclearly. Subtle sinking thought is a stable mind that holds the object of meditation clearly but lacks intensity. Sinking and scattering thoughts are the two main hindrances to shamatha. *See also* attachment-scattering thought; lethargy; scattering thought.

six perfections (satparamita; paröl tu chinpa druk). The practices of a bodhisattva. On the basis of bodhichitta, a bodhisattva practices the six perfections: charity or generosity, morality, patience, perseverance or joyous effort, concentration, and wisdom.

six powers. The powers that are developed while progressing toward shamatha. They are the power of study, used on the first stage of shamatha, the power of memory, used on the second stage, the power of mindfulness, used on the third and fourth stages, the power of awareness, used on the fifth and sixth stages, the power of effort, used on the seventh and eight stages, and the power of familiarity, used on the ninth stage. *See also* four attentions; nine stages of shamatha.

six root delusions (*mulaklesha*; *tsawat nyönmong*). Attachment, anger, ignorance, pride, afflicted doubt, and afflicted view.

six types of suffering. Nothing is definite in samsara, nothing gives satisfaction in samsara, you have to leave this samsaric body again and again, you have to take rebirth again and again, you forever travel between high and low in samsara, and you must experience pain and death alone.

spirits. Beings not usually visible to ordinary people; they can belong to the hungry ghost or god realms, and they can be beneficent as well as harmful.

stupa (*chörten*). A dome-shaped structure, often containing Buddhist relics, that represents the enlightened mind; stupas range in size from huge to a few inches in height.

subtle obscurations. See obscurations to knowledge.

sutra (*do*). A discourse of the Buddha recognized as a canonical text.

taking and giving (*tonglen*). The meditation practice of generating bodhichitta by taking on the suffering of others and giving them our happiness.

tantra (*gyü*). Also called *Vajrayana* or *Mantrayana*, the division of the Mahayana that is based on transforming impure vision into pure vision through deity practices where, in the higher tantras, you visualize yourself as the deity. Often called the resultant vehicle because you visualize the result now, as opposed to Sutrayana, which is the causal vehicle. A scriptural text and the teachings and practices it contains.

tantric vows. Vows taken by tantric practitioners.

Tara (*Drölma*). A female meditational deity who embodies the enlightened activity of all the buddhas; often referred to as the mother of the buddhas of the past, present, and future. The *Praises to the Twenty-One Taras* prayer is the most popular prayer for lay and ordained Tibetans alike.

ten bhumis (grounds or stages) (dashabhumi; sachu). The ten stages a bodhisattva progresses through once reaching the path of right seeing: the first level being during the path of right seeing, the second to seventh during the path of meditation, and the eighth to tenth during the path of no more learning.

ten directions. The four cardinal directions—north, south, east, and west—the four intermediate directions, and the zenith and nadir.

ten richnesses. Along with the eight freedoms, the defining features of the perfect human rebirth: being born as a human being; in a Dharma country and with perfect mental and physical faculties; not having committed any of the five heavy negative karmas without break; having faith in the Buddha's teachings; living at a time in which a buddha has descended, the teachings have been revealed, the complete teachings still exist, and there are still followers of the teachings; and having the necessary conditions to practice the Dharma, such as the kindness of others. *See also* eight freedoms.

thangka. Painted or appliquéd depictions of deities, usually set in a framework of colorful brocade.

Thirty-Five Buddhas. Also called the Thirty-Five Confession Buddhas, they are a group of buddhas visualized in a practice of confessing and purifying negative karmas done while reciting the *Sutra of the Three Heaps* and performing prostrations.

Thirty-Seven Practices of the Bodhisattva. A set of practices that embraces all the aspects of the bodhisattva's path to enlightenment, based on a text by Thokmé Sangpo.

Thokmé Sangpo. (1295–1371). Also known as Gyalse Ngulchu Thogme. A great master of the Nyingma and Sakya traditions and author of *Thirty-Seven Practices of the Bodhisattva* and a famous commentary on Shantideva's *Guide to the Bodhisattva's Way of Life.*

thought transformation (lojong). Also known as *mind training* or *mind transformation.* A powerful approach to the development of bodhichitta, in which the mind is trained to use all situations, both happy and unhappy, as a means to destroy self-cherishing and self-grasping.

three higher trainings. Ethics, concentration, and wisdom.

three kayas. Dharmakaya (truth body, *chöku*), sambhogakaya (enjoyment body, *longku*) and nirmanakaya (emanation body, *tulku*). The general way a buddha is described as emanating after enlightenment, the dharmakaya being a result of the wisdom side of the practice and the rupakaya (form body, *zukku*)—of which sambhogakaya and nirmanakaya are aspects—of the method side.

three poisons. Attachment, anger, and ignorance.

three principal aspects of the path. The three main divisions of the lam-rim: renunciation, bodhichitta, and right view (of emptiness).

Three Rare Sublime Ones (Triratna; Könchok Sum). Also called the *Three Jewels* or *Triple Gem*; the objects of Buddhist refuge: the Buddha, Dharma, and Sangha. Lama Zopa Rinpoche prefers "Three Rare Sublime Ones" as a more direct translation of *Könchok Sum.*

three realms. The desire, form, and formless realms.

three types of suffering. The suffering of pain (or suffering), the suffering of change, and pervasive compounding suffering.

tonglen. See taking and giving.

transmigratory beings. Sentient beings who pass from one realm to another, taking rebirth within cyclic existence.

tsatsa. A print of a buddha's image made in clay or plaster from a carved mold.

tsok. Literally, gathering—a gathering of offering substances and a gathering of disciples to make the offering.

Tsongkhapa Losang Dragpa, Lama Jé (1357–1419). Founder of the Geluk tradition of Tibetan Buddhism and revitalizer of many sutra and tantra lineages as well as the monastic tradition in Tibet.

union of clear light and illusory body. The final stage of completion stage of highest yoga tantra, where the practitioner is able to unite the clear light mind called the *meaning clear light* (a direct realization of emptiness) with the *pure illusory body*, the experience of the winds entering the indestructible drop at the central channel.

vajra (dorjé). Literally, "adamantine"; the four- or five-spoke implement used in tantric practice.

Vajrasattva (Dorjé Sempa). Male meditational deity symbolizing the inherent purity of all buddhas. A major tantric purification practice for removing obstacles created by negative karma and the breaking of vows.

Vajrayana (Dorjé Thekpa). Another name for *tantra*; the Adamantine Vehicle; the second of the two Mahayana paths. It is also called *Tantrayana* or *Mantrayana*. This is the quickest vehicle of Buddhism, as it allows certain practitioners to attain enlightenment within a single lifetime.

virtue. Positive karma; that which results in happiness.

virtuous friend. *See* guru.

vows. Precepts taken on the basis of refuge at all levels of Buddhist practice. Pratimoksha (individual liberation) vows are the main vows in the Hinayana tradition and are taken by monks, nuns, and laypeople; they are the basis of all other vows. Bodhisattva and tantric vows are taken in the Mahayana tradition, the latter is in association with a tantric initiation.

wisdom (prajna; sherab). Different levels of insight into the nature of reality. There are, for example, the three wisdoms of hearing, contemplation, and meditation. Ultimately, there is the wisdom of realizing emptiness, which frees beings from cyclic existence and eventually brings them to enlightenment. The complete and perfect accumulation of wisdom results in the dharmakaya.

wish-granting jewel. Also called *wish-fulfilling jewel*. A jewel that brings its possessor everything they desire.

wrong view. Any mistaken or deluded understanding that leads to suffering. In Buddhism there are various ways of defining wrong views. The most common is as the last of the ten nonvirtues, heresy (*mithyadrishti; lokta*), but it can also be either all five of the afflicted views among the unwholesome mental factors—the view of the transitory aggregates, extreme views, views of superiority of belief, the views of superiority of morality and discipline, and mistaken or wrong views—or the last one alone.

yama. A guardian of the hell realm.

Yama. The Lord of Death, seen on the Wheel of Life.

Yeshe, Lama (1935–84). Born and educated in Tibet, he fled to India, where he met his chief disciple, Lama Zopa Rinpoche. They began teaching Westerners at Kopan Monastery in 1969 and founded the Foundation for the Preservation of the Mahayana Tradition (FPMT) in 1975.

yidam. See deity.

yogi. A highly realized male meditator.

Zong Rinpoché (1905–84). A powerful Gelukpa lama renowned for his wrathful aspect who had impeccable knowledge of Tibetan Buddhist rituals, art, and science.

BIBLIOGRAPHY

Sutras

Arya Sanghata Sutra (*Arya Sanghatasutradharmaparyaya*; *Phakpa sunggi do chökyi namdrang*). Available in several languages at https://fpmt.org/education/prayers-and-practice-materials/sutras/#sanghata-sutra. Accessed 03/24/2023.

Dhammapada. Excerpted in FPMT 2021a, 79. Available in its entirety as Cleary 1995.

Diamond Cutter Sutra (*Arya Vajracchedikanamaprajnaparamitamahayanasutra*; *Phakpa sherabpa röltu chinpa dorjé chöpa sheja thegpa chenpö do*). Excerpted in FPMT 2021a, 79. Available as *Vajra Cutter Sutra* in several languages at https://fpmt.org/education/prayers-and-practice-materials/sutras/#vajra-cutter-sutra. Accessed 09/08/2023.

Great Nirvana Sutra (*Mahaparinirvanasutra*; *Yongsunya ngenla depa chenpö do*). Excerpts in English are available at www.nirvanasutra.net. Accessed 06/01/2023.

Heart of Wisdom Sutra (*Prajnaparamitahridayasutra*; *Sherab kyi pharöl tu chinpai nyingpö do*). Available in several languages at https://fpmt.org/education/prayers-and-practice-materials/sutras/#heart-sutra. Accessed 03/24/2023.

Perfection of Wisdom in Eight Thousand Lines (*Ashtasahasrika Prajnaparamitasutra*; *Sherab kyi pharöl tu chinpa trigyé tongpa*). Available as Conze 1995.

INDIAN- AND TIBETAN-LANGUAGE WORKS

Aryadeva. *Four Hundred Stanzas* (*Chatuhshataka shastranamakarika*; *Tenchö shi gyapa shejawai tsik leur jepa*). Excerpted in Pabongkha 2006, 623. Also available as Sonam 2008.

Atisha. *Lamp for the Path to Enlightenment* (*Bodhipathapradipam*; *Jangchup lamgyi drönma*). Available as Sonam 1997a.

———. *Bodhisattva's Jewel Garland* (*Bodhisattvamanyavali*; *Jangchup sempai norbü trengwa*). Available as Lhakdor 2020.

Chekawa Yeshé Dorjé. *Seven-Point Mind Training* (*Lojong dön dunma*). Available in Jinpa 2006.

Dharmarakshita. *The Wheel of Sharp Weapons* (*Thekpa chenpö dodé gyen*). Available as Ngawang Dhargyey 2002.

Kamalashila. *Stages of Meditation* (*Bhavanakrama*; *Gom Rim*). Available as Dalai Lama 2019.

Maitreya. *The Adornment of Mahayana Sutras* (*Mahayanasutralamkara*; *Thekpa chenpö dodé gyen*). Available as Jamspal, et al., 2004.

Maitreya. *Ornament of Clear Realizations* (*Abhisamayalamkara*; *Ngönpar tokpä gyen*). Available as Stcherbatsky and Obermiller 1992.

Shantideva. *A Guide to the Bodhisattva's Way of Life* (*Bodhisattvacharyavatara*; *Jangchup sempai jöpala jukpa*). Available as Gómez, forthcoming; Batchelor, 1979–2011; Wallace, 1997; Padmakara Translation Group, 2006.

Thokmé Sangpo. *The Thirty-Seven Practices of the Bodhisattva* (*Gyalsé laklen sodunma*). Available as Sonam 1997b.

Tsongkhapa, Jé. *Foundation of All Good Qualities* (*Yönten shyir gyurma*). Available in FPMT 2021a, 111–15, and as FPMT 2020a.

———. *The Great Treatise on the Stages of the Path to Enlightenment* (*Lamrim Chenmo*). Available as Lamrim Chenmo Translation Committee 2000–2004.

———. *Golden Garland of Eloquence* (*Lekshé sertreng*). Available as Sparham 2010.

———. *A Hymn of Experience* (*Lamrim nyamgur*). Available in FPMT 2021a, 124–31.

———. *Middle Length Lamrim* (*Lamrim dringwa*). Available as Quarcoo 2021.

———. *The Three Principal Aspects of the Path* (*Lamtso namsum*). Available in FPMT 2021a, 116–23, and as Zopa 2021.

English-Language Texts

Batchelor, Stephen. 1979–2011. *Guide to the Bodhisattva's Way of Life*. Dharamsala, India: Library of Tibetan Works and Archives.

Chöden Rinpoché, His Eminence. 2020. *Mastering Meditation: Instructions on Calm Abiding and Mahāmudrā*. Translated by Tenzin Gache. Boston: Wisdom Publications.

Cleary, Thomas, trans. 1995. *Dhammapada: The Sayings of Buddha*. London: Thorsons.

Conze, Edward, trans. 1995. *Perfection of Wisdom in Eight Thousand Lines and Its Verse Summary*. San Francisco: Four Seasons Foundation.

Dalai Lama, H. H. the. 2019. *Stages of Meditation: The Buddhist Classic on Training the Mind*. Translated by Venerable Geshé Lobsang Jordhen, Losang Choephel Ganchenpa, and Jeremy Russell. Boulder, CO: Shambhala Publications.

Foundation for the Preservation of the Mahayana Tradition. 1999. *The Sadhana of Samayavajra: Damtsig Dorje Depa*. Portland, OR: FPMT.

———. 2011. *Preliminary Practice of Prostrations to the Thirty-Five Confession Buddhas*. Translated by Lama Zopa Rinpoche. Portland, OR: FPMT.

———. 2020a. *The Foundation of All Good Qualities*. Portland, OR: FPMT.

———. 2020b. *FPMT Retreat Prayer Book*. Portland, OR: FPMT.

———. 2021a. *FPMT Essential Prayer Book*. Portland, OR: FPMT.

———. 2021b. *A Method of Practicing Ganden Lhagyma According to the Instructions of Lama Zopa Rinpoche*. Portland, OR: FPMT.

Gómez, Luis O., trans. Forthcoming. *Guide to the Bodhisattva's Way of Life*. Boston: Wisdom Publications.

Gyältsen, Losang Chökyi, and Jamphäl Lhundrub. 2016. *Lama Chöpa Jorchö*. Portland, OR: FPMT.

Gyatso, His Holiness Tenzin. 2019. *Stages of Meditation: The Buddhist Classic on Training the Mind*. Boston: Shambala Publications.

Gyatso, His Holiness Tenzin, and Bhikshuni Thubten Chodron. 2019. *Following in the Buddha's Footsteps*. Boston: Wisdom Publications.

Jamspal, Lozang, and Robert Thurman and the American Institute of Buddhist Studies. 2004. *The Universal Vehicle Discourse Literature: Mahayanasutralankara*. New York: American Institute of Buddhist Studies.

Jinpa, Thubten, ed. 2006. *Mind Training: The Great Collection*. Boston: Wisdom Publications.

———. 2008. *The Book of Kadam: The Core Texts*. Boston: Wisdom Publications.

Lamrim Chenmo Translation Committee. 2000–2004. *The Great Treatise on the Stages of the Path to Enlightenment* (*Lamrim Chenmo*). Three vols. Ithaca, NY: Snow Lion Publications.

Lhakdor, Geshé. 2020. *Atisha's Bodhisattva Garland of Gems*. Dharamsala: The Foundation for Universal Responsibility of HH the Dalai Lama. http://furhhdl.org/wp-content/uploads/2020/09/Text-for-E-Teaching-.pdf. Accessed 06/01/2023.

McDonald, Kathleen. 2005. *How to Meditate: A Practical Guide*. Boston: Wisdom Publications.

Ngawang Dhargyey, Geshé. 2002. *The Wheel of Sharp Weapons*. Dharamsala: Library of Tibetan Works and Archives. New Delhi: Paljor Publications.

Padmakara Translation Group, trans. 2006. *The Way of the Bodhisattva*. Ithaca, NY: Shambhala Publications.

Paltrul Rinpoché. 2010. *Words of My Perfect Teacher: A Complete Translation of a Classic Introduction to Tibetan Buddhism*. New Haven, CT: Yale University Press.

Pabongka Rinpoché. 2006. *Liberation in the Palm of Your Hand* (*Namdröl lakchang*). Translated by Michael Richards. Boston: Wisdom Publications. Also published in three parts as *Liberation in Our*

Hands, translated by Geshé Lobsang Tharchin and Artemus B. Engle, 1990–2001. Howell, NJ: Mahayana Sutra and Tantra Press.

Quarcoo, Philip. 2021. *The Middle-Length Treatise on the Stages of the Path to Enlightenment*. Boston: Wisdom Publications.

Rabten, Geshé. 2014. *The Essential Nectar: Meditations on the Buddhist Path*. Boston: Wisdom Publications.

Sonam, Ruth, trans. 1997a. *Atisha's Lamp for the Path to Enlightenment*. Commentary by Geshé Sonam Rinchen. Ithaca, NY: Snow Lion Publications.

———. 1997b. *The Thirty-Seven Practices of Bodhisattvas: An Oral Teaching by Geshé Rinchen Sonam*. Ithaca, NY: Snow Lion Publications.

———. 2008. *Aryadeva's Four Hundred Stanzas on the Middle Way*. Commentary by Geshé Sonam Rinchen. Ithaca: Snow Lion Publications.

Sparham, Gareth, trans. 2010. *Golden Garland of Eloquence*. Singapore: Asian Humanities Press.

Sopa, Geshé Lhundub. 2004–17. *Steps on the Path to Enlightenment*. Five vols. Boston: Wisdom Publications.

Stcherbatsky, T., and E. Obermiller. 1992. *Abhisamayalankara Prajnaparamita Upadesa Sastra: The Work of Bodhisattva Maitreya*. New Delhi, Sri Satguru.

Tsering, Geshé Tashi. 2005. *The Four Noble Truths*. Boston: Wisdom Publications.

Tsöndrü, Yeshé. 2019. *The Essence of Nectar*. Dharamsala: Library of Tibetan Works and Archives. Also published within Rabten 2014.

Wallace, Alan and Vesna. 1997. *Guide to the Bodhisattva's Way of Life*. Ithaca, NY: Snow Lion Publications.

Zopa, Lama Thubten, Ven. Jampa Zangpo, and Ven. Thubten Donyo. 2010. *Burning Offering to Dorjé Khadro*. Portland, OR: FPMT.

Zopa, Lama Thubten. 2001a. *Transforming Problems into Happiness*. Boston: Wisdom Publications.

———. 2001b. *Ultimate Healing: The Power of Compassion*. Boston: Wisdom Publications.

———. 2003. *The Yoga of Offering Food.* Boston: Lama Yeshe Wisdom Archive.

———. 2009. *Heart of the Path: Seeing the Guru as Buddha.* Boston: Lama Yeshe Wisdom Archive.

———. 2011. *Heart Advice for Retreat.* Portland, OR: FPMT

———. 2012a. *Bodhisattva Attitude: How to Dedicate Your Life to Others.* Boston: Lama Yeshe Wisdom Archive.

———. 2012b. *How to Practice Dharma: Teachings on the Eight Worldly Dharmas.* Boston: Lama Yeshe Wisdom Archive.

———. 2012c. *The Preliminary Practice of Dorjé Khadro.* Portland, OR: FPMT.

———. 2013. *The Perfect Human Rebirth: Freedom and Richness on the Path to Enlightenment.* Boston: Lama Yeshe Wisdom Archive.

———. 2016. *Wish-Fulfilling Golden Sun.* Boston: Lama Yeshe Wisdom Archive. Available as a download: https://www.lamayeshe.com/sites/default/files/wishfulfilling_golden_sun_c5.pdf.

———. 2017. *Abiding in the Retreat: A Nyung Nä Commentary.* Boston: Lama Yeshe Wisdom Archive.

———. 2019. *Bodhichitta: Practice for a Meaningful Life.* Boston: Wisdom Publications.

———. 2020a. *A Short Vajrasattva Meditation: Purification with the Four Opponent Powers.* Portland, OR: FPMT

———. 2020b. *Patience: A Guide to Shantideva's Sixth Chapter.* Boston: Wisdom Publications.

———. 2020c. *The Six Perfections: The Practice of the Bodhisattvas.* Boston: Wisdom Publications.

———. 2022. *The Power of Mantra: Vital Practices for Transformation.* Boston: Wisdom Publications.

Zopa, Lama Thubten, trans. 2019. *Eight Verses of Thought Transformation.* Portland, OR: FPMT.

———. 2021. *The Three Principal Aspects of the Path.* Portland, OR: FPMT.

INDEX

ABOUT THE AUTHOR

··

LAMA ZOPA RINPOCHE (1945–2023) is one of the most interna-
tionally renowned masters of Tibetan Buddhism, who worked
and taught ceaselessly on almost every continent for fifty years. He was
the spiritual director and cofounder of the Foundation for the Preservation of the Mahayana Tradition (FPMT), an international network
of Buddhist projects, including monasteries in six countries and meditation centers in over thirty; health and nutrition clinics, and clinics
specializing in the treatment of leprosy and polio; as well as hospices,
schools, publishing activities, and prison outreach projects worldwide.
Lama Zopa Rinpoche is the author of numerous books, including
*Patience, The Six Perfections, Bodhichitta, The Four Noble Truths, Trans-
forming Problems into Happiness, How to Enjoy Death, Ultimate Healing,
The Door to Satisfaction, How to Be Happy, Wholesome Fear, Wisdom
Energy,* and *Dear Lama Zopa,* all from Wisdom Publications.

ABOUT THE EDITOR

GORDON MCDOUGALL was director of Cham Tse Ling, the FPMT's
Hong Kong center, for two years in the 1980s and worked for Jamyang
Buddhist Centre in London from 2000 to 2007. He helped develop the
Foundation of Buddhist Thought study program and administered it
for seven years. Since 2008 he has been editing Lama Zopa Rinpoche's
teachings for Lama Yeshe Wisdom Archive and Wisdom Publications.

WHAT TO READ NEXT FROM WISDOM PUBLICATIONS

Patience
A Guide to Shantideva's Sixth Chapter
Lama Zopa Rinpoche

"Often in the West we think that patience is passive aggression: waiting for that horrible thing to go away. Lama Zopa Rinpoche shows us in great detail how to cultivate actual patience, the practice of the bodhisattva: wholeheartedly welcoming the problems. Rinpoche's powerfully experiential teachings give us the confidence to know that we can do it, too."
—Ven. Robina Courtin

The Six Perfections
The Practice of the Bodhisattvas
Lama Zopa Rinpoche

"A jewel of a book, containing much practical advice on how we can start working on these six precious practices, even if we are not yet bodhisattvas."
—Sangye Khadro (Kathleen McDonald), author of *How to Meditate*

Bodhichitta
Practice for a Meaningful Life
Lama Zopa Rinpoche

An accessible, inspiring book on one of the most important topics in Tibetan Buddhism, written by one of its renowned masters.

The Four Noble Truths
A Guide to Everyday Life
Lama Zopa Rinpoche

The Buddha's profound teachings on the four noble truths are illuminated by a Tibetan master simply and directly, so that readers gain an immediate and personal understanding of the causes and conditions that give rise to suffering as well as the spiritual life as the path to liberation.

How to Be Happy
Lama Zopa Rinpoche

"Rinpoche works with determination and great sincerity in the service of Buddha's teachings and sentient beings."
—His Holiness the Dalai Lama

Transforming Problems into Happiness
Foreword by His Holiness the Dalai Lama
Lama Zopa Rinpoche

"A masterfully brief statement of Buddhist teachings on the nature of humanity and human suffering. . . . This book should be read as the words of a wise, loving parent."
—*Utne Reader*

How to Face Death without Fear
A Handbook by Lama Zopa Rinpoche

"The reality of death is an important opportunity for spiritual transformation. Kyabje Lama Zopa Rinpoche's combined teachings and practices lead the reader to an understanding of this reality and help the person who is dying to achieve a better future life. Rinpoche's clarity and blessings will be tremendously beneficial."
—Yangsi Rinpoche, president, Maitripa College

Ultimate Healing
The Power of Compassion
Lama Zopa Rinpoche

"This truly is an awesome book."
—Lillian Too

Bliss of Inner Fire
Heart Practice of the Six Yogas of Naropa
Lama Thubten Yeshe
Foreword by Lama Zopa Rinpoche

"An impressive contribution to the growing body of Buddhist literature for an English-reading audience."
—*The Midwest Book Review*

How to Meditate
A Practical Guide
Kathleen McDonald

"Jewels of wisdom and practical experience to inspire you."
—Richard Gere

The Power of Mantra
Vital Practices for Transformation
Lama Zopa Rinpoche
Compiled and edited by Gordon McDougall

Beloved teacher Lama Zopa Rinpoche guides us through the most popular mantras in Tibetan Buddhism: Shakyamuni Buddha, Chenrezig, Manjushri, Tara, Medicine Buddha, Vajrasattva, and more.

About Wisdom Publications

Wisdom Publications is the leading publisher of classic and contemporary Buddhist books and practical works on mindfulness. To learn more about us or to explore our other books, please visit our website at wisdomexperience.org or contact us at the address below.

Wisdom Publications
132 Perry Street
New York, NY 10014 USA

We are a 501(c)(3) organization, and donations in support of our mission are tax deductible.

Wisdom Publications is affiliated with the Foundation for the Preservation of the Mahayana Tradition (FPMT).